Philosophy through Design

DESIGNING IN DARK TIMES

Responding to the current and wide ranging systemic, social, economic, political and environmental challenges we face, the aim of this new series is to bring together a series of short, polemical texts that address these crises and their inherent possibilities.

Understanding that the old division between the theoretical focus of the sciences and the practical stance integral to designing, making and shaping the world is dissolving, the series explores new ways of acting and knowing concerning the artificial. Identified by a refusal of resignation to what-is and by the equal necessity and urgency of developing new models of the possible, the books work to present both modes of thought (models, concepts, arguments) and courses of action (scenarios, strategies, proposals, works) at all levels from the local and the micro (the situation) to the global and the macro (the universal).

The aim is to push the boundaries of both design and thought, to make each more capable of opening genuine possibilities for thinking and acting otherwise and thus of better facing, and facing down, the myriad failures of the present. Re-thinking the relation between justice and making, and between material human needs and the means and modes of how these can be realized, these works are conceived as a contribution to the wider necessities of dealing with a vulnerable precarious world; of establishing project- not-profit as the basis of action; and of building the bases for wide-ranging emancipatory politics.

As the world descends into crisis these books seek to offer, in small ways, a counter view. Against the instrumental they use the fact that design is *also* a means of articulating hitherto unforeseen possibilities — for subjects as much as for the world — to show how at base it offers irreplaceable capabilities for thinking and acting well in the artificial. In so doing, they point us towards ways of reversing some of the negative and destructive tendencies threatening to engulf the world.

Published and Forthcoming

Politics of the Everyday
Ezio Manzini

Designing in Dark Times: An Arendtian Lexicon
edited by Eduardo Staszowski and Virginia Tassinari

Making Trouble: Design and Material Activism
Otto von Busch

Designing for Interdependence: The Poetics of Relating
Martin Ávila

Designing and the Social Imagination
Matthew DelSesto

Design Education and Democracy on the Edge of Collapse
Zoy Anastassakis and Marcos Martins

Philosophy through Design
Brian Dixon

How Designing Happens
Cameron Tonkinwise

Reconstrained Design
James Auger

Clive Dilnot
Eduardo Staszowski

'An essential read for anyone wanting to activate philosophy and close the gap between design practitioners and academics.'

DANIELLE LAKE, *Director of Design Thinking and Associate Professor of Human Service Studies, Elon University, USA*

'*Philosophy through Design* creates a bold proposal for designer philosophers who bring design and philosophy together to address existential concerns we are facing today. In his tour de force, Brian Dixon develops this urgently needed character through a study of design, pragmatism, feminism and eco-philosophy.'

ILPO KOSKINEN, *Professor of Design, University of New South Wales, Sydney, Australia*

'Some design practice has re-oriented to address today's urgent problems, their histories and their futures. But alongside this busy doing, new thinking is needed. This book contributes to that by charting a course for scholarship and practice in philosophy through design.'

LUCY KIMBELL, *Professor of Contemporary Design Practices, Central Saint Martins, University of the Arts London, UK*

Philosophy through Design: Rethinking Design Practice for a Changing World

Brian Dixon

BLOOMSBURY VISUAL ARTS
LONDON • NEW YORK • OXFORD • NEW DELHI • SYDNEY

BLOOMSBURY VISUAL ARTS
Bloomsbury Publishing Plc, 50 Bedford Square, London, WC1B 3DP, UK
Bloomsbury Publishing Inc, 1385 Broadway, New York, NY 10018, USA
Bloomsbury Publishing Ireland, 29 Earlsfort Terrace, Dublin 2, D02 AY28, Ireland

BLOOMSBURY, BLOOMSBURY VISUAL ARTS and the Diana logo are trademarks of
Bloomsbury Publishing Plc

First published in Great Britain 2026

Copyright © Brian Dixon, 2026

Brian Dixon has asserted his right under the Copyright, Designs and Patents Act, 1988,
to be identified as Author of this work.

For legal purposes the Acknowledgements on p. xi constitute an extension of this copyright page.

Cover design by Andrew LeClair and Chris Wu of Wkshps

All rights reserved. No part of this publication may be: i) reproduced or transmitted in any form,
electronic or mechanical, including photocopying, recording or by means of any information
storage or retrieval system without prior permission in writing from the publishers; or
ii) used or reproduced in any way for the training, development or operation of artificial
intelligence (AI) technologies, including generative AI technologies. The rights holders
expressly reserve this publication from the text and data mining exception as per
Article 4(3) of the Digital Single Market Directive (EU) 2019/790.

Bloomsbury Publishing Plc does not have any control over, or responsibility for, any third-party
websites referred to or in this book. All internet addresses given in this book were correct at the time
of going to press. The author and publisher regret any inconvenience caused if addresses have
changed or sites have ceased to exist, but can accept no responsibility for any such changes.

A catalogue record for this book is available from the British Library.

A catalog record for this book is available from the Library of Congress.

ISBN:	HB:	978-1-3504-2339-8
	PB:	978-1-3504-2338-1
	ePDF:	978-1-3504-2341-1
	eBook:	978-1-3504-2340-4

Series: Designing in Dark Times

Typeset by RefineCatch Limited, Bungay, Suffolk
Printed and bound in India

For product safety related questions contact productsafety@bloomsbury.com.

To find out more about our authors and books visit www.bloomsbury.com
and sign up for our newsletters.

To two boys who are growing up fast.
There's a love of wisdom in your exploring.

CONTENTS

List of Figures x
Acknowledgements xi
Preface xiii
Introduction: From Philosophy in Design to Philosophy through Design 1

1 Connecting Design and Philosophy through Dewey and Addams 37
2 The Technological Horizon: Digital Ontologizing 69
3 The Social Horizon: Association in Experience 97
4 The Ecological Horizon: Connecting Everything 129
5 Philosophy through Design: A Starting Point 167

References 203
Index 227

FIGURES

2.1 A printer that produced cards allowing for reflection on technological mediation as part of a ritual designed to explore the generative potential of philosophy at Eindhoven.   85

3.1 A novel interactive device termed the 'Energy Babble' produced through an ANT-inspired 'procomposition' process.   123

4.1 A shared drinking glass vessel produced as part of the Un/Making project.   147

4.2 The material used in developing the *Grounded* project outcome.   156

ACKNOWLEDGEMENTS

My academic career has been supported by a number of key individuals who generously offered guidance and advice and at just the right moment – whether it was pursuing a PhD, exploring a job posting or encouragement to consider writing a book. This allowed me to progress in ways I would never have imagined before I began. I am exceptionally grateful for that support. It literally made me who I am.

I reflect on this because more than any other work I've published, this book feels like a culmination of a process, the outflow of insights developed in my post-doctoral writing. It ultimately traces a vision for design practice that sees it engage with deep, open-ended methodological concerns along a spectrum that links research (as in my early writing) to the more general idea of the philosophical negotiation of meaning and value (as is the case here).

That is not to say that there is not more that can be done. There is much more to do both in terms of refinement of what is written as well as programmes of experimentation with the ideas and concepts that have been developed. There is work that lies beyond, of course, as well. Nonetheless, I see this book as completing that necessary arc of tracing that commenced in those early days.

As a result, an extended thanks must be provided for early guidance and advice. The two key individuals in this are Janet McDonnell and Ilpo Koskinen. They supported the opening of this tracing with their suggestions of writing a book and the additional input, most especially from Ilpo, allowed this to progress to this point.

In writing this book other voices have fed in and provided very helpful thoughts. This includes Clive Dilnot, Vanessa Patrycja Kaszynska, Cameron Tonkinwise, Cara Broadley, Lucy Kimbell and others. I am grateful to them for their time and the interest they showed.

My family are the ones I write for because although each text is ultimately an academic endeavour in the literal sense, there is a core of meaning that drives the underlying programme.

In writing about design, I am seeking to draw out values that extend beyond the discipline, pointing towards wider possibilities of who we can be and what we might do. It is the moments I spend with my loved ones that draw these to the surface. I thank you for your care and for your love.

PREFACE

Design is notoriously difficult if not impossible to define. Is it about form giving or meaning, problem solving or problem finding, or all of these combined? Are there standalone step-by-step design methods, a single design process, or is it simply a matter of attitude, of approaching situations and contexts in certain ways, which allow things to happen and change to come about?

Again and again, on each attempt to grasp design's boundaries, it appears to slip away, disappearing into vagueness and confusion. This is not helped by the field's seemingly continual evolution and transformation. At one point, in definition at least, design was simply a matter of aesthetics, ensuring that something appeared a certain way and gave rise to particular ideas and concepts.[1] This was succeeded by a focus on use, materials and technology – design as the process of drawing a perfect alignment between form and function.[2] More recently it has become a matter of experience,[3] working through the meaning of products and platforms, looking at what needs they meet and qualities they engender. Now, alongside all of these things, design is approached via systems drawing in the entire organizations and ecological networks, becoming the all-seeing discipline capable of realizing change at scale.

We are at a point where design's star is on the rise. It is rapidly entering previously closed disciplinary spaces, connecting to new audiences, entering contexts never previously entered, whether in government, well-being or the biological realm. This expansion carries great promise. Design, it is claimed, will allow humanity to address its ever-growing existential threats – threats that call the future into question, whether climate change, global

---

[1] David Pye, *The Nature and Aesthetics of Design* (London: Barrie and Jenkins, 1978).
[2] Horatio Greenough, *Form and Function: Remarks on Art, Design and Architecture*, edited by Harold A. Small (Berkeley: University of California Press, 1966 [1947]).
[3] James Robert Rossman and Mathew D. Duerden, *Designing Experiences* (New York: Columbia University Press, 2019).

poverty or hunger. Regardless of the context, we are promised that design can find a way.

Evidence of design's potential here exists but it is nonetheless limited.[4] The discipline cannot claim to be a panacea for all contemporary ills; there is not always a solution to every problem. Indeed, some question the unbounded optimism that commonly attaches to the field. It has been claimed that design thinking, for example, may work against the common good, with the possibility that outcomes may only serve to reinforce pre-existing power structures and, as such, perpetuate inequalities.[5] Here, in seeking to do good, design might well cause harm, stalling social progress and limiting the potential for change. This is where the question of responsibility comes into play.

Responsibility is not a new concern in design. In fact, it is a relatively old one. Since at least the late 1960s we can detect the emergence of what might be termed a 'responsibility consciousness' within the field. This has taken various forms, relating to the social world and the environment.[6] Today, it has also progressed to include an awareness of the responsibility to respect difference and diversity across cultures.[7]

---

[4] Roberto Verganti, Claudio Dell'Era, and Kenneth Scott Swan, 'Design thinking: Critical analysis and future evolution,' *Journal of Product Innovation Management* 38, no. 6 (2021): 603–22.

[5] Rebecca Anne Price and Peter Lloyd, 'Asking effective questions: awareness of bias in designerly thinking.' In *Handbook of Engineering Systems Design*, edited by Anja Maier, Josef Oehmen, Pieter E. Vermaas (Cham: Springer International Publishing, 2022,) 1–16.

[6] This emerges most substantially with Victor Papanek, *Design for the Real World* (London: Thames and Hudson, 1971) and Buckminster Fuller, *Utopia or Oblivion: Prospects for Humanity* (London: Allen Lane 1970).

[7] Two key horizons of note can be identified here. With regard to a need to celebrate diversity there is the pluriversal thought of Arturo Escobar; see, for example, Arturo Escobar, *Designs for the Pluriverse: Radical Interdependence, Autonomy, and the Making of Worlds* (Durham, NC: Duke University Press, 2017). Next to this, with regard to the need to acknowledge and practically work through cultural difference, there is the decolonizing design movement. See, for example, Tristan Schultz, Danah Abdulla, Ahmed Ansari, Ece Canlı, Mahmoud Keshavarz, Matthew Kiem, Luiza Prado de O. Martins, and Pedro J. S. Vieira de Oliveira, 'What is at stake with decolonizing design? A roundtable.' *Design and Culture* 10, no. 1 (2018): 81–101.

This book is also concerned with responsibility and, within this, criticality. I, along with a growing number of theorists in design and beyond,[8] take the view that if design and, more particularly, designers are going to respond to the overwhelming global challenges we face – and, in doing so, act *responsibly* – they cannot simply act *unthinkingly*. Rather, acting *and* thinking must be drawn into fuller and clearer alignment. This requires an evaluation of what design is at present – something that all those who argue that design must seek to address its responsibilities do. It also requires that design work to *reconstruct* what it is such that it can understand, better position and critically work through the responsibility it carries. This too is a relatively common position. Almost all theorists who argue for greater responsibility taking in design also argue for a reconstruction of sorts, though depth of reconstruction varies depends on the position taken.[9] Following some others, I will suggest that it is possible for design to develop a greater sense of how it can be more than it is, or, at least, more than it currently appears to be – a new thing, something as yet unformed and undefined.[10]

Here the key question is always what might this look like? How would design change?

In simple terms, mine is a proposal to turn to philosophy. Specifically I propose a philosophy *through* design

Why a turn to philosophy? The simple answer is that, conventionally, it is philosophy that has fostered and supported the particular structured approach to thinking required here, the sort that allows for questions of responsibility to be addressed and negotiated with criticality and self-awareness. Traditionally,

---

[8] I am thinking most particularly here of the work of Tony Fry, whose theories I will reference in due course. See, for example, Tony Fry, *Design as Politics* (Oxford: Berg, 2010).

[9] One might argue that while Papanek may have been radical in his time, he was very much preserving the basic conception and positioning of professional design, as the designing of *things*. If we compare this to Tony Fry's futuring, to be covered in Chapter 4, we can see that radical reimaginings are also possible beyond this.

[10] In calling for a reconstruction of sorts in design, alignment can be drawn to the work of Fry and Escobar.

it is the space in which questions of meaning and value, what matters, how it matters and what is good, have been explored and challenged. Equally, it is also a space (though not the only one) in which questions of good and bad, better and worse, right and wrong are queried. This, it is argued, is what design, in its twenty-first-century positioning, needs.

Why *through* design? This is because design is practice. Its responsibilities take shape in practice and, helpfully, to design is to engage in problem identification and the exploration of solutions or, from a philosophical standpoint, answers.

I am not the first to suggest a philosophy through design or, at least, a greater coming together of the two disciplines. In the technological space, there is already a proposal for a 'philosophy through design' from Jonne Van Belle and colleagues.[11] Equally, work is already underway in both Simon Fraser University in Vancouver and the Eindhoven University of Technology, where design researchers claim to be 'doing' philosophy (see Chapter 2). Beyond this, Tony Fry has positioned his theories of design, sustainability and the future[12] in deeply philosophical terms. In the philosophy of design work of Stéphane Vial, there is the suggestion that design practice – by virtue of the production of 'appearances' processes of making – can be understood as a form of phenomenology (a distinct early-twentieth-century approach), which he terms a creative phenomenology or phenomenology by practice.[13] Then there is the theoretical interrelating of the work of Gilles Deleuze and design by authors

---

[11] Jonne van Belle, Jelle van Dijk, and Wouter Eggink, 'Towards a Tangible Philosophy through Design; Exploring the question of being-in-the-world in the digital age.' In *Proceedings of the Academy for Design Innovation Management conference*, Loughborough University, 19–21 June 2019.

[12] Fry has proposed 'design futuring' as a means of developing a 'redirective' practice in design allowing for a true sustain-ablity, which, in turn, might enable humanity to have a future. The underpinning theories are noted throughout but covered most thoroughly in Chapter 4. See Tony Fry, *Design Futuring: Sustainability, Ethics and New Practice* (Oxford: Berg, 2009).

[13] Stéphane Vial, 'The effect of design: A phenomenological contribution to the quiddity of design presented in geometrical order.' *Artifact: Journal of Design Practice* 3, no. 4 (2015): 1–6.

such as Jamie Brassett,[14] where questions are asked for what design can become[15] through philosophy as well as what philosophy can become through design.[16] This is turn links to recent philosophic perspectives, which explore the integration of thought and action that seeks to explore the potential of philosophy – more especially, writing philosophy – next to creative practice.[17]

For my part, it is important to note in turning to philosophy – scoping a philosophy through design – I am not aiming to directly apply or impose philosophy on design, bluntly grafting one thing onto another. Rather, the aim is to offer paths by which philosophy might interweave and inflect design – support thinking in and beyond direct action – exploring what design could become when so positioned and, within this, what this becoming might offer. Returning to the idea of an aligned acting and thinking, the point is to work to understand how, by enfolding a philosophical angle, a novel design acting-thinking can seek to address the challenges of our time with sensitivity and understanding, as well as potentially produce insights of value for philosophy itself.

To work through this idea will require that we look to both design and philosophy. It will also require that we consider how both have already been drawn into alignment (or not) and what this has meant, particularly for design. However, it is important to note that no in-depth histories will be offered here – only brief

---

[14] Jamie Brassett, 'Poised and complex: The becoming each other of philosophy, design and innovation.' In *Deleuze and Design*, edited by Betti Marenko and Jamie Brassett (Edinburgh: Edinburgh University Press, 2015), 31–57.

[15] *Becoming* is a key Deleuzian (and by association Guattarian) concept. It is distinguished from the classical philosophical concept of 'being', which is seen as representing a fixed state, on the basis that it suggests an ongoing process, wherein transformation is a constant. For an overview see Todd May, 'When is a Deleuzian becoming?' *Continental Philosophy Review* 36, no. 2 (2003): 139–53.

[16] Betti Marenko and Jamie Brassett (eds), *Deleuze and Design* (Edinburgh: Edinburgh University Press, 2015).

[17] Erin Manning and Brian Massumi, *Thought in the Act: Passages in the Ecology of Experience* (Minneapolis, MN: University of Minnesota Press, 2014).

sketches of where we are, generally and in relation to specific areas. None of this will be definitive. Also, and importantly, my referencing will be non-exhaustive. I freely admit that some voices and arguments, whether from philosophy or design, will be absent. I regret that this may disappoint some readers, but full and comprehensive survey of fields is simply not possible in a text such as this. Nonetheless, I will seek to point and footnote as best as I can to highlight where further reading might progress understanding. All of this, it is hoped, will serve to initially situate what is eventually proposed as best as possible within a single text, as well as encourage others to follow on with other, finer-grained proposals.

This brings us to the positioning of *this* work. With philosophy, as with any theoretical referencing, positioning is, of course, very important. Here, my central anchoring is to classical pragmatism and, more particularly, to two late American pragmatist philosophers, John Dewey and Jane Addams. This alignment relies not only on an already deep relationship between design, Dewey and increasingly Addams but also on what I see as the value of Dewey's proposal for a reconstruction in philosophy based on practical, real-world experimentation and, next to this, Addams's example of how philosophizing can be a lifelong, practical, reflective and iterative project. Taken together, both can be understood, in their own way, to represent what I am terming prototypic 'designer philosophers' – that is, individuals who not only engage in philosophic debate but do so through an active participation in the world, paying special attention to the ethical dimensions of their work, seeking above all to ameliorate, to make better through thinking-acting.

It must be highlighted here at the outset that such a conception of philosophy is distinct and particular. It diverges markedly from contemporary understandings of the discipline's scope and role. In this vision, there is no formal logic, no focus on abstract arguments but, rather, a working through of things in context and furthering (ideally an enhancing) of experience beyond. And while this vision is based on historic references, I will argue that through design there is a future for it yet.

Distinct approaches aside, I must acknowledge upfront that by referencing pragmatism in this way, I am adopting a Western orientation perspective. Realistically, however, this is the only authentic position I can work outwards from. I was born in a small town in the Republic of Ireland. I hold two passports, one Irish and one Canadian. To my shame, I only speak English. I undertook university study in Ireland and in the UK. The proposals I set out here have their own disciplinary rationale (covered as I progress) but they are also undoubtedly the product of the cultural matrix within which I have lived and built up my experience. While potentially problematic, holding awareness of this allows me to see that I need be as expansive as possible – a subject I will tackle in due course as I begin to introduce pragmatism.

Our discussion will be framed, for the most part, by contexts. In particular, we will look at the areas of technology, the social and the ecological. These are identified as thematic domains in which the challenges of our age both take form and issue consequences and, as such, where design can be seen to hold special focus, in relation to its activities and their consequences. Of course, these domains do not function as discreet siloed subjects, they are relational interconnecting vectors from which all manner of entanglements move in and out of view.

The technological directly implies the social; it emerges from shared needs, concerns and desires and relies on our common enterprise and economic systems. It also directly calls up the ecological. There are no smartphones without rare earth minerals, without metal and the raw materials for glass and plastics. More directly, each internet search, each checking of social media or email or momentary watching of a video causes a distant server to power up as the data is drawn down. Mirroring this, the social, in turn, is also technological and, equally, ecologically bound, though the degree to which this is seen to be the case would depend on one's perspective. Then the ecological, when taken as a central concern, is all-encompassing. It involves all manner of activity, human and non-human. The technological ripples through as well, connecting us as living beings to natural resources (like, as noted, the rare minerals and energy required to build and use our smart devices). Each is related, each overlaps and all are interlinked within the complex web of challenges we face.

If this is the case, there is a reasonable question to be asked here at the outset as to why I have chosen to handle these areas separately at all. Isn't that a characteristically modernist trait, something someone from the twentieth century would do? Break things down into parts and forget about the relationships?

This is all true. It is modernist to break things down into parts, to see them as unrelated. However, I am not fully separating things out and am attending to relationships – constant cross-references are made outwards – for example, to the shared affordances of pragmatism and other philosophies. More significantly, I handle each area separately, not because they are seen as separate and separated but rather because the situations within which we might want to engage in philosophy through design would likely themselves have very specific qualities, unique focal points that cannot be ignored or overlooked. Sometimes we may observe technology as troubling. Other times social or political processes will have failed us. Almost always these days, we live in fear of the ecological and what our environmental and, accordingly, our general future portends. All such concerns remain related. It is where we start and finish that is at stake, and in starting and finishing with specific qualities and focal points, it is useful to be able to hone in on certain resources that might aid the structuring of a process of inquiry. By exploring these contexts in a focused manner, I intend to open up perspectives – theoretical resources, ways of seeing and specific insights – that a philosophy through design might build upon.[18]

Beyond the contexts there is the practice itself, of course. In the end, it is hoped that we can frame an early outline of a present-day designer philosopher and their notional practice.

---

[18] There will also be glimpses of practices that can be understood as prototypic philosophy through design, even if the work itself is not as yet being positioned as such.

This figure will not be fully defined – that is a longer-term project. Their practice, however, will be given a possible outline from which others might work outwards. More pointedly, it is hoped that what emerges is the clear overview of the potential of a designer-philosopher mindset. This relates not only to the impact of bringing designing and (a form of) philosophizing together but equally to the even greater potential impact of bringing other disciplines together via a design–philosophy interweaving.

Introduction: From Philosophy in Design to Philosophy through Design

At the quarter point of the twenty-first century, design has emerged as force for the age, capable of rising to the challenge of the seemingly endless waves of crisis and disaster. Reviewing the literature, it would appear that such a status has been posited for some time. Writing in 1971, Victor Papanek noted:

> We are beginning to realise that the main challenge for our society lies no longer in the production of goods. Rather, we have to make choices that deal with 'how good?' instead of 'how much?' But the changes, and our awareness of these changes, have been so highly accelerated that trying to make sense of them will become our basic industry. Moral, aesthetic, and ethical values will evolve along with the choices to which they have been applied. We may still consider religion, sex, morality, the family structure, or medical research to be remote from technology and design. But the margin is narrowing fast. With all of these changes, the designer (working as part of a multidisciplinary team) can and must involve himself.[1]

---

[1] Victor Papanek, *Design the Real World*, 3rd edn (London: Thames and Hudson, 2019), 277.

In many ways, some fifty years hence, this totalizing vision has been realized, at least to an extent, in the phenomenon of design thinking. Design thinking is often packaged as a benevolent gifting of knowledge from professional design to humanity – the missing toolkit by which all the world's ills can be both readily and rapidly solved through creativity. In reality, of course, design thinking ultimately functions as an abstract modelling of the design process, the process by which design claims to centre on humans proceeds. Within this modelling, design is presented as involving five distinct stages: empathize, define, ideate, prototype and test. It here becomes an activity that one progresses through (and may backtrack upon) in order to achieve shared goals. Generally, these goals relate to changing or transforming a given context (for example, the experience of being a patient in a hospital).

The modelling has its detractors. Most immediately, it is considered superficial; a short-term attempt to solve problems that are generations in the making can never hope to adequately address those problems, at least not in their totality. As a further, more serious criticism, some argue that it serves only to perpetuate stereotypes and biases.[2] If you gather people together uncritically around an issue, allowing them to believe in the power of process alone, then there is undoubtably a risk. Then, equally worrisome is the claim that in such scenarios, design is reinforcing existing power structures and economic models and, as such, actively preventing the emergence of alternatives.[3]

Design is of course much more than design thinking. Viewed in broad terms, design is deeply connected to tradition. It has a legacy as old as human history and a formal identity that can be traced back to the onset of the Industrial Revolution. Gradually emerging in the context of manufacturing and mass production, it evolved as a means of resolving aesthetic and eventually functional considerations. This carries a legacy that continues to the present

---

[2] Verganti, Dell'Era and Swan, 'Design thinking: Critical analysis and future evolution.'

[3] Rebecca Ackermann, 'Design thinking was supposed to fix the world. Where did it go wrong', MIT Technology Review, 9 February 2023, https://www.technologyreview.com/2023/02/09/1067821/design-thinking-retrospective-what-went-wrong/

day – for example, in the development of visual material such as advertising campaigns and printed literature and consumer products such as vacuum cleaners. Design, however, has, over the decades, also evolved to become something more, developing into an expanding programme that demonstrates an intriguing capacity to shapeshift when it comes into contact with novel economic and social contexts. Time and again, it has demonstrated that it can become what is needed in relation to situational demands. A useful example is the relatively recent emergence, in the 1980s/1990s, of user experience design, or UX for short, where design activity is redirected to the *process* of creating a digital product – for example, the process of creating a mobile app or a website – rather than being wholly focused on the eventual, singular standalone product itself. This approach emerged from within existing practices because it was needed within the discipline – i.e. practice demanded certain skills and abilities to address the problems being encountered. This, in turn, can be understood as a response to industry and, ultimately, market demands.

As design has encountered other novel contexts, it has adapted and responded to shape something that builds on what already existed but equally moves past this to establish something new. From here, novel communities of practice emerge, advocating for recognition and legitimacy. By way of example, we may point to areas such as service delivery and the processes of government.[4] Here, in recent years, we have seen the gradual establishment of practices such as service design and design for policy. With service design, the previously intangible spaces of customer experience (CX) and organizational structures have been opened to designers, keen on reimagining what could be. In design for policy, design has found a role in formal policy-making contexts in government departments and labs, where it offers a range of generative methods and, potentially, a means of reframing policy-making practice more widely.[5]

---

[4] Christian Bason, *Design for Policy* (London: Routledge, 2016).
[5] Lucy Kimbell, Catherine Durose, Ramia Mazé and Liz Richardson, *Design and Policy: Current Debates and Future Directions for Research in the UK: Report of the AHRC Design Policy Research Network* (London: University of the Arts London, 2023).

Beyond these examples other, more specifically social, approaches have also opened up across the field. There is the long-established area of participatory design, dating back to the 1960s, and the more recent area of social design proper. In the background, there is also the all-encompassing agenda of codesign, which sees people and groups drawn into the design process regardless of context or subject matter. Once recognition and legitimacy are granted to such approaches, another emergent horizon opens up. At present, a relevant example might be ecological or regenerative design, an approach which seeks to align design with natural biological processes, responding to concerns related to the climate emergency and biodiversity loss.[6] Following the conventional trajectory, in time, it too will achieve recognition and legitimacy.

As has been noted, this expansionist programme places a considerable burden of responsibility on design. It is to this concern which we initially turn.

DESIGN'S DEEPENING RESPONSIBILITIES

Design has always held responsibility: designers have designed things and these things have and have had definite social and environmental impact. Sometimes this impact has been overtly positive; for example, many groups have benefitted from dedicated efforts to support their particular need, whether that relates to improved accessibility for the visually impaired through better digital design or enhanced quality of life for those who suffer from acute illness through, for example, the development of specialized medical devices. Here, design responds well to the challenges presented; things are better and responsibilities have been met. In direct contrast, at other times, design's impact has been overtly negative. A key global example here is of course the devasting pollution – on land, in rivers and seas – that follows

---

[6] See for example, Daniel Christian Wahl, *Designing Regenerative Cultures* (Axminster: Triarchy Press, 2016).

on from the disposal of plastic waste, a process to which design has both directly and indirectly contributed.

In large part, this is a matter of scope and scale. When design is seen to operate at a level of aesthetics and functionality, the associated risks appear foreseeable and, as such, can notionally be identified and addressed in straightforward terms. From this point of view, a product may simply be ugly, lacking beauty and meaning and, as such, detracting from the overall qualitative bearing of daily experience. A product might also be dangerous or dysfunctional (e.g. faulty electronics or a tin opener that does not open tins). In these cases, the solution is improved design, a making good on abject failure.

When the scope and scale are redefined, however, so too is the level of risk. Perhaps most strikingly, we see this in relation to the ever-expanding presence and potency of digital technology generally and, increasingly, artificial intelligence in particular. In this context, design is contributing to a gradual redrawing of our understanding of selfhood and social interactions. Its role here positions it at the very heart of deep and troubling ethical questions relating to the type of futures we wish to see come about.

Alongside this, we can also note design's entry into the ecological domain. Here, practitioners are seeking to develop new ways of recognizing and relating both to environmental need and processes within their designs. This is a matter not only of changing patterns of production and consumption but, potentially, also of reorientating the entire economic system, exploring radical alternatives to the status quo. The risks here are again profound. Indeed, they are existential in the sense that the continuation of human and planetary life more generally now depends on the realignment of our economies and lifestyles – the ultimate design challenge.

If designers are to play a significant role in relation to such issues, they must be extremely well-informed, deeply self-aware and uncompromising in their criticality.

Unfortunately, the field has historically struggled to work through this. Concerns regarding how action can and should be directed via a coherent methodological knowledge base have bedevilled the discourse since at least the 1960s.[7] Decade after decade, proposals have been developed, progressed and subsequently, through challenge and progress, have fallen away. The same goes for theoretical alignments, where most often the domain of psychology is referenced. Though this delivers value it can, again, be difficult to move from theory to practice.[8] Ethics too has been a long-term challenge for the field. While there is a strong legacy of ethical discourse in design[9] and much theoretical progress has been made in recent years, it has not yet become fully established within the field.[10] Most glaringly, it is absent from many design curricula and, accordingly, remains an under-discussed topic in professional practice.[11] A robust and easily shared design ethics framework could open up possibilities for designing for emerging contexts more responsibly, offering a means or set of protocols for approaching the responsibilities of design directly, both existent and new-found.

These perennial gaps have led to much ongoing commentary in the field, with various frameworks being proposed as a means of addressing the challenges faced. A common thread that runs

---

[7] Here, in terms of specific labels, simple well-known examples would include the agendas of design science, the design methods movement, and more recently the efforts to formalize design logic. On each occasion both designers and design researchers have encountered difficulty when trying to appropriate abstract principles into practice, i.e. in moving from one person's vision to neat real-world application. See for example Nigel Cross, 'Developing design as a discipline.' *Journal of Engineering Design* 29, no. 12 (2018): 691–708.

[8] Initially, it was cognitive psychology in particular that formed the touchstone reference within disciplinary agendas in design. Here, the human mind is approached as symbolic processing system. See Don Norman, *The Design of Everyday Things* (New York: Basic Books. 2013 [1986]). Having moved past the latter orientation, the field is today exploring the potential of behavioural science, which may yet yield value of both practice and research.

[9] The spearhead here was Papanek, *Design for the Real World*.

[10] This is changing. See Emma Felton, Oksana Zelenko and Suzi Vaughan (eds), *Design and Ethics: Reflections and Practice* (Abingdon, Oxon: Routledge, 2012).

[11] Time and again, commercially driven design has demonstrated that it is simply not capable of such self-regulation. Accordingly, the shaping of an ethical framework demands something more than a commercial mindset. This is already apparent in Papanek, *Design for the Real World*.

through all of this work is a deep recognition of the need for change, not only in the discipline but more generally across the social, political and economic domains. For example, writing on the need to design for resilience, design academic Stuart Walker contextualizes the issues as running as deep as the philosophical question of how we should live.[12]

As one would expect, some proposals are incremental, others more radical. The radical side tends to take up wide-ranging, all-encompassing perspectives. We may here note the important work of Tony Fry, who seeks to tackle what he terms our 'defuturing' – that is, the endangerment of human and planetary life – through the establishment of a redirective practice in design, what he calls a 'futuring'.[13] Then there is the pluriversal proposals of Arturo Escobar, who envisages an approach to design that centres and honours ecologically bound, indigenous ways of experiencing and knowing.[14] There is the design justice work of Sasha Costanza-Chock, who argues that design must work to act as liberating force for the marginalized and oppressed, directly confronting social, political and environmental inequalities head on.[15] And, as another last example, there is Gui Bonsiepe who, in discussing design's role next to the various proliferating crises we face, highlights its 'disobedience'[16] – that is, how it can find ways to address the challenges meaningfully.

In linking to this general agenda, rather than present a final proposal for reconstruction of design, the present book suggests an ongoing process of evaluation that might in turn eventually lead to a reconstruction. Ultimately, its envisaged programme of reform is directed towards an exploration of the possibilities

---

[12] Stuart Walker, *Design for Resilience: Making the Future We Leave Behind* (Cambridge, MA: The MIT Press, 2023).

[13] See Fry, *Design Futuring*.

[14] Arturo Escobar, *Designs for the Pluriverse: Radical Interdependence, Autonomy, and the Making of Worlds* (Durham, NC: Duke University Press, 2018).

[15] Sasha Costanza-Chock, *Design Justice: Community-Led Practices to Build the Worlds We Need* (Cambridge, MA: The MIT Press, 2020).

[16] Gui Bonsiepe, *The Disobedience of Design*, edited by Lara Penin (London: Bloomsbury, 2022).

of philosophy next to the areas of focus noted above, i.e. technology, the social world and the ecological. Some might view this turn to philosophy as taking a step back from methodology and theory – i.e. considering first principles before last so that the latter can be enhanced – but this is not the intention. Instead, the turn towards philosophy is positioned as taking a *step away* from traditional methodological and theoretical questions, moving beyond them to something other. In positive terms this means exploring how design can become an approach to thinking-acting which allows for a direct and iterative exploration of meaning and value in real terms, in and beyond context. This would be titled a *philosophy through design* and would allow for problem identification and the exploration of solutions/answers *in* practice where design's responsibilities take shape.

It is important to note that I am not alone in drawing lines to philosophy in this way. Much of the above work is deeply philosophical in character. Equally, as we will begin to cover below and beyond through the forthcoming chapters, design and philosophy interface and interact in a number of intriguing and often complicated ways – not least in the domain of technology where, as we will see, researchers in Eindhoven and Vancouver explore 'doing' philosophy through design.

DESIGN AND PHILOSOPHY: SOME STARTING POINTS

Any attempt to link design and philosophy soon becomes complicated. The two draw together and pull apart in numerous ways and no one way of relating them can claim to take precedence over any other. The pulling apart will be obvious enough for many. Design has conventionally been defined as a discipline that eschews theory and formal philosophies. Designers are seen as resistant to the abstractions of argumentation and sequenced logic.[17] Their focus is directed towards doing, not thinking.

---

[17] See, for example, Anne Gentes, *The In-Discipline of Design: Bridging the Gap between the Humanities and Engineering* (Cham: Springer 2017).

When it comes to how the two draw together, the picture becomes more complex. At least three key points of connection can be identified. There is, first and foremost, the emergent domains of the philosophy of design and design philosophy.[18] Both present what might be characterized as developing areas of study, which, at their core, focus on progressing a rigorous philosophic understanding of design and its outcomes. The terms – philosophy of design and design philosophy – can be divided on the basis of the former generally being seen to focus on 'what' professional design is and means,[19] and the latter representing a more open-ended questioning of design's social and political meanings and responsibilities, as well the potential scope of the discipline generally.[20]

Design theorist Anne-Marie Willis sees this latter area of work as sharing some of the interests of the philosophy of technology, but distinct from both it and formal design research in that it 'opens design to be interrogated and theorized'. Within this strand of work we may locate some of the discipline's most prolific contributors – for example, Tony Fry, Cameron Tonkinwise[21] and Clive Dilnot, as well as individuals such as Anne Marie Willis who have explored ideas around design's ontological role.[22] Alongside these figures, it is also arguable that the work of some prominent design theorists can also be found to fit into this

---

[18] Within this general grouping, one might also draw a line to what could be termed philosophies of designing. These are generally issued by designers themselves, offering reflections on their approach to designing and what it means to be a designer. See e.g. Norman Potter, What Is a Designer: Things, Places, Messages (London: Studio Vista, 1969).

[19] See for example Pieter E. Vermaas, Peter Kroes, Andrew Light and Steven Moore (eds), *Philosophy and Design: From Engineering to Architecture* (Dordrecht: Springer, 2007); Pieter E. Vermaas,and Stéphane Vial (eds), *Advancements in the Philosophy of Design* (Cham: Springer, 2018).

[20] Anne-Marie Willis, 'Introduction.' In *The Design Philosophy Reader*, edited by Anne-Marie Willis (London: Bloomsbury, 2019), 6.

[21] Tonkinwise provides the field with a deeply philosophical critical commentary on such themes as sustainability and technology. Like Fry, his work has been informed by Heidegger.

[22] See Anne-Marie Willis, 'Ontological designing.' *Design Philosophy Papers* 4, no. 2 (2006): 69–92.

category – for example, Richard Buchanan's extensive explorations of how design can be understood as a modern form of rhetoric.[23] From 2003 to 2017, work here was supported by the existence of the *Design Philosophy Papers* journal, which gave space for the philosophical scoping within the design.[24] Issues were arranged thematically, covering areas such as technology, ethics, beauty and materiality, among many other domains. Though this journal has now ceased,[25] all contributions remain available to download from an online archive.[26]

As a second special category of design and philosophy being drawn together, we can identify philosophically informed design work. Here, a philosophy or philosophical concept acts as a reference point, giving context to the design process and its outcome. Perhaps the most prominent example of such an approach is the critical design work of Antony Dunne, Fiona Raby and others, where questions are asked of existing technological and social values with a view to exploring an alternative vision for how we might live.[27] This also links in to speculative design,[28] design futures and design fiction work,[29] which tend to focus on

---

[23] Here, Buchanan links to the work of the late philosopher Richard McKeon, a one-time student of Dewey's. See Richard Buchanan, 'Design and the new rhetoric: Productive arts in the philosophy of culture.' *Philosophy & Rhetoric* 34, no. 3 (2001): 183–206.

[24] Anne-Marie Willis, 'Editorial.' *Design Philosophy Papers* 15 no. (2017): 95–7. doi:10.1080/14487136.2017.1390193.

[25] In the final editorial, Willis comments that the increasingly standardized and designed approach to knowledge production was 'obstructing critical thinking and normalizing the absence of a politics of intellectual work'. The journal was seen to be supporting this framework and, as such, the view was taken that it was better to support critical thinking in design studies in ways extending beyond journal formats.

[26] The Studio at the Edge of the World, 'Edgewords', accessed 18 November 2024, https://www.thestudioattheedgeoftheworld.com/archive1.html

[27] Antony Dunne, *Hertzian Tales Electronic Products, Aesthetic Experience, and Critical Design* (Cambridge, MA: The MIT Press, 2008).

[28] Antony Dunne and Fiona Raby, *Speculative Everything: Design, Fiction and Social Dreaming* (Cambridge MA: The MIT Press, 2013).

[29] Tony Fry, *Writing Design Fiction: Relocating a City in Crisis* (London: Bloomsbury, 2021).

envisaging (i.e. designing) potential beyond-the-present social, political, economic scenarios giving material form to the potential meanings and values that could arise within these. Most often, the design process is not based on abstract theorizations or arguments but rather on prototyped material artefacts, photographic representations, visual scenarios and general possibilities which are accompanied by narratives. Outputs usually take the form of images and text in publications, but exhibitions and physical displays are also common.[30] This is not to say that writing on its own is prohibited; it too is a possible outcome.[31] All of these approaches can be seen to have much in common with a philosophical method referred as 'thought experiments', where particular conditions, along with their consequences and meanings, are scoped out and envisaged. A key link between all of these is an implicit or explicit reliance on logic to carry propositions forward: if then, if then, guides the way.

Next, as a third category of drawing towards, there are a number of strands of philosophy that draw in design and design-led concerns. These include what is referred to as 'object-orientated ontologies' and postphenomenology.

Object-orientated ontologies (OOO) decentre traditional human perspectives on 'being' in favour of the relationships that can be drawn between human and non-human things.[32] Working across disciplines, OOO-based theorists focus on tracing the form of these relationships and the networks they form, seeking to productively examine the meaning of these relationships/networks, surfacing new ways of seeing activities and processes. Perhaps the most impactful voice here for design has been the late Bruno Latour, who, alongside his highly cited work on actor

---

[30] Matt Malpass, *Critical Design in Context: History, Theory and Practice* (London: Bloomsbury 2017).

[31] Fry, *Writing Design Fiction* is an example.

[32] Graham Harman, *Object-Orientated Ontology: A New Theory of Everything* (London: Penguin, 2018).

network theory (ANT),[33] examined the role of design directly from a philosophical perspective (see below).

Next to OOO work, postphenomenology[34] is centrally concerned with the use and experience of technology. Ultimate focus is directed towards asking ethical questions of technology's role within our lives. While still peripheral to the discipline of design, the approach has gained increasing attention, with a number of leading theorists drawing explicit alignment with the perspective.[35] Intriguingly it is via this route that Jonne van Belle and collaborators[36] have proposed a philosophy through design via design research (see Chapter 2).

Beyond these categories, as an additional link, I would argue that design and philosophy also come together in a research context, through a series of varied approaches that directly involve practice. These approaches are sometimes referred to as research through design, or practice-based or -led research[37] or, alternatively, constructive design research.[38] Through all, design practice ultimately comes to play a part in the process of knowledge production. This may take the form of design being applied directly within the research, in the context of specific techniques or methods (e.g. as a means of framing workshops) or, equally, within the process of making a contribution (e.g. producing a made artefact which demonstrates a given idea or concept).

---

[33] Actor network theory can be understood as a distinct object-orientated approach to sociology. Both humans and non-humans are seen to hold agency and collectively form networks of relationships, which carry power dynamics. See Bruno Latour, *Reassembling the Social: An Introduction to Actor Network Theory* (Oxford: Oxford University Press, 2005).

[34] A key text is Peter-Paul Verbeek, *What Things Do: Reflections on Technology, Agency and Design* (University Park, PN: Pennsylvania State University Press, 2005).

[35] Ron Wakkary, *Things We Could Design: For More than Human-Centered Worlds* (Cambridge, MA: The MIT Press, 2021).

[36] van Belle et al. 'Towards a Tangible Philosophy through Design.'

[37] Laurene Vaughan (ed.), *Practice-Based Design Research* (London: Bloomsbury, 2017).

[38] Ilpo Koskinen, John Zimmerman, Thomas Binder, Johan Redström and Stephan Wensveen, *Design Research Through Practice: From the Lab, Field, and Showroom* (Amsterdam: Elsevier, 2011).

As we will be discussing, there is no fixed method or prescribed way of researching defined here. Most contributors align such work to existing methodological discourse as well as broader disciplinary theories beyond design. Equally, sometimes, philosophy too will be referenced. The form this takes will vary. At times, philosophy will support the methodological framing. Other times, it may provide a context to open an investigation, where a project might be framed in relation to particular theoretical insights that derive from philosophy. For example, a researcher might question the extent to which particular forms of representation are possible or how particular aesthetic experiences might be shaped.

As will be progressively explored through the coming chapters, it is the argument of this book that such enfoldings of design within research can act as reference point in the development of a novel approach to philosophy – what will here be termed a philosophy through design – that opens up a path by which design might begin to address the depth of our present and future challenges with rigour and optimism.

However, to begin to trace this out, we have some preliminary ground to cover. To get started, it will be useful to tease out design and philosophy relationships a little further. After briefly exploring this, I will highlight the present book's positioning and link to the work of the pragmatists John Dewey and Jane Addams, with whom this text will move to draw an alignment. Thereafter, we will look in a little more detail at how a philosophy through design could potentially evolve from design research involving practice. Finally, as a close to this chapter, we consider the structure of the text as a whole.

A SENSE OF PHILOSOPHY NEXT TO DESIGN

Philosophy, like design, evades easy definition. Although it is many things, it is perhaps best described as a means of asking and answering questions. These questions could relate to any manner of concerns ranging from the nature of knowledge, to how the mind works, to what it means to be happy, to the moral bearing (i.e. the rightness or wrongness) of a given issue. As with design, these questions arise from an identification of a problem. Not unlike design, the process of answering a philosophical question can be conceived of as a form of problem solving. One identifies a philosophical problem; aims to give it form and clarity; explores possible answers; begins to tease these out; returns to the problem; potentially revises or redefines it; and, again, reverts to exploring possible answers. Gradually, through refinement and iteration, what is termed an argument – the main outcome of philosophical inquiry – is developed. As with a design outcome, this too will be refined and iterated over time, gradually given form. That is not to draw too close a likeness, however. A philosophical argument will be text-based or verbal, something which is set out in words. Design, on the other hand, can take any number of forms, material and immaterial.

Another point of intersection between philosophy and design is philosophy's deep commitment to precedent and legacy. In a Western context, philosophy carries a direct history that extends as far back as ancient Greece.[39] Indeed, the history of Western philosophy is one of cultural evolution: the history of how the West conceived of the world over time, of knowing and being and doing. Through philosophy, we can trace how classicalism gave way to Christianity; how Christian perspectives gradually yielded to those of science; and how these gradually fragmented into the disciplinary channels we know today.

Unlike design, present-day philosophy is not regularly positioned as a means of responding to contemporary global crises. As we will see, this is partly a matter of subject focus. At present, the field can be understood to divide into two loosely defined alignments.

---

[39] There are many compelling histories of Western philosophy. One recent broad-ranging example is found in Antony C. Grayling, *The History of Philosophy: Three Millenia of Thought From the West and Beyond* (London: Penguin, 2019). An intriguing, if brief, contextualizing from a design perspective is offered by Anne-Marie Willis in her Introduction to the *Design Philosophy Reader*, where she stresses the inevitably interactions between the Greeks and other cultures – including 'Persia, India, China and Africa' – that will have informed their particular approach to, and conception of, philosophy. See Willis, 'Introduction', 6.

These alignments are titled analytic philosophy and what is generally referred to as continental philosophy. The first aims to uncover truth via an *analysis* of language and meaning. Its adherents are mostly found in anglophone countries such as the United States and the UK. The second, the continental, refers to a crude, somewhat uncomfortable grouping of several traditions which can be related in so far as they are concerned with surfacing perspectives on human and non-human experience and existence. Key authors here are generally non-anglophone Europeans, with strong traditions existing in countries such as France, Germany and the Netherlands.

Both of these alignments offer theoretical resources, ways of seeing and insights that might support and progress understandings of the world but, as we will explore in the next chapter, currently neither is especially well equipped (nor positioned)[40] to offer tools for practical action – that is, means to respond directly to the current global challenges we face. Nonetheless, we can begin to locate philosophy's direct relations (or not) next to these traditions and perspectives and values that ground them.

As noted above, philosophy directly interfaces with design through the strands of the philosophy of design and design philosophy. Philosophy of design work can be seen to align with both the analytic tradition as well as the continental tradition. With regard to the analytic, we might, by way of example, turn to texts such as Glen Parsons's *The Philosophy of Design*, which offer arguments that draw together understandings of the design process, its histories, its key concepts and how these link to aesthetics and ethics.[41] This is an approach to design as it is

---

[40] One might argue that it is not philosophy's job to change the world. Nonetheless, that does not preclude the possibility that it could, nor that it might be desirable. In the modern era such a sentiment can be traced back at least to Marx, when he famously commented that 'philosophers have only interpreted the world, in various ways. The point however is to change it.' Karl Marx 'Thesis on Feuerbach'. In *Ludwig Feuerbach and the Outcome of Classical German Philosophy*, edited by Frederic Engels (New York: International Publishers, 1941 [1888]), 84. John Dewey, as we will see, would agree.

[41] Glenn Parsons, *The Philosophy of Design* (Cambridge: Polity, 2015).

commonly understood and, within this, an analysis of what this means. Other contributions here take in subject areas such as the intentionality of design[42] and modellings of design as a communication process.[43] With regard to continental references, recent work has drawn links to phenomenology[44] and discourse theory.[45]

Within design philosophy, there is a strong tendency to reference continental philosophy, especially the work of Martin Heidegger. Here, Tony Fry's work in particular is noteworthy. His texts are threaded through with Heideggerian concepts. There is a general emphasis, for example, on the idea of being – both humanity's being as well as the being of a designer – and regular reference to the central Heideggerian expression 'being-in-the-world'. He also links to the deeply Heideggerian concepts of care and dwelling. Technology is contextualized in terms of resource appropriation and the negative environmental impact that follows.[46] Time, the extending of time for humanity and ecological systems generally, undergirds the idea of futuring.

This leads us to some of the wider design philosophy connections found in OOO and postphenomenology.[47] Both can be seen as

---

[42] Per Galle, 'Design as intentional action: a conceptual analysis,' *Design Studies* 20, no. 1 (1999): 57–81.

[43] Nathan Crilly, David Good, Derek Matravers and P. John Clarkson, 'Design as communication: exploring the validity and utility of relating intention to interpretation.' *Design Studies* 29, no. 5 (2008): 425–57.

[44] Søren Bolvig Poulsen and Ulla Thøgersen. 'Embodied design thinking: a phenomenological perspective.' *CoDesign* 7, no. 1 (2011): 29–44.

[45] Katherine Hepworth, 'Governmentality, Technologies & Truth Effects in Communication Design.' In *Advancements in the Philosophy of Design*, edited by Pieter E. Vermaas and Stéphane Vial (Cham: Springer, 2018), 497–522.

[46] Fry, *Design as Politics*, 22. This vision was crucial to Heidegger's later understandings of technology where the environment was positioned in terms of Gestell, or 'enframing', a source from which to draw on. See Martin Heidegger, *The Question Concerning Technology and Other Essays*, translated by William Lovitt (New York: Harper and Row, 1977), 3–34.

[47] As will be covered in Chapter 2, postphenomenology presents itself as an 'after' phenomenology, building on the tradition with a distinct perspective. For an early presentation see Don Ihde, *Technology and Lifeworld: From Garden to Earth* (Bloomington, IN: Indiana State University Press, 1990).

deriving from continental philosophy. Among other connections, both also trace lines to Heidegger's work. As with Fry, there is special reference to his perspective on technology. Indeed, postphenomenology, as the name suggests, has a foundational source in classical European phenomenology. Alongside this, building a direct bridge to OOO, there is also reference the work of Bruno Latour[48] and, more recently, to aspects of classical pragmatism, all of which will be covered below.

Both perspectives – OOO and postephenomenology – in their own way, open up ways of seeing design that allow for a surfacing of complex relationships. We are able to ask questions of how the things we design lead to specific actions and outcomes, ultimately affecting our experience and framing particular realities. Equally, through both, we can also examine how these things have an impact on the non-human world (e.g. on animal life or specific ecologies). Additionally, postphenomenology, through its focus on morality, opens up a robust ethical horizon for the discipline, whereby the desirability of specific technologies and their experiential impact can be questioned and appraised.[49]

While postphenomenologists such as Peter-Paul Verbeek have directly addressed design in their moral discussions,[50] it is perhaps the OOO-informed work of Bruno Latour that has had the most impact in the field through his ANT work noted above. As we will see, the perspectives of ANT have allowed for design theorists to formulate particular visions for how the design process might be understood as a wide-ranging, less human-centred activity, which carries deep social and political meanings.

---

[48] This comes through in Verbeek's work. Verbeek, *What Things Do*.

[49] See e.g. Verbeek, Peter-Paul. 'Materializing morality: Design ethics and technological mediation.' *Science, Technology, & Human Values* 31, no. 3 (2006): 361–80; Merlijn Smits, Geke Ludden, Ruben Peters, Sebastian J. H. Bredie, Harry Van Goor and Peter-Paul Verbeek. 'Values that matter: a new method to design and assess moral mediation of technology.' *Design Issues* 38, no. 1 (2022): 39–54.

[50] Verbeek, *What Things Do*.

Latour's direct discussions on design appear in his well-known 'Cautious Prometheus' paper.[51] Here, he questions what the concept of design has come to mean, how it can be best understood and how it can be seen to link to contemporary philosophical positions, focusing, in particular, on the work of Peter Sloterdijk as an example of a philosopher who can be understood to address the meaning of design in philosophical terms. Design is seen to work with what is (designers are always seen to *re*design and rarely, if ever, radically transform); to be inherently flexible; and also inherently ethical (i.e. there is good and bad design). Layering on top of this, for Latour, Sloterdijk's Heideggerian explorations of humanity's inherent 'thrownness'[52] within its material situation – i.e. that we cannot understand humanity without also attending to humanity's materiality – offers a compelling account of design's existential positioning. Here, we are to recognize that design always relies on design, on and on; we are always bound within it and on what has come before.

Reference to Sloterdijk here points to the existence of a wider European philosophy of technology tradition, which, as yet, has not attracted much attention from design theorists. Here, over the course of the twentieth century and into the twenty-first, contributors have reflected on the meaning of technology and creative practice in our lives. Alongside Sloterdijk, we can note the work of such philosophers as Vilém Flusser,[53] Günther

---

[51] Bruno Latour 'A cautious Prometheus? A few steps toward a philosophy of design (with special attention to Peter Sloterdijk)'. In *Networks of Design: Proceedings of the 2008 Annual International Conference of the Design History Society*, edited by Fiona Hackney, Jonathan Glynne and Viv Minton (London: Design History Society, 2009), 2–10.

[52] Thrownness is a key Heidegger concept presented in *Being and Time*. It refers to how we are always already here, within our situation. See Martin Heidegger, *Being and Time*, translated by Joan Stambaugh (Albany, NY: State University of New York Press, 2010 [1927]), 133.

[53] Of the listed authors, Flusser, known as philosopher of media, is the most direct in his handling of the subject of design. This, along with photography and writing, is given focused attention in dedicated texts. In relation to design, his key work in English is the posthumously published Vilém Flusser, *The Shape of Things: A Philosophy of Design* (London: Reaktion Books, 1999). Photography is handled in Vilém Flusser, *Towards a Philosophy of Photography* (London: Reaktion Books, 2000).

Anders,[54] Hans Jonas,[55] Bernard Stiegler,[56] Yuk Hui[57] and Byung-Chul Han.[58] As with the postphenomenological perspective, many of these contributors work to draw out our relations with the world that are shaped technologically or through design and the economic concerns that sit behind and alongside these domains. Some of this material places a particular emphasis on the ethical,[59] noting what needs to be done in order to address the challenges posed by modernity and the outworkings of our technologically mediated existence. Flusser, for note, is the most design-orientated of this grouping. His *The Shape of Things* offers an analysis of the discipline, tracing and surfacing the otherwise unarticulated meanings of common design terms and values and, from this, reflecting on design's wider role within human life. For Cameron Tonkinwise, this work can show 'designers and design students the philosophising that they are doing without knowing it'.[60]

Beyond such work, it is also worth drawing attention to the myriad diverse, sometimes tangential, but nonetheless valid references to design that have emerged in the field in recent

---

[54] For an overview see Babette Babich, *Günther Anders' Philosophy of Technology* (London: Bloomsbury, 2022).

[55] A compelling overview of Jonas's work contextualized in relation to principle of responsibility in a way that aligns with the present text is found in Lewis Coyne, *Hans Jonas: Life, Technology and the Horizons of Responsibility* (London: Bloomsbury, 2022).

[56] Stiegler traces the socio–political meanings of technological development and capitalistic economics, arguing for potential responses to the challenges faced. An overview of his work is available in Ross Abbinnett, *The Thought of Bernard Stiegler: Capitalism, Technology and the Politics of Spirit* (Abingdon, Oxon: Routledge, 2018).

[57] See e.g. Yuk Hui, *Art and Cosmotechnics* (Minneapolis: University of Minnesota Press, 2021).

[58] See, for example, Byung-Chul Han, *Psychopolitics: Neoliberalism and New Technologies of Power*, translated by Erik Butler (London: Verso, 2017), which explores the relationship between capitalism, technology and power.

[59] One of Jonas's key works is Hans Jonas, *The Imperative of Responsibility: In Search of Ethics for the Technological Age*, translated by Das Prinzip Verantwortung (Chicago: University of Chicago Press, 1984).

[60] Cameron Tonkinwise, 'Designing Philosophically: Review of Vilem Flusser, 'The Shape of Things: A Philosophy of Design', Design Philosophy Papers 1, no. 6 (2003), 368.

years. Perspectives here cover such topics as the relationship between drawing, form and design, as well as the meaning of these terms;[61] creativity as a method of inquiry;[62] and the question of what it means to be contemporary.[63] The feminist perspective of Sara Ahmed, in particular, stands as a compelling example of work that explores a concern – in this case, the idea of use – sitting at the centre of the current disciplinary structure.[64] Her inquiry traces the various meanings of use through such contexts as the use of things; the biological aspects of use; the relationship between technique and use; and the concept of queer use.

These voices take aspects of design, highlighting potential points of focus and positionalities that call our attention to the potentialities of the discipline's social and political meanings. The key challenge presented is that of the possibility of interrogation: the opportunity to take account of given ways of seeing and work through their possible implications such that we might begin to recognize and address that which is otherwise unrecognized and unaddressed.

Having set out the above, we will now move to consider how we link to philosophy here.

LINKING TO PHILOSOPHY HERE

The starting point for the vision of a philosophy through design set out in this book finds its source in the work of John Dewey and Jane Addams, two prolific twentieth-century classical pragmatist philosophers. Dewey was an academic philosopher who maintained close contact with the social and political concerns of his time,

---

[61] Jean-Luc Nancy, *The Pleasure in Drawing* (New York: Fordham University Press, 2013).
[62] Alva Noë, *Strange Tools: Art and Human Nature* (New York: Farrar, Straus and Giroux, 2016).
[63] Giorgio Agamben, *What is an apparatus? And other essays* (Redwood City: CA: Stanford University Press, 2009).
[64] Sara Ahmed, *What's the Use? On the uses of use* (Durham, NC: Duke University Press, 2019).

advocating for and campaigning on issues that he believed in. Addams, by contrast, was a social reformer who maintained close contact with the academy, lecturing and publishing regularly. Despite some differences, they had much in common, not least their commitment to making things better through a form of solution-seeking problem solving grounded in understanding and experimentation.

There are a number of key reasons for linking to their work in the context of a philosophy through design. First, as we will see, their work aligns strongly to design with a number of strong pre-existing connections already established within the discourse.[65] While focus tends to concentrate on Dewey, references to Addams's work now sit at the forefront of contemporary discussions in design practice and theory.[66] These alignments/connections allow for the drawing of a direct and immediate link between design and philosophy that can be progressed and expanded upon.

Second, leading on from this, there is the sheer breadth of their contributions. Dewey's work links up logic, metaphysics, social and political theory, ethics, as well as aesthetics and religious perspectives. Addams provides examples of profoundly impactful real-world engagement which allowed for special reflections on ethics and democracy, along with a multiplicity of social thematics. Combined, these allow for a wide outlook in relation to how a philosophy through design might attend to given issues.

Third, a values-led commitment to transformation and reform was key to both Dewey's and Addams's agendas. Dewey was unconventional in that he spent most of his long career arguing for change not only within his discipline but also beyond (e.g. in the US political system). While this took several guises over the years, the particular agenda that concerns us here is his vision for what he termed a 'reconstruction in philosophy', originally set out in the 1920s. It was here proposed that through practical, real-world experimentation, philosophy could act as a means of responding to the social and moral concerns of the present. As will be explored in the next chapter, I affirm that, despite its age,

---

[65] See e.g. Dixon, *Dewey and Design*.
[66] See e.g. DiSalvo, *Design as Democratic Inquiry*.

this vision of reconstruction still holds relevance today, particularly in relation to the framing of a philosophy through design. Next to this, Addams's work, along with the feminist pragmatists more generally, demonstrates that when it comes to change, positioning yourself on the ground in immediate relation to given challenges and opportunities not only opens up paths to transformation and reform but, if reflected upon and reported, can also allow for the framing of valuable philosophic perspectives.

By referencing their work here, I am ultimately framing this text in pragmatist terms, or, to be more particular, in *productive* pragmatist terms. That is to say, I see it as practically bound, as seeking to devise a means to respond to the challenges of the present and the issues we face. More than anything else, Dewey's and Addams's work promotes an experimental attitude and, within this, directs concerns towards the consequences of action as opposed to theoretical abstraction in and of itself. This is seen to provide the undergirding for a possible philosophy through design, making Dewey and Addams what I term 'proto designer philosophers' – that is, individuals whose lives and work provide a loose historical model for how a philosophy through design might be pursued and enacted.

Before moving on, it is important to note that this text is by no means limited to the perspectives of Dewey and Addams. Here, three key points are worth noting. First, I do not lift what Dewey and Addams say and expect it be applied as a direct guide. Their proposals and insights are highlighted so as to inform a much wider inquiry. Second and following on, design work, drawn mostly from research, is referenced throughout. In this referencing we will see how design concerns lead to questions and how questions are asked and answered practically in and through designing. These questions are seen to hold philosophical register, and as such the work can be understood to act as guide to the context of framing a philosophy through design. Third, as I move through the themes of the discussion – which will draw together the technological, the social and the ecological – I will reference many present-day philosophers working in areas such as postphenomenology and environmental ethics and beyond. This opens up productive links to contemporary discourse and, accordingly, offers a wider sense of the potential range of perspectives that might come to bear on any philosophy through design.

However, further discussion of this will have to wait until the next chapter. For now, as a final step within this Introduction, we will consider how design research involving practice might inform a philosophy through design.

A SPACE BEYOND DESIGN RESEARCH INVOLVING PRACTICE

The proposal that design practice might be enfolded in research first appeared in the 1990s, gaining strong currency through the 2000s. Here, as noted, some talk of 'research through design'[67], others of practice-based and practice-led[68] research. In mainland Europe, the term 'constructive design research'[69] is commonly used. Regardless of the term applied, early methodological discourse was largely directed towards the legitimization of the approach, i.e. arguing for its validity as a means of knowledge production. Alongside this, parallel discussions focused on the structuring of the method and whether or not design outcomes could be understood to function as standalone contributions to knowledge. Such concerns are now largely settled. The idea of design in research has gained legitimacy; individuals undertake practice-based/led doctorates, academics frame and deliver design-based research programmes and, increasingly, countries such as the UK, the Netherlands and many Scandinavian countries are beginning to integrate design as a key pillar with their national research agendas.[70] In relation to questions of method and outcomes,

---

[67] Christopher Frayling, 'Research in art and design.' *Royal College of Art Research Papers* 1 (1993): 1–5.

[68] Chris Rust, Judith Mottram and Jeremy Till, *Review of Practice-led Research in Art, Design and Architecture* (London: The Arts and Humanities Research Council: 2007).

[69] Koskinen et al., *Design Research Through Practice*.

[70] We can see this in the establishment of the UK's Design Observatory for example. See AHRC, 'Design Research', accessed 9 November 2024, https://www.ukri.org/what-we-do/browse-our-areas-of-investment-and-support/design-research/

design practice now stands as a wide horizon of methodological possibility, offering a spectrum ranging from a strong emphasis on creative practice through to blending of design activity within conventional research approaches.[71]

Across the board, there is now a willingness to accept the premise that the creative activities of design – the thinking, imagining, prototyping – can drive research; that in generating knowledge, *things* can be generated too; research can be more than description and explanation but also a process of making real what was not before, i.e. real*izing*.[72]

In so far as the approach can be given definition as a process, it is possible to note the following potential characteristics.

1. Design research involving practice will likely emerge from a specific motivational context. Here, an individual or group will be inspired to either respond to a real-world issue (such as the need to design a product for an otherwise neglected context) or, alternatively, a conceptual concern that would benefit from a practical exploration (e.g. a future-focused investigation of a particular technology such as generative AI).[73]
2. It will likely be based on contextual, creative experimentation. Experiments here may take a number of forms. They might function as a direct test of an idea (i.e. seeking to appraise whether x or y is possible). They might be open-ended and reflective (i.e. investigating whether a particular technique or

---

[71] Boudewijn Boon, Ehsan Baha, Abhigyan Singh, Frithjof E. Wegener, Marco C. Rozendaal and Pieter Jan Stappers, 'Grappling with diversity in research through design'. In *Synergy – DRS International Conference 2020, Volume 5: Situations*, edited by Stella Boess, Ming Cheung and Rebecca Cain (London: The Design Research Society 2020), 139–151.

[72] Koskinen et al. *Design Research Through Practice.*

[73] Anne Louise Bang and Mette Agger Eriksen, 'Experiments all the way in programmatic design research.' *Artifact: Journal of Design Practice* 3, no. 2 (2014): 4–11.

possibility can be realized in practice as driven by design). Either way, it is likely that things – artefacts, plans, proposals – will be developed, tested and evaluated iteratively in particular situations.[74]

3. This could be a collaborative process, whereby partners are involved in the creative activities through co-design or participatory design or, simply, the limited application of co-creative techniques. These partners might be community groups, organizations or experts from other disciplines. They might equally be individual citizens, who can provide particular insights that might not otherwise be available. Regardless of who is involved, the point would be that, to varying degrees, all would have an opportunity to creatively shape what emerges.

4. As has already been suggested, such work may be prospective or speculative in focus. A project may seek to look ahead to the possibilities of a point in time beyond the present as a means of either exploring what could be (that currently is not) or, alternatively, as with the generative AI example above, that latent or near-horizonal possibilities of existent technological capabilities be appraised and evaluated.

5. Research involving design practice is likely to result in a made artefact or other design-based outcome, such as plans or proposals. Though these designs may be seen to function as contributions to knowledge and practical responses to research question in their own right, there is general consensus that such objects will need to be accompanied by a text that explicitly qualifies the argument presented such that it can be understood both in relation to its overall claims

---

[74] There is an important qualifier here in relation to the idea of testing in 'particular situations'. It is possible that tests of particular design outcomes might take place in decontextualized lab-based settings, with statistical data being captured as a means of testing and evaluating these outcomes.

(i.e. what the final conclusions are) as well as how these claims were reached. In this text, I will refer to these aspects as the criteria of communicability (i.e. that there is clarity of the final claims) and retraceability[75] (i.e. that the means by which these claims were reached can be retraced, as a step-by-step process).[76]

6. It is unlikely that design research involving practice will result in anything approximating generalizable conclusions, i.e. findings that can be characterized as universal laws or seen to represent an objective truth. Though there are often clearly defined epistemological reasons underlying this, the non-generalizability of the work can be linked to two

---

[75] These criteria are proposed here as possible criteria for design research involving practice. This proposal relates to (and extends into) the transferability discussion offered in a point below. The underpinning concepts loosely align to the concepts present in the criteria of credibility and confirmability as discussed in Yvonna Lincoln and Egon Guba, *Naturalistic Inquiry* (London: Sage, 1985), where the pair discuss the evaluations of qualitative research in particular and specifically focus on how these diverge from standard scientific evaluations of quality. Credibility is alignable to my communicability, in so far as it is said to relate to whether the argument is seen to hold internal validity. In qualitative research this often requires a triangulation of methods (i.e. seeking multiple sources of data in order to reach a conclusion). In design research, however, this may not always be possible and a case for the reasonableness and quality of the argument may need to be made. Confirmability relates to checking for whether independent data analysis (by another researcher) results in similar conclusions being reached. Retraceablity functions in a similar way but relates to the representation of the process as a whole and not just the collection and analysis of the data.

[76] A useful study of possible quality frameworks in 'research through design' is available from Isabel Prochner and Danny Godin, 'Quality in research through design projects: Recommendations for evaluation and enhancement.' *Design Studies* 78 (2022): 101061. An initial discussion of a dedicated approach here is offered in John Zimmerman, Erik Stolterman and Jodi Forlizzi, 'An analysis and critique of Research through Design: Towards a formalization of a research approach.' In *Proceedings of the 8th ACM Conference on Designing Interactive Systems* (2010), pp. 310–19.

key factors that will likely be characteristics of the research. First, participant numbers are often low compared with the sample sizes of science. As such, it will not be possible to develop statistical overviews of how given populations will act/interact or how phenomena will occur. Second and related, given that projects are generally undertaken in specific contexts, the conclusions are mapped to the given space and time, when particular conditions applied. These may or may not relate to the conditions that will prevail in another space and time.

7. Following from the latter point, the research will often aim to meet the criterion of *transferability* rather than generalizability. In this text, this is seen to rely on criteria of communicability and retraceablity noted above relating to the presentation of the research claims and how these claims were arrived at. For a project to be transferable, its claims and process will be sufficiently well articulated that others might seek to reapply the process elsewhere, in another context, in order to appraise whether the same results emerge.[77]

8. The results of design research involving practice diverge from the norms of conventional knowledge production (in, for example, the social sciences) in that it not only investigates what is but also what could be and, in this, often demonstrates the thing that could be. A project, therefore, often not only results in new knowledge but also ontological transformation, i.e. something which did not exist now does. As a straightforward example, researchers might develop a product with a novel functionality

---

[77] A discussion of transferability can be found in Dixon, *Dewey and Design*, 179. A contexualization of this in a wider discussion of quality criteria for 'research through design' can be found in Prochner and Godin, 'Quality in research through design projects.'

and test this, noting the situational dynamics that result from its use. Insights here might relate to both the value of the technological capabilities as well as to the new experiential horizons these allow for and, as such, the new reality that opens up in relation to them.[78]

Following on from the above, though design research involving practice is positioned exclusively as a form of knowledge production – i.e. a research approach that may be applied in the process of generating novel disciplinary and interdisciplinary insights – it can, at times, function as more than that. One may note a highlighting of concerns and interests that extend beyond the purely disciplinary, veering into, for example, a questioning of social or technological meanings and values[79] and even ethics.[80] These are areas that traditionally one might consider the domain of philosophy. This focus might be attributable to the tendency of designer researchers to work directly in specific contexts, engaging with real people living in real places on real projects. In such circumstances it is perhaps unsurprising that wider concerns such as the ethical aspects of given objects or processes creep into the frame as core motivational concerns.

To illustrate this, we might turn to the work of Anne Louise Bang and colleagues. Through the mid-2010s, Bang and others including Peter Krogh, Martin Ludvigsen and Thomas Markussen undertook extensive reflections on the structure and contexts

---

[78] With regard to design and knowledge production, this proposal is put forward in Dixon, *Dewey and Design* and Dixon, *Design, Philosophy and Making Things Happen*. The proposal also relates to an emergent conceptualisation of design practice as having the capacity to shape existence through the creation of new things/experiences, which is referred to as ontological design; see Willis, 'Ontological designing.'. This latter idea is covered in Chapter 2.

[79] See e.g. Dalsgaard, Peter. 'Pragmatism and Design Thinking.' *International Journal of Design* 8, no. 1 (2014), 143–55.

[80] Philip Ross, 'Ethics and aesthetics in intelligent product and system design.' PhD diss. (Eindhoven: University of Technology Eindhoven, 2008).

of design experiments.[81] Within this, they paid special attention to the typology of underlying motivations. Referring to specific project examples, they identified a number of complex motivational interweavings which it is possible to characterize as veering towards the philosophical.[82] These included:

- 'An ethical approach combined with a practice-based and artistically inclined approach'
  This motivational context is demonstrated with reference to Otto Von Busch's dissertation, 'Fashion-able. Hacktivism and engaged fashion design',[83] which, through a philosophical framing, is said to ask ethical questions of the 'passivity and disengagement of users or recipients of high-fashion products' and seeks to address this through 'explorations of what it could take to reformat the relationship between consumer, product, and industry'.
- 'An ethical approach combined with a technologically provoked approach'
  The work drawn on here is Philip Ross's dissertation 'Ethics and aesthetics in intelligent product and system design',[84] which questions the apparent value-neutrality of new technology through a focus on what it means to embed 'modes of conduct in products'.
- 'An ethical approach combined with a political approach'
  This example relates to Ambra Trotto's dissertation, 'Rights through making',[85] on the potential of making

---

[81] Anne Louise Bang, Peter Krogh, Martin Ludvigsen and Thomas Markussen, 'The Role of Hypothesis in Constructive Design Research.' Paper presented at *the 4th The Art of Research: Making, Reflecting and Understanding*, Aalto University School of Arts, Design and Architecture, Helsinki, Finland, 28–29 Nov 2012.
[82] Ibid, 8.
[83] Otto von Busch, 'Fashion-able. Hacktivism and engaged fashion design.' PhD diss. (Gothenburg: University of Gothenburg, 2008).
[84] Ross, 'Ethics and aesthetics in intelligent product and system design.'
[85] Ambra Trotto, 'Rights Through Making.' PhD diss. (Eindhoven: Eindhoven University of Technology, 2011).

processes to revitalize human rights. Here, through workshops, designers were asked to 'articulate human rights concerns and ideals' that can be applied in everyday decision making.

While philosophical concerns may be at play in design research involving practice, as in these examples, it must be noted that, intriguingly, the general approach does not, as a matter of course, hold any fixed philosophical bearings. No one specific philosophy or orientation is identified as *the* methodological alignment. Each researcher or group of researchers must inscribe their own path, find their own way. This is demonstrated by the necessarily broad reach of the literature on the subject. For example, design theorist Ilpo Koskinen has spoken of there being three core methodologies within practice-based research (relating to science, sociology and the arts)[86] and four epistemological traditions within design more generally.[87] On the positive side, one might describe this situation as representing a flexible, open-ended plurality, whereby the discipline is seen to allow for correspondence, exchange and interdisciplinarity. On the negative side, one might equally argue that the field is trapped in a 'methodological mire'[88] wherein it is difficult to identify which alignments might be preferable and what the benefits of a specific selection might be.

Leaning towards a positive view, it is perhaps through its flexibility and open-ended plurality that design research involving practice holds the potential to function as more than knowledge production, to become more than a means of simple data collection and analysis. This is the thread from which we will explore the possibilities of framing a philosophy through design.

As will likely be apparent from the above, the framing that will emerge here will centre upon design*ing*, a 'doing' founded

---

[86] Ilpo Koskinen et al., *Design Research Through Practice*.
[87] Ilpo Koskinen and Peter Gall Krogh, *Drifting by Intention: Four Epistemic Traditions from within Constructive Design Research* (Cham: Springer, 2020).
[88] Ben Matthews and Margot Brereton, 'Navigating the Methodological Mire: Practical Epistemology in Design Research'. In *The Routledge Companion to Design Research*, edited by Paul A. Rodgers and Joyce Yee (Abingdon, Oxon: Routledge, 2015) 151–62.

in experience. Though I reference design research involving practice, I am not promoting 'research' as such but, rather, a philosophical responding to real-world social and moral concerns in and through practice.

What would this look like?

In so far as an outline can be offered here in advance of engaging with the work of Dewey, Addams or other perspectives from philosophy, design or elsewhere, the following can be said.

The starting point for a philosophy through design project would be felt situational concerns or points of intrigue which encourage further reflection – in other words, things we see as problematic and deserving of our attention and focus. These elements would not just be concerning or intriguing in direct terms (i.e. noting that something is broken or seeing a particularly striking colour) but rather they would be troublesome or in some way especially compelling and complex. We would have an urge to better understand, to work through both practically and reflectively.

It might be a matter of speculating on the potential of a particular technology (our generative AI example) or a trying-to-understand how a present situation can be improved upon, ameliorated. The aim would be to formulate viable questions – these would likely be questions about meaning, value and/or ethical matters – and, through design, progressively experiment with possible responses. In doing so, as has been noted, one would reference the approach of design research involving practice. However, as this is philosophy, there would not be an expectation that this would involve formal data collection as a foundational activity. For example, it is unlikely that one's focus would be directed to interviews or the framing of any statistical analysis. The process as envisaged would centre on design, on action and reflection, doing and thought. It is possible that there would be reference to existing insights, whether philosophical or disciplinary; these might inform and thread through the practice, but attention would remain on the situation and its transformation. One would act and work through the overall outcomes of action reflectively, whether textually and/or visually – whatever modalities are preferred – and then act and reflect again.

When eventually, through design, one arrives at what is deemed to function as a useful answer, it becomes possible to confirm an endpoint. This might be a well-realized speculation into the potential of a technology under scrutiny or a robust set of insights into a problematic situation and how it can be improved upon/ameliorated. Either way the outcome must map to or, alternatively, be returned to and tested in its original situation. This will demonstrate its viability, the meaningfulness of the answer it provides. It is important to note that this would not and could not be an answer for all time but rather would function as an answer for *now*, a working through of the concern or intrigue. As with design research involving practice, what emerges would need to be represented in an accessible way. This would involve text, a communication of what has been achieved, and depending on the answer arrived at, it might also involve made artefacts, plans or proposals. The whole of what is presented would function as an argument, a position that is put forward in relation to a situation, which may or may not have bearings on other similar or, indeed, dissimilar situations.

This is a different form of philosophy from the one we have come to know through the twentieth and twenty-first centuries. It is, in essence, a novel framing of an approach that relates to the discipline of philosophy but functions as a materially bound artful dialogue with the world, a deliberate forward and back in the asking and answering of a question and demonstration of an answer. As we will see, this links, to a degree, to past philosophic positions and approaches (i.e. that of Dewey, Addams and other pragmatists) but, equally, strikes out and sketches a novel vista. What is novel is the explicit drawing in of design and, from this, the commitment to direct situational change: a response, in context.

Through the remainder of this text will I aim to progressively trace this out.

THE STRUCTURE OF THIS BOOK

Taking the first steps towards giving form to a philosophy through design, the next chapter will open up with a deeper discussion on philosophy. It will first consider the work of John Dewey, looking in particular at his 1920s proposals regarding a reconstruction in philosophy. Next to this, we will look to the work of the feminist pragmatists such as Jane Addams, who, through their socially engaged work in inner-city Chicago, demonstrated an absolute commitment to contextual engagement, i.e. living and working within the situations they sought to change through participative action. The chapter will round out with a consideration of how these threads, i.e. Dewey's reconstruction proposals and the feminist pragmatist work, align with the concerns of philosophy today. Here, we note a brewing disciplinary malaise within philosophy and highlight how a 'philosophy through design' might be framed via a coupling of Dewey–Addams's work to the needs of design.

From here, the following three chapters will give form to this approach by sequentially exploring how insights can be drawn out in relation to our three key areas of focus: technology, the social, and the ecological. Within each chapter, the frame of reference will switch back and forth between philosophy and design, design and philosophy; equally, links drawn between both domains in the form of concluding points that trace the contours of a philosophy through design.

To begin, then, Chapter 2 turns attention to technology. To open, a brief overview of Dewey's and Addams's technological perspectives will be offered. From here, we will examine how particular philosophies of technology – in the form of postphenomenology, pragmatism, Marxism and increasingly feminism – have, to varying degrees, already gained recognition and become established within design. This leads into examples of what might be characterized as philosophy through design work, currently being undertaken at the University of Technology Eindhoven and Simon Fraser University. Thereafter, the possible meaning of these philosophies/examples for a philosophy through design will be considered directly, with focus being directed on the way that when related to technology, design appears to open up a space in which we can consider human experience anew.

Building upon these threads, Chapter 3 will consider the social horizon directly. Focus will initially turn to the work of

Dewey and Addams here and, from this, to the above-noted social aspects of design, with reference being made to the processes of designing with others and design for social contexts. Linking to the last chapter, attention will also be directed towards Bruno Latour's actor network theory, a perspective aligned to science and technology studies, which can be seen to bridge philosophy, technology and social theory. This leads into an overview of communication and culture as additional threads, which hold relevance here. Issues of decolonializing design will be picked up at this point. Broadly, the chapter will aim to give form to a basic strategy that allows for a flexible way of approaching social concerns in a philosophy through design, noting general problems at the same time as being able to mount specific responses.

In Chapter 4, we turn away from singularly human concerns and consider what is perhaps the most critical horizon within this discussion: the ecological. This thematic draws broad-based existential questions into focus, wherein not only is the future of humanity at stake but, equally, the future of planetary life itself. The chapter thus functions as an urgent call for action.

It opens with a brief overview of pragmatism's treatment of the ecological before moving to sketch out design's expanding ecological agenda. Here, particular attention is paid to the ways in which design, both practically and theoretically, has sought to respond to growing ecological concerns. It is noted that there is some way to go before design can claim a properly ecological positioning. Following on, a case study considers the work of Kristina Linström and Åsa Ståhl, which explores design in the context of the climate crisis. This is then followed by a brief consideration of some key ecological perspectives in philosophy, linking some conventional and lesser-known perspectives. An exploration of the area of ecofeminist design is offered. Lastly, by way of close, the two strands of design and philosophy are drawn together. In this, we will trace a more robust ecological positioning for design based on ecological ways of seeing, which, it is proposed, can give rise to ecological ways of being.

Finally, to close, in Chapter 5 we group the insights of the earlier chapters to set out the structure of a possible philosophy through design. This amounts to a process-based overview of how such forms of inquiry might commence, progress and finally conclude. Next to this, the characteristics of new a figure – the designer philosopher – will be profiled. From here, we will look at some areas for further consideration, including how connections might be drawn between what has been set out and perspectives that extend beyond the Euro-American Global North. Finally, to close, a general case will be made for the overarching value of a philosophy through design, looking not only at its possible impact for the field of design and its stakeholders, but also its potential to support developments in philosophy itself.

1 Connecting Design and Philosophy through Dewey and Addams

Having set out the present challenge for design in the last chapter, with its intensive, expanding range of responsibilities, this chapter will function as a first step in the process of giving form to a philosophy through design linked to a design research involving practice approach.

At the outset, it must be acknowledged that a philosophy through design could take many forms – there is no one form, no essential way being proposed here. I have, of course, noted design's and philosophy's ways of coming together through the philosophy of design and design philosophy, philosophically informed design work such as critical design, and through the areas of object-orientated ontology and postphenomenology. This is where design research involving practice was highlighted as a possible fourth category of connection but, as has been noted, this particular form of research is inherently pluralist, almost explicitly (if not quite) embracing philosophical non-alignment.

Thus, in moving out from a design research involving practice perspective, we have options when drawing on philosophy – there is no one way that this might be done. In beginning to propose a specific strategy here, I turn (as I have before)[1] to the work of

---

[1] Brian Dixon, 'Constructing a Reconstructed Philosophy: A Deweyan Philosophy-Through-Design.' *Design Issues* 39, no. 4 (2023): 77–88.

the twentieth-century American philosopher John Dewey, but also look beyond him to his contemporaries, the feminist pragmatists, who include the famous Chicago social reformer Jane Addams among their ranks. I will not only draw on Dewey and Addams, however. The philosophy through design I seek to give form to goes further. There is, of course, the need to consider contemporary voices in philosophy and other feminist perspectives, as well as point to non-Western perspectives.[2] These will be offered gradually, in stages, as we progress through the text.

To start the progression, I will first offer a brief rationale for why Dewey and Addams (along with the feminist pragmatists generally) have been selected as key reference points. The general contributions of Dewey, Addams and the feminist pragmatists are then discussed. From, here, the following section will consider how these positions align to the problems and disaffections of both historic and present-day philosophy, something which is both relevant and useful when considering a philosophy through design. Then, closing this chapter and looping back to the previous, a brief, final section will note the alignments that can be drawn between Dewey, Addams and the feminist pragmatists, contemporary philosophic concerns, and design and design research involving practice. Taken together, this will set us on a path to sketching a philosophy through design through the remainder of the book via technology, the social and ecological domains. For now, however, we turn to the question of why Dewey and Addams.

WHY DEWEY AND ADDAMS? THE PROTO-DESIGNER PHILOSOPHERS

If we leave Jane Addams aside for a moment, opening with a reference to John Dewey (1859–1952), a white, male, North

---

[2] The verb point is used here as I am working outwards from my own cultural starting position as both an Irish and a Canadian citizen, who has lived exclusively in anglophone countries.

American philosopher of the late nineteenth and early twentieth centuries, may seem an odd place from which to begin to map a potential philosophy through design for the twenty-first century. Decolonizing is now a key agenda not only for design but for almost all disciplines. Equally, just as in any field of study or practice, there is a need to ensure that wherever possible non-male voices are given equal presence and weighting. Yes, there are the feminist pragmatists and Addams, but how will one ensure that a superficial linking is avoided here?

These concerns are not to be ignored. Though my orientation is Western (I am white, male and European, after all), I recognize and fully acknowledge the profound need to drive for greater plurality in our discourse; the wider the range of perspectives and voices, the stronger the field. This is an imperative for our age.

Following on, the key point I must make here is that Dewey's and Addams's philosophy, pragmatism – which we explore as we advance through the text – allows for this, offering a perspective that not only embraces diversity but also one which can accommodate difference and alternative perspectives. As we shall see, this is because it is democratic in spirit. The point is to open up communication and, in this, to experiment. Accordingly, the present text is positioned as the beginning of a conversation and process of trial and error, testing the possibilities of envisaging and revisioning.

With regard to the non-male voice, our turn to Jane Addams and the feminist pragmatists will not be a for-the-sake-of-it, one-off referencing but a positive opening up aimed at rebalancing design's understanding of pragmatism. In the end, the insights that emerge will not just inform our eventual philosophy through design proposals but frame them in way that extends beyond anything Dewey's perspective alone could allow. It is important for designers and design theorists to realize that Addams and Dewey are not easily separated. To know the work of one without the other is to lack significant contextual understanding. Their intellectual and activist work entangles in multiple ways and careful scholarship positions Addams's work (theoretical and practical) as a key source for Dewey's own theories.[3]

Equally, we are not restricting ourselves to simply the feminist pragmatists; many other non-male philosophers and designers will be drawn upon in the following chapters. This not only includes other feminist perspectives but also the more-than-human perspective, where non-human life and being is considered alongside the human.

The key reason for turning initially to Dewey relates to his call for a reconstruction in philosophy – one which, as will be discussed, proposed a new approach and direction in the field. The proposal was ultimately unsuccessful; philosophy was not reconstructed in the way proposed. Nonetheless, I will suggest that it still bears relevance today, arguably for philosophy but, with regard to our present concerns, more especially for design as it seeks to mobilize in relation to challenges (and opportunities) of the twenty-first century.

In the end, both individuals (along with many of their contemporaries) offer us a glimpse of how prototypic designer philosophers – the figure we will eventually scope at the end of the text – might position themselves. They do this through the examples they both provide as individuals who, though philosophical active in the conventional sense (e.g. they regularly published philosophical works), also explored their concerns directly in the socio-political realities of their time. Addams stands as the clearest example of this – through her Hull House settlement initiative, discussed below, she engaged in city-wide social reform projects, as well as getting involved in national political campaigns.[4]

---

[3] These links will be surfaced as we proceed, but the crucial point to make here is that Addams appears to have inspired Dewey's key democratic ideas – that is, democracy is firstly communal. It is founded on how we act and interact as social beings and how, within this, we envisage and decision a collective future. See Chapter 3.

[4] Addams was an avowed pacificist and campaigned in relation to this. She was awarded the 1931 Nobel Peace prize. Elizabeth N. Agnew, 'A will to peace: Jane Addams, World War I, and 'pacifism in practice."' *Peace & Change* 42, no. 1 (2017): 5–31.

Her efforts also enabled dozens, if not hundreds, of other individuals to do similarly, building a community of practice that was not only action-orientated but also deeply intellectual (i.e. there was a clarity of purpose and process attached to the work being undertaken).

While Dewey was most certainly a conventional philosopher in so far as he was a working academic attached to university philosophy department, he also regularly forged relationships beyond academia and was politically active throughout his life. His work also crossed over into the civic realm, particularly when he oversaw an experimental elementary school at the University of Chicago. Here, he investigated the direct application of specific teaching models and, in doing so, developing globally impactful pedagogic philosophy and theory.[5]

Thus, Dewey's and Addams's was a living philosophy – one that took form in practice, looping back and forth between action, thought and insight. The philosophy they offer was based on abstract argument alone but argument forged through real-world reflection, where things had been experienced, were tried and tested, had failed or succeeded, progressed or did not. Their work is also long-term; it built up literally over a lifetime and would simply not be possible to deliver ready-made.

In saying all of this, it is important to point out that neither Dewey nor Addams (and their pragmatist contemporaries) are positioned as perfect and without failings. Their work is not beyond criticism or freed from any need for revision and adaption. There are the decolonial and feminist concerns already highlighted above, but there are also areas of their thought that, from our current standpoint, can be progressed and built upon, knowing what we know now both historically – a hundred years of history have passed, after all – and critically, with wholly new branches of philosophy having opened up through this period.

---

[5] Laurel Tanner, *Dewey's Laboratory School: Lessons for Today* (New York: Teachers College Press, Columbia University, 1997); Michael Knoll, *John Dewey's Laboratory School: The Rise and Fall of a World-Famous Experiment* (London: Palgrave Macmillan, 2024).

The philosophy through design that I eventually outline will thus link to their thought and the example they offer but will also move beyond it. In terms of linking, I take Dewey's reconstruction proposals and Addams's approach to situated, participative inquiry seriously; I also draw on their ethical approaches. In terms of moving beyond them, by linking to both design research and other philosophic voices, I will map several paths (plural) by which we might formulate a design-based response to the challenges we, in the twenty-first century, collectively face – that is, a general approach to philosophy through design that enfolds connections to the technological, the social and the ecological allowing for movement in, across, around and beyond.

Further details will follow as we progress. For now, we will turn to look at Dewey and Addams directly.

A DEWEYAN STARTING POINT

John Dewey stands as one of the twentieth century's most prolific philosophers, having made profound contributions in areas such as education and democracy as well as logic, ethics, social theory, art and religion. The broad sweep of Dewey's work can be attributed at least partly to the fact that he operated at a time when philosophic, along with disciplinary boundaries more generally, were not as sharply defined as today. Indeed, during the early phase of his career, it was possible for Dewey to engage with subject matter we would today characterize as fitting within highly specialized domains beyond philosophy, whether pedagogy, psychology or political science.

However, despite this apparent broadness, he was not unthinking in drawing together his interests. Underpinning his work was a special systematic perspective centring on a novel experiential understanding of logic that he based on the insights of William James and Charles Sanders Peirce, often identified as the founders of pragmatism.[6] This perspective amounted a human-level

---

[6] Ralph Sleeper, *The Necessity of Pragmatism: John Dewey's Conception of Philosophy* (New Haven, CT: Yale University Press, 1986).

understanding of experimentation or, more specifically, 'inquiry'. In it, through what was termed 'a pattern of inquiry', humans are seen to move from a doubtful situation to one that is resolved via identifying the problem, envisioning a possible solution and iteratively testing this solution until an evidencable conclusion has been reached. By highlighting such an approach in the context of philosophy in particular (as opposed to inquiry generally), Dewey is essentially playing traditional philosophy's abstraction off against the empirical accountability of science and research strategies more generally. Ultimately, through this experiential perspective, he was able to bring his theories together. We – humanity – are ultimately seen as creative beings who inquire (informally and, at times, formally) in all areas of life, whether in education, politics, ethics, broader social contexts, art or religion, moving from doubt to resolution(s), doubt to resolution(s), on and on in cycle.[7]

Dewey made a first attempt to capture the wider meaning of this developmental arc – his pattern and the many appending theories/areas of interest – in *A Reconstruction in Philosophy*,[8] a book that was published during an overseas visit to east Asia in the early 1920s. In it, Dewey calls for a fundamental, first-principles shift in philosophy's ultimate aims. Here, rather than focus on the progression of specifically disciplinary concerns (i.e. the problems of philosophers), the field would become a means of problem solving in the context of widely held social and moral concerns. As often happened, Dewey pointed to the method he referred to as 'intelligent action' as the means by which such a philosophic programme could progress. For him, intelligent action was to be understood in terms of well-framed

---

[7] It is worth noting here that the pattern is already well established as a reference point within design, aligning well with ideas of design and how inquiry works in this context, where the viability of a concept is explored iteratively through experimentation; see Brian Dixon, 'Experiments in Experience: Towards an Alignment of Research through Design and John Dewey's Pragmatism.' *Design Issues* 35, no. 2 (2019): 5–16.

[8] Dewey, John, *The Middle Works, 1899–1924, Volume 12: 1920, Essays, Miscellany, and A Reconstruction in Philosophy*, edited by Jo Ann Boydston (Carbondale, IL: Southern Illinois University Press, 1982 [2008]).

experimentation, grounded in the logic of experience – his pattern of inquiry undertaken with rigour. One was to address a problem in context with a willingness to iterate through successive cycles of trial and error such that eventually one arrives at a desired result, even if there are several intermediate moments of failure.

Moving beyond *A Reconstruction*, Dewey continued to advance this vision through the remainder of the 1920s. It is arguable that this can be linked to his east Asian experience.[9] Certainly, there was a shift in his outlook. Writing to a friend, he remarked: 'Nothing western looks quite the same anymore, and this is as near a renewal of youth as can be hoped for in this world.'[10]

1925's *Experience and Nature*[11] goes some way to demonstrating the meaning of this for his work. Here we encounter a bolder, wider, more consolidated vision. Indeed, many see the text as *the* definitive work of his career. As with *A Reconstruction*, the guiding proposal is again that philosophy might operate as a form of direct experimentation – what is here referred to as the denotative method – where questions would be directly addressed in active inquiry.

The first chapter of the text, which was originally entitled 'Experience and Philosophical Method', is dedicated to outlining the characteristics and meaning of the experimental aspect or denotative method. At its core, the chapter functions as a plea that philosophers acknowledge the need to work with and in a broadly defined 'experience'. While this includes the notion of

---

[9] While it is difficult to appraise the extent to which this can be attributed to his Asia visit, there does appear to have been an impact. In attempting to characterize the change, it is possible to claim that post-Asia, he developed a bolder and more wide-ranging agenda, but equally, and importantly, it began to consolidate, with many strands being drawn together. A comparison of the vagueness of *A Reconstruction* and the surety of *Experience and Nature* goes some way to demonstrating this.

[10] John Dewey to John J. Coss, 22 April 1920. Quoted in George Dykhuizen, *The Life and Mind of John Dewey* (Carbondale, IL: Southern Illinois University Press, 1973), 205.

[11] John Dewey, *The Later Works, 1925–1953, Volume 1: 1925, Experience and Nature*, edited by Jo Ann Boydston (Carbondale, IL: Southern Illinois University Press, 2008 [1981]).

'experiencing' (i.e. matters of passive perception such as seeing light or colour), focus is also directed outwards to the role of the person within the wider environment, as well as the intricacies of the social and cultural realities in which individuals reside; experience is here all that is in and of the world, whether feelings, things, or what we as beings with agency *do*, especially collectively. As Dewey puts it, it is 'the whole wide universe of fact and dream, of event, act, desire, fancy and meanings, valid or invalid'.[12]

Working within this unending context, the denotative method would amount to a form of 'pointing'. Things – whether facts, dreams, events, acts, desires, fancies or meanings – would be noticed, identified and thereafter act as the material by which philosophic inquiry would proceed. Inquiry in this regard would still be a matter of reflection, of working through in thought, problems and possibilities. However, it would be distinct from traditional forms of argumentation in that it would, by necessity be ill-formed and undefined at the outset. Experience in all its disclarity would both set and shape direction. The working through of an outcome would, by necessity, involve a return to experience, wherein ideas would be tested. Here, the methods and products of philosophy can be 'traced back their origin' and equally 'conclusions [would also] be brought to the things of ordinary experience, in all its coarseness and crudity, for verification'.[13] This is not about truth, however. Dewey's pragmatism is keen to avoid this idea; instead favouring the idea of evidence and persuasion.[14] We share our findings and have them confirmed or not. Accordingly, thereafter, there would be a reporting of the process and its conclusions. This would provide 'a map of the road that has been travelled', which others could 'retravel' to 'inspect for themselves'.[15]

---

[12] Dewey, *The Later Works, 1925–1953, Volume 1 1925, Experience and Nature*, 371.

[13] Ibid, 39.

[14] Dewey suggested concepts such as knowledge and belief might be replaced by the idea of warranted assertability. See John Dewey, *The Later Works, 1925–1953, Volume 12: 1938, Logic: The Theory of Inquiry*, edited by Jo Ann Boydston (Carbondale, IL: Southern Illinois University Press. 2008 [1986]), 15.

[15] Dewey, *The Later Works, 1925–1953, Volume 1*, 389.

Summing the method up, Dewey writes that through experience as method is that 'to settle any discussion, to still any doubt, to answer any question, we must go to some thing pointed to, denoted and find our answer in that thing'. In short, '*denotation* comes first and last'.[16]

Beyond the denotative method, there is also a second, broader and more significant proposal set out in *Experience and Nature*. Here, Dewey can be seen to be drawing out a far-reaching statement regarding questions of reality and existence – traditionally referred to by philosophers as metaphysical questions. To this end, the text also offers a sprawling account of what it means to be in the world, move within its currents and thrive. Chapter by chapter, Dewey works through a series of reflections on areas such as patterns within experience, experience more broadly, and the means by which one can come to better appreciate the complexities of being. Key themes include nature, the body, communication, language, art, science, knowledge and philosophy itself.

As a key general positioning in relation to these themes, Dewey draws the areas of language, communicating and acting all into alignment in relation to the shaping of reality, on the basis that how the reality is understood is itself an aspect of reality. For him, language is the 'naturalistic link between experience and nature'.[17] Here, our reality is contained within the meaning things carry for us, what we, together, say, think and do in relation these meaning.[18] New ideas, new meanings, new things give rise to new realities.[19] This is an especially compelling proposition in the context of design.[20]

Leading on from this, with philosophy, he is again looking to reconstruct or, at the very least, reform his primary discipline. Indeed, he works to extend *A Reconstruction*'s proposals by

---

[16] Ibid, 372.

[17] Ibid, 7.

[18] Ibid, 147.

[19] Sleeper, *The Necessity of Pragmatism*, offers a comprehensive overview of this perspective on Dewey's work and how it links together across his theories.

[20] This is outlined in Dixon, *Dewey and Design*.

scoping an additional, more expansive future role for the field. Here, beyond attending to social and moral problems, philosophy would come to function as an interdisciplinary organ, opening up communication across fields that would otherwise not enter into communication. Philosophy would in essence become a messenger.[21]

The ultimate aim of such a philosophy would be cultivating a form of wisdom that is guided by the evidence of the disciplines being drawn together in concert, a focusing on what we know and what this means. To enable this, philosophy would act as a form of criticism, supporting communication and sharing between disciplines, with all their various languages. As various findings were gradually consolidated and integrated over time, it would become possible to identify what Dewey referred to as the generic traits of existence,[22] the core elements that make experience what it is. Equally, and more importantly, he also suggested that, through this process, it would be possible to identify how and in what ways 'goods' could be created and sustained. This latter aspect of the proposal is important in that it pushes disciplinary agendas beyond the mere reporting of 'insights' into a space where the value of those insights are to be considered and curated within a wider system concerned with general well-being and welfare. Taken as a whole, this return-to-wisdom[23] vision for philosophy positions the field as an ongoing conversation on the search for the good life as set against the findings of robust inquiry; it is not only a conversation about what is good, but also how we can attain it.[24]

---

[21] Dewey, *Experience and Nature*, 306.

[22] Ibid, 388

[23] Philosophy literally means 'love of wisdom' and historically – in the ancient world at least – its purpose would have been directed towards identifying the key principles that might best guide human conduct and decision making. See James A. Harold, *An Introduction to the Love of Wisdom: An Essential and Existential Approach to Philosophy* (Oxford: University Press of America, 2004).

[24] The proposals of *Experience and Nature* were again built upon in *A Quest for Certainty*, a final noteworthy text from the 1920s, originally delivered as the Gifford Lectures in Edinburgh in 1928. Its focus was directed towards

Across all of these works, we can understand Dewey as both calling for a reconstruction in philosophy while also seeking to give it form. While his proposals may sound more or less compelling in and of themselves, the question arises as to what they mean practically for a philosophy through design and whether the concerns and ideas can offer any meaningful insights for philosophy today. This is something we will pick up later in the chapter. Equally, before moving on, it is important to also to note how a non-Western link is drawn in Dewey's work via his east Asian experience – a point that will be noted again at the end of the text.

From the above, we will now turn to consider the work of the feminist pragmatists, contemporaries of Dewey, who provide a strong exemplar of how philosophy can respond directly to social and moral concerns.

ADDAMS AND THE FEMINIST PRAGMATISTS

Pragmatism has traditionally been positioned as a male-dominated movement, driven by a relatively small group of academic philosophers, active from the mid-nineteenth to the mid-twentieth century. Most often, the names of Charles Sanders Peirce, William James, John Dewey and George Herbert Mead are drawn together as its core figures. Peirce is said to have founded the movement,

> the general character of knowledge, with the call for a more generous action-orientated understanding of what it meant to come to know and understand. Again, Dewey considers philosophy's role and function within this. If it was to have a future, it would need to move past its historic agenda of claiming access to an absolute sense of the certain and definite, to act as the guarantor of knowledge, something more than science. As with *Experience and Nature*, he suggested, it would, instead, become a form of criticism, a discipline allowing for interdisciplinary communication and the identifying 'goods' or value. This time, however, it was not just about communication, value or hosting a conversation on the goods/values, but also about identifying the *use* that knowledge should be put to, exploring how problems might be addressed. John Dewey, *The Later Works, 1925–1953, Volume 4: 1929, The Quest for Certainty*. Edited by Jo Ann Boydston (Carbondale, IL: Southern Illinois University Press, 2008 [1984]), 247–50.

James popularized it and Dewey, with the help of Mead, the one who ultimately consolidated key positionings (the latter two were colleagues at the University of Chicago through the 1890s). This overview can be useful as far as it goes. Regrettably, however, it overlooks the many, many other persons who were integral to pragmatism's development and progress over the decades. This is most especially the case with a group of women, who are now commonly referred to as the *feminist pragmatists*.

While these individuals did not necessarily explicitly align to either a feminist or pragmatist label, viewed historically their work can be understood in such terms.[25] Some prominent figures here include Jane Addams, Ellen Gates Starr, Julia Lathrop[26] (who were all involved in Hull House) and Mary Parker Follett[27] (who was not), among many others. Key among this grouping is Addams who, along with Ellen Gates Starr, founded Hull House in Chicago. Hull House was established as a 'settlement house', a concept that had first appeared in England in the late nineteenth century.[28] The aim was to draw together citizens from different socio-economic classes and backgrounds (i.e. those that were privileged and those that were not) in the same space to engage in shared activities. This translated to a remarkably broad programme spanning, but not limited to, the provision of education, accommodation, enterprise, philanthropy, physical activity, politics and philosophy, as well as various arts including drama.[29] As

---

[25] For a detailed overview of this grouping see Charlene Haddock Siegfried, *Reweaving the Social Fabric: Pragmatism and Feminism* (Chicago: University of Chicago Press, 1996). It is important to note that scholarship remains unresolved here, with much work remaining to surface previously forgotten figures.

[26] Jane Duran, 'Ellen Gates Starr and Julia Lathrop: Hull House and Philosophy.' *The Pluralist* 9, no. 1 (2014), 1–13.

[27] Mary Parker Follett, *Prophet of Management: A Celebration of Writings from the 1920s*, edited by Pauline Graham (Washington, DC: Beard Books, 1995).

[28] John Gal, Stefan Köngeter and Sarah Vicary (eds), *The Settlement House Movement Revisited: A Transnational History* (Bristol: Policy Press, 2021).

[29] Jane Addams, *Twenty Years at Hull House, with Autobiographical Notes* (Chicago: University of Chicago Press, 1990 [1910]).

Addams's biographer, James Weber Linn put it, the aim was 'not to provide a higher civic and social life for anybody; it was to provide a *center for the development* of such a life'.[30]

While the Hull House operational model is difficult to characterize succulently, it can be understood as context-based, activist-led, participatory programme aimed at change making; self-electing individuals took up residence at the house and could propose and, thereafter, pursue socially orientated, transformative projects. Rightly, this work is increasingly being read in design-based terms, specifically in relation to alignments that can be drawn to the social design of today.[31]

In the end, Hull House had incredible longevity, surviving Addams's death in 1935 to take on new forms through the twentieth century and beyond into the twenty-first. Viewed retrospectively, the programme as a whole can be judged a success in so far as it had prolonged, lasting impact for the communities it served and set a leading example of how embedded social work might be conducted, with and within communities. A key to its success is perhaps the emergent open-ended approach taken.[32] Addams was not herself a social worker or designer, rather she has been characterized as a 'brilliant convener of participatory design communities'.[33] It was the Hull House community who set the agenda. This community, in turn, had no fixed approach to problem solving; members did not know at the outset what course an investigation or project might take, or indeed, what outcomes might emerge.

---

[30] James Weber Linn, *Jane Addams: A Biography* (Chicago: University of Illinois Press, 2000), 110–11.

[31] See Danielle Lake, 'Jane Addams, Social Design, and Wicked Problems: Designing in, with, and across.' In *The Oxford Handbook of Jane Addams*, edited by Patricia M. Shields, Maurice Hamington and Joseph Soeters (Oxford: Oxford University Press, 2022); and Carl DiSalvo, *Design as Democratic Inquiry: Putting Experimental Civics into Practice* (Cambridge, MA: The MIT Press, 2022).

[32] This thesis is advanced by Erik Schneiderhan, 'Pragmatism and empirical sociology: the case of Jane Addams and Hull House, 1889–1895.' *Theory and Society* 40 (2011): 589–617.

[33] Danielle Lake and Judy Whipps, 'Feminist Pragmatist Design: Evolutionary Systems Change.' *Design Issues* 39, no. 4 (2023): 21–34.

As a result, a specific Hull House way of working is perhaps best understood in progressive terms (i.e. as something that developed over time). Charlene Haddock Siegfried presents it as a special 'experimental approach' that relied on listening to the communities and groups the Hull House residents were working with. This listening allowed for a 'process of coming to understand' and, in turn, a responding. There were two modes of response: 1) the creation of new political/government institutions that somehow met previously unmet needs; and 2) empowering those they collaborated with to undertake this work themselves. Siegfried notes that all work would be evaluated on the basis of whether or not the 'proposals and practices' resulted 'in more rather than less suffering for those they were supposed to benefit'.[34]

Over time, such activity gave rise to a series of theoretical and philosophical contributions from Addams. This work is said to have relied on a personal 'pragmatist method' that has been characterized as 'autobiographical, contextual, pluralistic, narrational, experimentally fallibilist, and embedded in history and social movements'.[35] To put it another way, the method can be understood to rely on the accumulative store of work from Hull House and its historical and pollical contexts (i.e. the social movements it linked to), but also the shifting of the personal within that (i.e. the autobiographical), the feeding in of perspectives of many others (i.e. the pluralistic) and storytelling (i.e. the narrational). Perhaps Addams's best-known philosophic contribution is her special care-based perspective on ethics, offered in *Democracy and Social Ethics*. This can be characterized as offering an ethical position centred upon the group or community as opposed to the individual and their conduct. It is, as we will explore in Chapter 3, ultimately a practical and democratic ethics, based on learning and collaboration.[36] In many ways, it can be seen as *the* foundational principle of the Hull House model.

---

[34] Charlene Haddock Siegfried, *Reweaving the Social Fabric: Pragmatism and Feminism* (Chicago: University of Chicago Press), 199.
[35] Charlene Haddock Siegfried, 'Introduction.' In Jane Addams, *Democracy and Social Ethics* (Urbana: University of Illinois Press, 2002 [1905]), xiv.
[36] Jane Addams, *Democracy and Social Ethics* (Urbana: University of Illinois Press, 2002 [1905]).

This a useful point at which to return to Dewey in relation to Addams and feminist pragmatists.

LINKING AND COMPARING DEWEY AND ADDAMS AND THE FEMINIST PRAGMATISTS

Addams, her Hull House contemporaries and indeed the Hull House model generally acted as a key source of inspiration for Dewey,[37] something he acknowledged (both implicitly and explicitly) on several occasions within his work.[38] Recent feminist pragmatist scholarship has begun to surface some of the precise threads underpinning this. Perhaps most fundamental is Dewey's attribution of his key concept of 'democracy as a way of life' to Addams.[39] This concept holds that rather than taking form singularly as a political system, democracy should be understood as the basis of community life itself. Here, our daily cooperative coming together as citizens is seen as a democratic practice. As we act and interact, we are involved in a collective shaping of our shared values and ideals. Political democracy – with Parliaments and voting and so on – extends outwards from this. It is a follow on, not an origin.

As a further intriguing point, it has also been suggested that Addams's views here may have informed Dewey's ethics, which he understood as contextually bound, relating to social norms

---

[37] There is an absence of focused scholarship on the Dewey–Addams relationship. However, helpful accounts do exist in Charlene Haddock Siegfried (ed.), *Feminist Interpretations of John Dewey* (University Park, PN: The Pennsylvania University Press); and Siegfried, *Reweaving the Social Fabric*.

[38] An example of the implicit acknowledgement is an extensive quoting of Addams in the opening of the third part of his *Ethics*, John Dewey, *The Later Works, 1925–1953, Volume 7 1932, Ethics*, edited by Jo Ann Boydston (Carbondale, IL: Southern Illinois University Press, 2008 [1985]),

[39] Jane Dewey, 'Biography of John Dewey.' In *The Philosophy of John Dewey*, edited by Paul Arthur Schilpp (Evanston: Northwestern University Press, 1939), 30.

and costumes and something which was best explored in action.[40] This alignment will be picked up in Chapter 3.

Beyond Addams, Dewey was also deeply inspired by other contemporary feminist pragmatists. For example, with regard to his pedagogic theories, Charlene Haddock Siegfried has detailed how he drew deep inspiration from Ella Flagg Young, a student and eventual colleague of his in the experimental Laboratory School at the University of Chicago.[41] Young is said to have helped Dewey appreciate the centrality of reflection in this work, as well as the deep importance of the social within psychology.[42]

What is especially striking about the Dewey–Addams–feminist pragmatists connections such as these is how Addams and others can be seen have to *practised*, and drawn out from practice, the values that Dewey would eventually foreground within his work. As noted above, Dewey himself was a practitioner in the context of his own academic work (e.g. the Laboratory School).[43] However, one may still draw a distinction between Dewey, Addams and other feminist pragmatists in so far as Addams and the others

---

[40] The extent of Addams's influence on Dewey's ethical theories is difficult to pinpoint. What can be said is that Dewey sees the democracy-as-a-way-of-life concept in ethical terms and that Addams's perspective is foregrounded within his *Ethics*, first published in 1908. Marilyn Fischer notes this difficulty, stating that through his 'close association with Addams in the 1890s, he no doubt noticed the pattern of her reasoning and the power of her method'. Marilyn Fischer, *Jane Addams's Evolutionary Theorizing: Constructing 'Democracy and Social Ethics'* (Chicago: University of Chicago Press, 2019), 66.

[41] Siegfried, *Reweaving the Social Fabric*, 79–82.

[42] Ibid, 80. The social aspect of psychology is something that Dewey would have explored at length with Mead as well.

[43] It is arguable that Dewey was also an activist. He took on several political roles through his lifetime, particularly in relation to the People's Lobby, which advocated for stronger democratic citizenship in America; see Mordecai Lee, *The Philosopher Lobbyist: John Dewey and the People's Lobby, 1928–1940* (Albany NY: State University of New York Press, 2015). He also paid particular attention and commented on political developments such as the Pullman workers' strike of 1893. An overview of Dewey's role and position in this latter concern (in the context of Addams's involvement) is available in Cheryl Hudson, 'The 'Un-American' Experiment: Jane Addams's Lessons from Pullman.' *Journal of American Studies* 47, no. 4 (2013): 903–23.

directed themselves primarily to achieving change in context, improving the here and now in the here and now. She and her colleagues literally *placed* themselves in the social context (i.e. they lived there) and sought to enact change via situated, participative action. Philosophy followed on, with Addams's perspectives emerging gradually over time *out of* action.

While Dewey's understanding of inquiry allows for such an approach,[44] it does not insist upon it; one can notionally inquire in Deweyan terms without a deep commitment to listening and responding via creating institutions and/or empowering citizens. The feminist pragmatists, then, through their situated model, demonstrate how this is both possible and desirable; their example urges a level of integration that Dewey as a standalone example cannot match (even with such examples as the Laboratory School).

Having covered pertinent insights from both Dewey's and Addams's work, it is important we now turn to consider the Dewey–Addams position map to the concerns of philosophy generally, both historically and in contemporary terms. As we will see, doing so will reveal the aspects that suggest an enduring relevance. We look first to where their concerns emerged from.

WHERE DEWEY'S CONCERNS CAME FROM

As has been alluded to in relation to Dewey's work, through the late nineteenth century philosophy was able to engage directly with the then-emergent fields of psychology, pedagogy and sociology, among other areas. This engagement centred on the scoping out of the future of progressive democratic societies and, ultimately, of human potentiality.[45] Alongside Dewey, other pragmatists, such as William James, George Herbert Mead and, of course, Addams, were also spanning disciplines. Each, in their own way, seamlessly blended together social and political questions

---

[44] Dixon, *Dewey and Design*, see Chapter 3, in particular.
[45] James T. Kloppenberg, *Social Democracy and Progressivism in European and American Thought, 1870–1920* (Oxford: Oxford University Press, 1986).

in their theorizing and civic work. They were philosophers but also psychologists, social practitioners, people making change and reflecting upon it.

In and around this movement, there was strong focus on what was referred to as 'public philosophy' within the field. Here it was expected that philosophers would seek to share their insights with those beyond their immediate professional circles. This often took the form of presentations and lectures but was also advanced through book publications aimed at a non-academic readership. There was also an emphasis on what might now be referred to as media engagement. Dewey, for example, routinely wrote for the press commenting on political and social matters of the day. Addams, too, regularly gave public lectures and positioned Hull House as a hub for intellectual exchange. In this context, philosophy had a role to play in the advancement of public discourse and contemporary political concern. Philosophers, in other words, maintained a *relationship* with the public, through philosophy.[46]

Things changed – so much so that, from our twenty-first-century vantage point, it is now perhaps difficult, if not impossible, to recover a sense of this general approach and agenda. Many attribute the change to the emergence of a new university model centred upon disciplinary specialization and the pursuit of original research, which gradually established itself in Germany, starting in the 1810s.[47] This model influenced developments in United States, which, along with Europe, was seeing a rapid expansion of its higher education system at the time.[48] In this new model, disciplines began to steadily peel away from philosophy and science came to predominate the university system.

---

[46] A brief sketch of the history of public philosophy is offered in Adam Briggle, 'The Professionalization of Philosophy from Athens to the APA and Beyond'. In *A Companion to Public Philosophy*, edited by Lee McIntyre, Nancy McHugh, Ian Olasov (London: John Wiley and Sons, 2022), 9–17.

[47] William Kirby, *Empires of Ideas: Creating the Modern University from Germany, to America to China* (Cambridge, MA: Harvard University Press, 2022).

[48] See Harold S. Wechsler, Lester F. Goodchild and Linda Eisenmann (eds), *The History of Higher Education* (Boston, MA: Pearson, 2006).

Set against such a backdrop, philosophy's survival depended on the establishment of its own programme of professionalization and, from the 1870s, steady advances were made in this direction. Philosophy became a prescribed activity with dedicated departments and doctoral programmes. Within this mix, the American Philosophic Association (APA) was founded in 1900.[49] Concurrent with these developments, public philosophy began to fall away – a point that can be registered in the 1916 address of the then President of the APA, Arthur Lovejoy, who called for an end to such efforts to speak to the masses, stating that it was time for philosophy to turn inwards and make progress in its own terms.[50]

Perhaps unsurprisingly, given this context, classical pragmatism is said to have entered a terminal decline from the 1920s onwards. While presentations of this decline vary, some argue that it did not fade away entirely but rather was gradually subsumed into a then strident movement known as logical positivism, which focused on surfacing objective truth through the framing of logical propositions.[51] What is certain is that instead of mounting a programme of experimental problem solving in the context of widely held social and moral concerns as per Dewey's reconstruction proposals, philosophy, along with the other disciplines with which it had previously held close association (e.g. psychology), gradually narrowed in and, some would argue, became siloed.

This extends into the present.

SOME SIMILAR CONCERNS IN PHILOSOPHY TODAY

It would be possible to argue that contemporary philosophy is in reasonable if not rude health. Philosophy departments still hold an important place in the composition of major global

---

[49] James Campbell, *A Thoughtful Profession* (Peru, IL: Open Court, 2006).
[50] Ibid, 281.
[51] A detailed historical overview is offered by Cheryl Misak, *The American Pragmatists* (Oxford: Oxford University Press, 2013).

universities.[52] Philosophic texts, aimed at both academic and popular markets, continue to be published by major publishing houses. Newer perspectives such as those presented by postphenomenology and object-orientated ontology continue to open up exciting horizons for the field. Digital communication makes it easier to access and share philosophic ideas than ever before. Then there are countries such as France, where the subject is still embedded in national curricula and taught each week to young citizens.[53]

Be this as it may, it is also possible to argue the opposite point. For one, there is the large-scale threat posed to the humanities by what might be perceived as an instrumentalist agenda (i.e. a general focus on economic value and efficiency) that favours subjects such as science, technology, engineering and maths (commonly referred to as STEM).[54] This emphasis has seen a sharp decline in philosophy departments within universities, especially in the United States and the UK.[55] Underpinning this is a general sense that philosophy's contemporary relevance has greatly diminished in the last half-century. Reflecting on the state of the discipline in 2016, Peter Boghossian notes that the 'most

---

[52] Such departments will admittedly likely rely on the historic reputations of both the institutions and past faculty. Nonetheless, many of these can still claim to be performing well. To take the University of Cambridge as an example, it can presently claim 150 undergraduate students, 50 postgraduate students and 30 academic members of staff. 'About Us Overview', University of Cambridge, Faculty of Philosophy, accessed 9 November 2024, https://www.phil.cam.ac.uk/aboutus

[53] Ghislaine Gueudet, Laetitia Bueno-Ravel, Simon Modeste and Luc Trouche, 'Curriculum in France: A national frame in transition.' In *International Perspectives on Mathematics Curriculum*, edited by Denisse R. Thompson, Mary Ann Huntley and Christine Suurtamm (Charlotte, NC: Information Age Publishing, 2017), 41–70.

[54] See for example, Maja Bacovic, Zivko Andrijasevic and Bojan Pejovic, 'STEM education and growth in Europe.' *Journal of the Knowledge Economy* 13, no. 3 (2022): 2348–71.

[55] Brian Ball and Patrycja Kaszynska, 'We should lament the demise of philosophy departments', Times Higher Education, 24 June 2024, https://www.timeshighereducation.com/blog/we-should-lament-demise-philosophy-departments

interesting thing' about the field is 'how uninteresting and largely irrelevant it has become'.[56] Approaching the issue from a historical angle, Stephen Gaukroger argues that the field 'seems to have lost its bearings'.[57] Others go further still and speak of the philosophy having entered a crisis,[58] reached an end,[59] or even died.[60]

This requires some working through. As has been alluded to above, in the anglophone world a large portion of contemporary philosophy is operating within the analytic vein, which emerged from logical positivism. In keeping with logical positivism emphasis on truth, the aim of such work is to support the structuring of scientifically orientated logic, sometimes via the manipulation of symbols (i.e. the use of alphanumeric code to represent given arguments). Approached in this way, the activity can be understood as a wholly technical enterprise, a programme of working through how philosophy can be bettered for the sake of philosophers and not the public. Herein, social, ethical and environmental questions are often ignored on the basis that they do not fit with the strict rigour demanded by both the general agenda (i.e. the concerns of analytic philosophy) and the logical-symbolic frameworks of the method. This is limiting and has, over time, massively reduced the scope of the field. Indeed, so great is the reduction that some have even cast doubt on the future viability of the analytic method itself.[61]

Such challenges are by no means confined to analytic philosophy, however. Though continental philosophy still offers commentary

---

[56] Peter Boghossian, 'Philosophy that matters,' *The Philosophers' Magazine* 72 (2016): 29–30.

[57] Stephen Gaukroger, *The Failures of Philosophy: A Historical Essay* (Princeton, NJ: Princeton University Press, 2020, 287.

[58] Mario Bunge, *Philosophy in Crisis: The Need for Reconstruction* (Buffalo, NY: Prometheus Books, 2001).

[59] Steven Burik, *The End of Contemporary Philosophy and the Task of Comparative Thinking: Heidegger, Derrida, and Daoism* (Albany, NY: State University of New York Press, 2009).

[60] Isabelle Thomas-Fogiel, *The Death of Philosophy: Reference and Self-Reference in Contemporary Thought* (New York: Columbia University Press, 2011).

[61] Aaron Preston, *Analytic Philosophy: The History of an Illusion* (London: Continuum: 2007).

and reflection on daily life without reference to technical logic or symbol systems – for example, perspectives can be seen to extend into the realm of psychoanalysis, cultural studies, sociology and literary theory – this work is, again, generally pitched at a level far removed from the concerns and understanding of the wider public. Equally, as with analytic philosophy, there is also a question of focus, of where philosophers direct their efforts in doing philosophy. Here again, a number of continental programmes have been criticized over the decades for attending more to the progression of idiosyncratic agendas than the quotidian – for example, deploying specific approaches in the interrogation of abstract subject areas such as reason, language, subjectivity or power.[62]

Here, in its abstraction, philosophy's potency is blunted. It is no longer a ready resource for individuals seeking to critically examine their own personal circumstances or wider social or cultural challenges. Worse still, some would suggest that such discourse has contributed to a loss of 'any notion of universal

---

[62] This can be illustrated through the trajectory of the concept of deconstruction, which was first proposed by French philosopher Jacques Derrida, as set out in Jacques Derrida, *Of Grammatology* (Baltimore: The John Hopkins University Press, 1997 [1974]). While difficult to define, deconstruction allows for a critical exploration of textual meanings, wherein concepts are literally broken down (deconstructed) in order to displace firmly held assumptions regarding categories and hierarchies; things are thus seen in a new light; see Jonathan Culler, *On Deconstruction: Theory and Criticism after Structuralism (25th Anniversary Edition)* (Ithaca, NY: Cornell University Press, 2007 [1982]), While popular through the 1970s and 1980s, especially in the context of literary criticism, the approach foundered in the 1990s. At this point, commentators note that it appeared to arrive at what some have referred to as 'deadend', with energy and enthusiasm dissipating and academic attention, ultimately, turning elsewhere. For an overview see Jeffrey Williams, 'The Death of Deconstruction, the End of Theory, and Other Ominous Rumors', *Narrative* 4, no. 1 (1996), 17–35. Accordingly, though the approach yielded an extensive legacy and opened up further inquiry, its contributions have been described as amounting to little more than 'methodological reform'. In other words, it has resulted in an intellectual game rather a progressive horizon by which positive insights might be garnered. See Jeffrey Nealon, *Double Reading: Postmodernism After Deconstruction* (Ithaca, NY: Cornell University Press, 2019 [1993]), 4.

knowledge, objective criteria, or foundation',[63] with no meaningful alternative being proposed by way of replacement.

Returning to the underlying concerns of Dewey's 1920s reconstruction calls (i.e. that the field has lost course and extracted itself from the quotidian), it is thus possible to note an alignment with the philosophical commentators of today.

SOME CONTINUED CALLS FOR PHILOSOPHIC RECONSTRUCTIONS

Intriguingly, many present-day commentators who express concerns for philosophy's future often offer proposals not dissimilar to Dewey's. There is of course a variation in form and emphasis, but at their core we may detect a call for a return to daily life. This is not so much about returning to pragmatism or a version of it (though in some cases it is); rather, it is more a call for a return to a general *meaningfulness*.

While many names might be highlighted here, Mario Bunge stands out on the basis that he also specifically calls for a 'reconstruction' in philosophy. In this, like Dewey, he holds that the major philosophic schools, analytic, continental and other, all lie in 'ruins' and the only way out is a return to first principles based on a how philosophy can support the asking and answering of fundamental life questions.[64]

Another example can be found in Philip Kitcher, who explicitly turns to Dewey's reconstruction work in his own questioning of contemporary philosophy.[65] Following on from Dewey's earlier position, Kitcher bemoans, in particular, the untethered, overly technical emphasis of much present-day philosophic work,

---

[63] Arleen Dallery, Charles E. Scott and P. Holley Roberts, 'Introduction.' In *Crisis in Contiential Philosophy*, edited by Arleen Dallery, Charles E. Scott and P. Holley Roberts (Albany, NY: State University of New York Press, 1990), x.

[64] Bunge, *Philosophy in Crisis*.

[65] Philip Kitcher, *What's the Use of Philosophy* (New York: Oxford University Press, 2023).

suggesting that the situation has worsened since Dewey's time. In terms of offering his own proposals, like Dewey, he sees a need to engage in methodological clarification and synthesis via a process of deep cross-disciplinary communication and sharing. Also, and importantly in the context of the present text, he sees a need for philosophy to engage directly in the problems of the world, working to provide immediate solutions to pressing challenges. We will return to Kitcher's proposal briefly in the final chapter.

A further example, and one we will also return to later, comes from eminent Dewey scholar Thomas Alexander,[66] who explores contemporary philosophy's divergence from the ideas underpinning Dewey's vision as set out in *Experience and Nature* – i.e. that it could support a broad programme of inquiry into value and what it means to live a good life. His key concern is how the discipline might adapt as set against the challenges of modernity.

In line with Dewey, Alexander foregrounds the philosophy's notional origin as the practice of the love of wisdom. For Alexander, wisdom is 'manifested in the relation of life to the world in which it is lived'. Philosophy as a practice of wisdom, then, would support 'living well in such a way that a distinctly human excellence is achieved through our capacity for intelligent action'. This is contextualized as 'action that consciously realizes ends that fund existence with reflective meaning and value'. While Alexander acknowledges that the discipline no longer embodies this ideal,[67] following Dewey again, he nonetheless proposes that this should be the directive aim of a present-day reconstruction – one that would lead to a radically different modelling of what philosophy is.

Taking wisdom – i.e. the oversight of the quality of life-world relations – as a central focus, the point would be to investigate

---

[66] Thomas M. Alexander, *The Human Eros: Eco-ontology and the Aesthetics of Experience* (Carbondale, IL: University of Southern Illinois Press, 2017).

[67] He accepts that the ideal of wisdom, literally the love of wisdom or being a friend of wisdom (which is a more accurate translation of philosophy), was only ever a brief focus for Western philosophy during its early period, Ibid, 73.

the furtherance of value in all its forms. This would be founded upon an attending to the world. There would be no 'substitute for experience'. Additionally, there would also be a need to play a critical role in diagnosing 'the deeper underlying problems of civilization so that these problems may be intelligently overcome'.[68] This in part requires ontological interrogation, i.e. an examination of how we understand our existence and tell stories about who we are and what we do. Equally, it also requires inquiry into 'the possible meanings of the situations in which we find ourselves' – that is, speculative reflection on what could be. Combining ontological and speculative inquiry, transformation through intelligent action is opened up. I take the view that if properly realized, this would be as much a design project as a philosophical project – a true philosophy through design.

Beyond such examples, it is also possible to detect a renewed push to reinstate a public philosophy within the field.[69] At present, activity here is largely centred upon extending philosophical work into political and social contexts. Here, on the political side, it is argued that a stronger, more informed public discourse can enhance democratic societies,[70] while socially, it is proposed that philosophic processes might support greater understanding among citizens.[71]

The movement includes academic philosophers experimenting with novel forms of engagement, as well as non-academic philosophers exploring how philosophy can be practised in ways

---

[68] Ibid, 76–7.

[69] This is not simply a matter of offering an overview of philosophical 'findings' to a public. Rather, it is all-encompassing. As Myisha Cherry sees it, there is a need to 'rethink how we do philosophy, where we do philosophy, and with whom we do philosophy'. See Myisha Cherry, 'Coming Out of the Shade' In *Philosophy's Future: The Problems of Philosophical Progress* (London: John Wiley and Sons, 2017), 21–30.

[70] Michael Sandel, for example, argues that a politically orientated public philosophy is necessary 'to repair the civic life on which democracy depends'. Michael J. Sandel, *Public Philosophy: Essays on Morality in Politics* (Cambridge, MA: Harvard University Press, 2005), 34.

[71] The work of Ask a Philosopher and Community Philosophy organizations, discussed below, offer two clear examples of this.

that move beyond academic norms. Across the board, rather than civic lectures and talks, increasing emphasis is being placed on fostering direct one-to-one and group dialogues, working through issues together such that a greater level of clarity and understanding is arrived at. This has included approaches such as 'Ask a Philosopher', an outdoor pop-up where a philosopher, Ian Olasov, made himself available to ask and answers questions at outdoor locations across New York.[72] Another complementary example in the UK, Community Philosophy operates as a facilitative organization, which aims to work through concepts such that '[p]ower shifts, minds change and preconceptions are discarded'.[73] Their methods include 'philosophy walks', where ideas are explored outdoors, on foot, to 'stimulate reflection'.[74] There have also been live projects – for example, with philosophers engaging with parents in a primary school, with the aim of enhancing their 'democratic voice'.[75]

This brings us back to Dewey and Addams and their referencing here.

LINKING TO DEWEY AND ADDAMS HERE

Collecting the above together, the key question here then becomes: how does the work of Dewey and feminist pragmatists such as Jane Addams begin to point to a framing of a philosophy through design, which acknowledges (and potentially connects to) ongoing concerns and developments within philosophy?

---

[72] Ian Olasov, *Ask a Philosopher: Answers to Your Most Important and Unexpected Questions* (London: Hachette Press, 2020).

[73] Community Philosophy, 'What is Community Philosophy', accessed 26 November 2024, https://communityphilosophy.co.uk/what-is-community-philosophy/

[74] Community Philosophy, 'Philosophy Walks', accessed 26 November 2024, https://communityphilosophy.co.uk/philosophy-walks/

[75] Charlotte Haines Lyon, 'Exploring Community Philosophy as a tool for parental engagement in a primary school.' *International Journal for Transformative Research* 2, no. 2 (2015), 39–48.

As has been shown, there is a general alignment between Dewey's and Addams's work and those who are concerned for philosophy in the present. In both instances, issue is being taken with what is seen as an undue focus on singularly disciplinary agenda (e.g. technical questions). From this, there is also concern regarding a general lack of engagement with lived experience. Then, as now (for those who hold such concern), the prescription is to return to the everyday, working to problem solve via direct experimentation.

An empirical, experimental philosophy, like that framed by Dewey, would move past the philosophy-as-technique and philosophy-for-philosophers framings we have touched on above. Equally, the necessary societal engagement and impact is embedded in the work itself. Here, in the exemplar of Addams and the feminist pragmatists' direct engagement approach, there is a notional model to follow, at least as a starting point. Further, Dewey's and Addams's deep commitment to public philosophy provides an early strategy for how outward dissemination might be supported such that society could better avail of the outcomes of such work. (On this latter point, we will return to the potential of public philosophy in the final chapter.)

Beyond these alignments, there is of course the opportunity to look outwards from both Dewey and Addams. In Dewey's case, this relates to the non-Western outlook. For Addams and the feminist pragmatists, there is a direct line to be drawn to social inequalities and direct, democratic work via the Hull House model.

This links up Dewey–Addams in relation to contemporary philosophy. But what of Dewey's and Addams's alignment to design?

As will likely be apparent, a Dewey–Addams modelling of philosophy such as that set out would also readily align to design and more particularly to design research involving practice.

As been noted, the connections between Dewey and design already exist – Dewey has long been identified as a philosopher who can speak to design. He himself established direct links to design at least as far back as 1930s when he contributed to the establishment of the Chicago Bauhaus[76] and curriculum development at North Carolina's famous Black Mountain College.[77] Indirectly, starting in the 1970s, his work emerged again, for example, as a key reference underpinning Donald Schön's famous reflective practice proposals, as well as early user experience work in Xerox Palo Alto. More recently, he has been directly referenced in the areas of HCI, participatory design and design thinking, through his work on aesthetic experience, political action and logic respectively.[78]

Alongside this, there has been a drawing of links between Dewey's work and design research practice, especially to design research involving practice. Here, as an entry point many have noted the correspondence between design practice, research practice and Dewey's model of inquiry.[79] Additional work has been done, exploring the extent to which his logical theory aligns with the open-ended, situational logic of design research involving practice.[80] A further series of contributions have sought to demonstrate how the whole of Dewey's philosophy – drawing in his theories of experience, inquiry, aesthetics as well as his social and political theory and ethics – can apply to design research involving practice and design research more generally.[81] Within these mappings, Dewey's work is shown to allow for ontological

---

[76] Alain Findeli, 'Moholy-Nagy's design pedagogy in Chicago (1937–46).' *Design Issues* 7, no. 1 (1990), 4–19.

[77] Helen Molesworth and Ruth Erickson, *Look Before you Leap: Black Mountain College 1933–1957* (New Haven, CT: Yale University Press, 2015), 33.

[78] Brian Dixon, Anna Rylander Eklund and Frithjof Wegener, 'Introduction: Pragmatism, Dewey, and Design Inquiry.' *Design Issues* 39, no. 4 (2023): 3–8.

[79] Guido Stompff, Ties van Bruinessen and Frido Smulders. 'The generative dance of design inquiry: Exploring Dewey's pragmatism for design research.' *Design Studies* 83 (2022): 101136; Marc Steen. 'Co-design as a process of joint inquiry and imagination.' *Design Issues* 29, no. 2 (2013): 16–28.

[80] Brian Dixon and Tara French, 'Processing the method: Linking Deweyan logic and design-in-research.' *Design Studies* 70, (2020): 100962.

[81] Dixon, *Dewey and Design*; Rabah Bousbaci, *L'Homme comme un «être d'habitude». Essai d'anthropologie et d'épistémologie pour les Sciences du design* (Québec City: Presses de l'Université Laval, 2020).

transformation, which, of course, is key to design research involving practice's change-based approach. Equally, the principles of researcher participation, uncertainty and difference and diversity, often central to design research involving practice work, are all accommodated within his philosophy.[82]

Dewey, it would seem, is a philosopher whom designers can understand (at least, if translated appropriately).

As has been alluded to, Jane Addams and the feminist pragmatists have not received the same level of attention in design studies to date, but there is a growing interest in building these linkages such that the Hull House model can act as an inspiration to designers and design researchers. In so far as work has been undertaken on this subject, what emerges is a set of proposals for a stronger participatory and democratic approach to design. We see this vividly relayed in the recent work of Carl DiSalvo whereby, in aligning with both Addams and Dewey, design is framed as 'democratic inquiry'.[83] Similarly, Matthew DelSesto profiles Addams's work as he explores the possibilities of aligning a contemporary social change agenda with the affordances of design.[84] In another example, taking a systemic design perspective, Danielle Lake and Judy Whipps draw on Addams and the feminist pragmatists as they highlight the need for designers to directly engage, situationally and relationally, with diverse communities and, here, to work flexibly and iteratively over longer temporal periods to prototype solutions to problems.[85] While an in-depth design research involving practice-Addams/feminist pragmatists mapping has not yet taken place, there would be significant value in scoping such an alignment. Nonetheless, from the above, it is evident that Addams's position has much to offer design.

---

[82] Dixon, *Design, Philosophy and Making Things Happen*.

[83] DiSalvo, *Design as Democratic Inquiry*.

[84] Matthew DelSesto, *Design and the Social Imagination* (London: Bloomsbury, 2022).

[85] Lake and Whipps, 'Feminist Pragmatist Design: Evolutionary Systems Change.'

Further analysis of the relationships that can be drawn between Dewey, Addams and design and design research will be explored as we advance to the chapters.

From now, having linked their work to design and design research involving practice, as well as concerns of contemporary philosophy beforehand, we are at last able to approach the task of progressively framing a philosophy through design in direct terms, through our areas of focus (i.e. technology, the social and the ecological). Based on the above discussion, there is not only the possibility of reshaping design by philosophy but also philosophy by design.

2 The Technological Horizon: Digital Ontologizing

It's early 2023 and the world is changing. It always is but this feels more intense than I've experienced previously. It feels as though a fundamental shift is taking place. A few months ago, a series of high-performing open-source AIs were launched. You offer a prompt, be it a request for a specific block of text, an image, lines of computer code or a recipe or poem. The AI, of course, responds immediately with the text, image, code, recipe or poem. Sometimes it is dazzling in its accuracy and precision, meeting and exceeding the expectations of the task that's been set. Other times, it's surprisingly off key, apparently failing to grasp even the slightest detail of what's been requested.

Despite this variability, the technology has rapidly entered public imagination and is now widely perceived as the next step, the thing that will change everything. There is a sense within this that this is an existential moment where a clear before and after will emerge and that life will never be the same.

This is troubling and while new technologies always seem to trouble, there's a marked difference with AI. The possibilities it hints at are more than the simple progression of already-established capabilities but rather a complete upending of what it means to learn, hold expertise and, ultimately, what it means to be human. Around the edges, there is also the suggestion of particularly dark scenarios emerging. For example, AI will likely accelerate the spread of disinformation, something which is already a very pressing challenge for democratic societies globally. As a further concern, already some individuals appear to be developing unhealthy parasocial relationships with AI-enabled technology – with chatbots, in particular, becoming a point of romantic or quasi-interpersonal focus. In some emerging cases, these relationships become so intense that the individuals begin to neglect loved ones in favour of the AI.

While issues such as these cannot be ignored, not all of the speculation and commentary is negative. Many, happily, project more hopeful AI-enabled futures where solutions to wicked problems will reveal themselves as if by magic, productivity will increase, supporting economic growth, and routine jobs will be improved. Here, humans will be able to get on with the driving of intent and creative decision making, while 'mindless' tasks will be handed over to the AI.

To get to this point, however, seems elusive. The whole world is grasping in the dark and events are vastly outpacing any opportunity for reflection. It seems all we can do, if we want a chance to reflect, we must do while acting, navigating through the uncertainty we face.

A question here that could guide us, if we were engaging in philosophy through design, might be: how to progress a positive AI, one that enriches rather than degrades life?

This chapter is the first in a series of three that will sequentially consider what I am here calling thematic horizons or areas of focus for an eventual philosophy through design: technology, the social and the ecological. As will become clearer as we advance, each, in their own way, calls up questions relating to meaning, value and ethics. Equally, as has been noted in the Preface, they also very directly intersect and overlap. There is no pretence here that anything other is the case; each is given an individual focus so as to align with likely situational concerns, our philosophical 'pointings' as it were. From these pointings, readers are thus able, through each chapter, to hone in on thematic references to pragmatism, design and philosophy more generally. As they progress, relationships, potential and actual, will gradually emerge.

In the present chapter, our focus is directed on the technological. This has always been an important area for design – a point that is furthered below. Philosophy, for its part, has long grappled with this thematic. As we have seen, there is a whole subdiscipline functioning as a philosophy of technology that links to, and builds on, classical and modernist accounts of its meaning for humanity. Perspectives offered here carry ontological, ethical, political and ecological bearings, with some commentors hopeful as to technological meanings/values and others distinctly pessimistic.[1]

Picking up on the above vignette, AI is, at present, an example of a technology that has in many ways outpaced not only our planning and legal systems but also, apparently, our capacity for general foresight. We are without register as to the meaning and consequences of scaling such a technology; its likely impact is difficult to envisage and assess; and its ultimate form unknowable. In a scenario like this, our only recourse is creative, speculative thought, a mapping ahead as to what could happen, what potentials – positive or negative – the technology might open up. This is where a philosophy through design can support efforts to quickly look ahead and understand what could be, how reality could change and what the consequences – desirable or undesirable – of such a change would involve.

Dewey would, in the round, agree with this stance. For him, technology was not to be understood as inherently good or bad in and of itself. Rather, the issue lay with the uses to which it was put and the (largely economic) value systems driving its design and development.[2] It was also to be seen as culturally embedded. In this view, while a specific technological artefact, e.g. a smartphone, is on its own, 'a particular thing',[3] i.e. a fixed object, it can also be understood to extend beyond this, to carry

---

[1] For a grouped range of key texts see David M. Kaplan (ed.), *Readings in the Philosophy of Technology* (Plymouth, UK: Rowman and Littlefield Publishers).

[2] John Dewey, *The Later Works, 1925–1953, Volume 5: 1925–1927, Essays, The Sources of a Science of Education, Individualism, Old and New, and Construction and Criticism*, edited by Jo Ann Boydston (Carbondale, IL: Southern Illinois University Press, 2008 [1984]), 87.

[3] Dewey, *The Later Works, 1925–1953, Volume 1: 1925, Experience and Nature*, 101.

meanings, which are 'relational, anticipatory and predictive'.[4] The smartphone, in other words, is understood as a phone, the basis of what it is seen to enable. Approached from this perspective, it comes to be seen as a means of connecting, of further action. *Through* the phone, we can make calls, consume social media, purchase items with one's digital wallet and navigate via maps. Over time, all such actions become patterns of activity, practices that configure and reconfigure things. This configuring/reconfiguring has consequences.

Following on from the last chapter, this relates to Dewey's view of reality, of how the meaning things carry for us (as expressed in language, communication and action) defines our existential understandings. In simple terms, new technologies, here, equals new realities.

Dewey was also alert to technological consequence as a particular thing. Some of his most powerful writing on the subject emerges in *The Public and its Problems*,[5] a 1927 text in which he reflected on what was perceived to be a crisis of governance in the United States in the mid-1920s. For Dewey, modern, complex societies such as the United States had become fractured and unwieldy due, in part, to industrial and technological expansion. New industries and technologies had opened up new forms of experience, leading to new problems. The more new industries/technologies, the more new experience, the more new problems.[6]

Dewey believed that such challenges required constant ongoing inquiry, where problems could be explored, understood and potentially addressed.[7] This was how his ethics – which will be covered in the next chapter – worked. On encountering a novel

---

[4] Ibid, 146.
[5] John Dewey, *The Later Works, 1925–1953, Volume 2: 1925–1927, Essays, Reviews, Miscellany, and The Public and its Problems*, edited by Jo Ann Boydston (Carbondale, IL: Southern Illinois University Press, 1984 [2008]).
[6] New problems, in turn, led to what Dewey termed new 'publics' – that is, distinct politically active, organized groups – which required representation. Ironically, this was further complicated by the distractions of popular culture and mass media, themselves reliant on technologies, being seen as barriers to these publics cohering. Ibid, 321.
[7] Larry Hickman, *Tools for a Philosophical Culture: Putting Pragmatism to Work* (Bloomington, IN: Indiana University Press, 2001).

ethical context centred on a problematic situation, one was to look ahead, inquire, imagine what could have happened and, in this, seek to determine through this imagining what was desirable or not. In many ways, this conforms to the general template set out in some design research, as in the examples that follow.[8]

Addams, for her part, did not reflect directly on the role of technology in her writings as such. She was, however, deeply concerned with seeking to ameliorate the rampant industrial exploitation of her time, where the labour movement was in its infancy and there were only limited workers' protections. While technology might be understood to play a tangential role in the distressing, unequal social conditions that she and her Hull House fellows encountered in the early twentieth century, her focus was directed towards the human–economic relationships between those that were seen to underpin worker exploitation. In this, her response was to seek to engender a greater social understanding and, from here, to encourage the exploration pathways from which challenges could be jointly addressed (between employers and employees). She envisaged a scenario where rather than employers aiming to be good 'to' their employees, they might be good 'with' them – that is, come to understand their needs on the basis of cooperative endeavour.[9]

We will briefly pick up again on Dewey's and Addams's perspectives at the end of the chapter.

Before launching in, it will be worth briefly noting two key reasons behind the selection of technology as a starting point for the discussion. First, it forms the core of contemporary design practice, a centre point around which designers currently work. It is arguable that this has always been the case; we have already noted how industrial manufacturing and mass production gave rise to design as we know it. However, the present-day situation is markedly different from this notional point of historic origin. Today,

---

[8] One example is the Everyday Design Studio, which will be considered later in the chapter. Here, the possibilities of human–technology relations are explored prospectively, by creating artefacts which do not exist to understand what their impact might be.

[9] Addams, *Democracy and Social Ethics*, 70.

the widespread adoption of digital devices by large swathes of the world's population, both in the Global North and Global South, means that designers now not only design for technological form and function (i.e. physical products and what they do) but also for technological experiences – that is, the realities that accompany the use of a particular product. Moreover, design outcomes are increasingly *digital* outcomes and, to a greater or lesser extent, hinge on digital systems (e.g. service design project work), which in turn underpin what we, as a species, can do. Then there are the emergent concerns such as those expressed through the AI vignette above, whereby we do not yet know what eventual form a technology might take or indeed what the consequences will be.

Second, more so than the other two horizons/areas – i.e. the social and the ecological – it is possible to claim that, through technology, philosophy and design have *already* come together in a definite, meaningful way. As we will see later in the chapter, this is perhaps best exemplified through the postphenomenological work mentioned in Chapter 1. Here, arguably, a philosophy *through* design has in fact begun to take shape, even if is, as yet, not widely labelled as such.

This will be picked up on again here when, to open the chapter, I will briefly explore how a series of distinct philosophical positions, including postphenomenology, Dewey's pragmatism, Marxism and feminism have each inspired specific approaches to designing for technology. Following on, to give illustration to this, I will turn to look at the pioneering work of the Department of Industrial Design at the Technological University of Eindhoven. Beyond, I then consider the potential value of progressing these positions/examples within the context of a philosophy through design, with particular attention being paid to the ways that, when related to technology, design appears to open up a space in which we can consider human experience anew.

THE TECHNOLOGICAL PHILOSOPHIES OF DESIGN

From the late 1990s onwards, the exponential rise of digital technology – from personal computers, to laptops, to mobile phones and, later, smartphones – marked a new phase for design. Increasingly, designers were called on to design dynamic as opposed to static outcomes. Interactive websites, software interfaces and apps demanded a new logic – a new way of seeing, being and acting – within the design process. As noted in Chapter 1, it is here we can register the emergence of approaches such as user experience. Initially, user experience work was integrated within a wider suite of human–computer interaction practices which referenced the frameworks of cognitive psychology. Here, the human mind is positioned as a part of wider system of parts which come together in specific activities, where there are inputs (symbols) and outputs (actions). Actions can be successful, leading to the achievement of desired goals, or unsuccessful, leading to errors.[10] To design well was to design out the errors. In so far as the human has presence within this framing, it is in relation to a discrete set of faculties such as perception, attention and memory.[11]

Over time, the frameworks of cognitive psychology came to be viewed as overly restrictive and inflexible, obscuring the richness of everyday lived experience and, as such, stunting creative potential.[12] However, escaping cognitive psychology was not as straightforward as simply selecting an alternative theory by which to design; there were no immediate alternatives. Instead, escape required a dedicated engagement with philosophy.

Work in this direction was gradual, only beginning in earnest in the 1990s. Nonetheless, a range of alternatives eventually surfaced, slowly reorientating design–technology relations over the ensuing three decades.[13] There was activity theory, which envisaged a particular subject-object-action framework.[14] There

---

[10] Margaret A. Boden, *Mind as Machine: A History of Cognitive Science, Volume 1* (Oxford: Oxford University Press, 2006).

[11] Norman, *The Design of Everyday Things*.

[12] Yvonne Rogers, *HCI Theory: Classical, Modern, Contemporary* (San Rafael: Morgan and Claypool, 2012).

[13] For a history see Rogers, *HCI Theory*.

[14] Victor Kaptelinin and Bonnie A. Nardi, *Acting with Technology: Activity Theory and Interaction Design* (Cambridge MA: The MIT Press, 2009).

was phenomenology, which offered a centring of situated embodiment and perception.[15] Then there was the classical pragmatism of John Dewey, in particular his theory of aesthetic experience, which was picked up by a number of scholars and gained popularity in the early 2000s.

This latter work focused on Dewey's proposal that aesthetic experience is distinguishable from prosaic experience on the basis that it holds distinction and definite structure. We have a great meal, witness a powerful storm, or are party to a particularly awful argument. There will be a beginning, a middle and an end to such experiences. For example, we will have prepared for our meal, got ready, journeyed to the restaurant, taken our table. There is the time at the restaurant: the waiting to be served, the being served, the moment the meal arrives and, of course, the act of eating the meal itself. This will be followed by the winddown, the slow leaving, the going home. Afterwards, we will be able to claim: that was '*an* experience'. In the context of designing for technology, this theory provides a template by which experience can be understood in holistic terms, where qualitative feeling can be considered, addressed and worked with.[16]

In design terms, the referencing of such material opened up a new perspective for the framing of enhanced, more human technological experiences grounded in an absolute attendance to *situation* and *feeling*. Designers were called upon to consider the 'threads' of experience – including the sensual, the emotional, the compositional, and the spatio-temporal – as a means of exploring and evaluating design possibilities.[17] Further, linking to other pragmatist work, there was also a proposal that the social aspect of experiences be approached in its own distinct

---

[15] Paul Dourish, *Where the Action Is* (Cambridge, MA: The MIT Press, 2001).

[16] Peter Wright and John McCarthy, 'Experience-centered design: Designers, users, and communities in dialogue.' *Synthesis Lectures on Human-Centered Informatics* 3, no. 1 (2010): 1–123.

[17] John McCarthy and Peter Wright, *Technology as Experience* (Cambridge, MA: The MIT Press, 2004), 80–94.

terms via such frameworks.[18] This general position eventually came to be termed experience-centred design, a wide-ranging perspective which not only seeks to address the experiential element of designing for technology but also the necessary democratic, ethical dimensions of such work.[19]

The progressive movement away from cognitive psychology outlined above was not the first time that philosophy had informed technologically orientated design work, however. Scandinavia's famous participatory design movement also drew on philosophical tenets. First emerging in the 1960s, it initially developed through a series of trade union-funded research projects addressing the challenges of the increased automation and technological input in the workplace. Drawing on the Marxist principles of worker emancipation and the need for creative agency within the context of work, the key idea was that those who were to use the technology should have a say in its design. This translated into a democratic creative process, where possibilities were jointly developed and solutions collectively arrived at.[20]

Critical to this was the technique of prototyping, i.e. the modelling of a proposed outcome that allows for its progressive testing and evaluation. While the Marxist-workplace orientation faded gradually over time, the democratic commitment and prototyping approach was maintained.[21] In this respect, participatory design stands as an example for how philosophy might, even tangentially, inform design strategies in the real world. As we

---

[18] Jodi Forlizzi and Katja Battarbee, 'Understanding experience in interactive systems.' In *Proceedings of the 5th Conference on Designing Interactive Systems: Processes, practices, methods, and techniques* (New York: ACM, 2004), 261–8.

[19] Wright and McCarthy, 'Experience-centered design: Designers, users, and communities in dialogue.'

[20] For a comprehensive edited text see Jasper Simonsen and Toni Robertson (eds), *Routledge International Handbook of Participatory Design* (Abingdon, Oxon: Routledge, 2012).

[21] Pelle Ehn, 'Learning in participatory design as I found it (1970–2015).' In *Participatory Design for Learning*, edited by Betsy DiSalvo, Jason Yip, Elizabeth Bonsignore and Carl DiSalvo (Abingdon, Oxon: Routledge, 2017), 7–21

will see in the next chapter, this has continued into the present, where participatory design has again drawn fresh links between design and philosophy, this time in relation to social concerns.

Another important philosophical line of design–technology work relates to feminism. Though this has been a somewhat marginal concern over the decades, feminist design–technology perspectives have appeared sporadically and more recently feminism has become a key pillar within the field's wider critical theory agenda.[22] In seeking to give a framing to this position, Shaowen and Jeffery Bardzell argued that a feminist approach to interaction design would foreground human, alongside scientific, concerns, at the same time as enfolding empathy, co-design and reflexivity within the process, all of which would, in turn, be underpinned by a pluralist outlook.[23]

Current feminist contributions tend to cohere around notion of challenging what has been referred to as the 'heterodoxy'[24] of digital outcomes and systems. Here, emphasis is placed on the ways in which technology might be better designed to ensure a greater inclusivity, allowing for alternative modes of being that align to the experience of womxn. An example of such work is the Feminist Server Stack,[25] a speculative design project that explored a feminist internet future based on a co-designed agonistic approach that enfolded not only technical concerns but also biological, geographical and political ones.

---

[22] Shaowen Bardzell, 'Feminist HCI: taking stock and outlining an agenda for design.' In *Proceedings of the SIGCHI conference on Human Factors in Computing Systems* (New York: ACM, 2010), 1301–10.

[23] Shaowen Bardzell and Jeffrey Bardzell, 'Towards a feminist HCI methodology: social science, feminism, and HCI.' In *Proceedings of the SIGCHI conference on human factors in computing systems* (New York: ACM, 2011), 675–84.

[24] Ann Light, 'HCI as heterodoxy: Technologies of identity and the queering of interaction with computers.' *Interacting with Computers* 23, no. 5 (2011): 430–8.

[25] Nancy Mauro-Flude and Yoko Akama, 'A feminist server stack: co-designing feminist web servers to reimagine Internet futures.' *CoDesign* 18, no. 1 (2022): 48–62.

Beyond the above, another final significant philosophical perspective must be attended to here: postphenomenology, which we encountered in the Introduction. As noted, postphenomenology forms an important, indeed perhaps the strongest, contemporary link between the fields of design and philosophy.

The key to understanding postphenomenology is that it is ultimately a philosophy of technology, which, as the word suggests, takes reference from classical phenomenology, in particular the work of Edmund Husserl, the founder of phenomenology, and Martin Heidegger. From the former (Husserl), there is an attention to the theorizing of human perception or, more particularly, the process of perceiving and how this might inform methods of philosophic enquiry.[26] From the latter (Heidegger), there is also an attendance to the process of meaning making or interpretation (referred to as hermeneutics) as it arises from within perception. The technological aspect of postphenomenology enters in via the 'post' prefix. Specifically, *post*phenomenology aims to link phenomenology's careful framing of perception-meaning to the areas of technology and science – referred to as technoscience – drawing out the ways in which both enhance and transform the processes of perception-meaning.

The general idea of a *post*-phenomenological perspective was first proposed by philosopher Don Ihde in the early 1990s.[27] In this, Ihde was primarily concerned with the concept of technological mediation, elaborating a taxonomy of human–technology relations as a means of better qualifying the ways in which technology frames experience.

Ihde's proposals were later extended by the Dutch philosopher Peter-Paul Verbeek. Verbeek worked outwards from a critique of classical philosophies of technology presented by key individuals such as Martin Heidegger and Karl Jaspers, claiming that such

---

[26] The methods of phenomenology, most especially those first defined by Edmund Husserl, are notoriously difficult to understand and have confounded many over the last century. For an outline, see Dermot Moran, *Introduction to Phenomenology* (Abingdon, Oxon: Routledge, 2000).

[27] Ihde, *Technology and Lifeworld*.

work tended to wrongly focus on the abstract idea of technology as opposed to its qualitative, material impact within lived experience. In developing an alternative, Verbeek pitches a renewed philosophy of technology – his own particular version of postphenomenology – that would focus on the concrete role of technology in our lives, with particular attention being paid to its moral dimension.[28] For Verbeek, technology could not be seen to carry moral intent, i.e. the conscious framing and evaluation of action and its consequences. However, he does claim that technology, 'things', could be seen to shape morality because 'they shape the way people experience the world and organize their existence'.[29]

In this view, the design of technology becomes a moral endeavour, with responsibility being placed on those involved in the design process, i.e. designers, in particular. Here, Verbeek takes the view that it is important that designers seek to anticipate the 'future mediating roles that products will play'.[30] To better enable this, Verbeek proposes a novel ethical framework that recognizes the role of things in the shaping of morality.[31] This is ultimately a posthumanist framework in that morality is no longer to be seen as singularly a matter of human intention and action but would now enfold technological agency as well.

Running in parallel to Verbeek, Ihde continued to progress his own strain of postphenomenology by drawing alignment with the classical pragmatism of John Dewey.[32] In this, he links to Dewey's relating of knowledge to action and experimentalism, highlighting how this allows for an overcoming of any concerns relating to phenomenology's individualist focus on perception-

---

[28] Peter-Paul Verbeek, *What Things Do: Reflections on Technology, Agency and Design* (University Park, PN: The Pennsylvania State University Press, 2005).

[29] Ibid, 216.

[30] Ibid, 234.

[31] Peter-Paul Verbeek, *Moralizing Technology: Understanding and Designing the Morality of Things* (Chicago: University of Chicago Press, 2011).

[32] Don Ihde, Postphenomenology and Technoscience: The Peking University Lectures (Albany, NY: State University of New York Press, 2009).

meaning, e.g. that it may result in subjective relativism.[33] His postphenomenology thus forms a phenomenology–pragmatism hybrid, enriching phenomenology with non-subjective understanding of knowing and pragmatism with a means by which experience might be rigorously analysed.[34] This positioning differs markedly from Verbeek's work on the basis that Ihde does not envisage a posthumanist framework but rather retains a mapping to what he refers to as the human embodied hermeneutic. Nor is he overly concerned with morality; postphenomenology for Ihde is broad-based means of understanding technological relations in the context of experience and knowledge production.

Returning to the context of design, postphenomenology – particularly, Verbeek's postphenomenology – has, in recent years, increasingly drawn the attention of both researchers and theorists and is now firmly established as a key philosophical perspective within the field. Indeed, it drives the programmatic agenda in at least two major global design research centres. The first and longest-running is the Department of Industrial Design at Eindhoven University of Technology in the Netherlands. The second is the Everyday Design Studio at Simon Fraser University in Vancouver in Canada. What sets apart at least the latter centre's use of postphenomenology from the theoretical engagement of others is their claim that in pursuing a postphenomenology in design, they are, in effect, 'doing' philosophy. Further, as has been noted, some Eindhoven graduates have already presented a philosophy through design proposal. We will explore these ideas directly in the next section.

---

[33] Phenomenologists have long struggled to provide an adequate response to the question of how to ensure validity in inquiry, i.e. to demonstrate that their methods can produce accurate and transferable results. See Cheryl Beck, Tatano, Barbara A. Keddy and Marlene Zichi Cohen. 'Reliability and validity issues in phenomenological research.' *Western Journal of Nursing Research* 16, no. 3 (1994): 254–67.

[34] Ihde is particularly keen on foregrounding phenomenological analysis within his work. He holds that phenomenological analysis allows us to better understand perception, embodiment and more generally the notion that our experience is formed within a lifeworld, i.e. a set of existential conditions that frame our being. Ihde, Postphenomenology and Technosciencer, 11–19.

'EMPIRICAL PHILOSOPHY' THROUGH A DESIGN–PHILOSOPHY CORRESPONDENCE

The Designing for Quality Interactions (DQI) Group at Eindhoven was established in the early 2000s under the leadership of Kees Overbeeke. Pursuing an agenda of 'How to design for . . .'[35] in the context of the experience of digital products, it operated into the mid-2010s. As was the case for many design–technology research programmes at time, the group gradually shifted their alignment from the models of cognitive psychology noted above to explore the possibilities of a fine-grained qualitative analysis, which in their case took on a phenomenological focus. Within this, attention was directed to the two figures of Maurice Merleau-Ponty, a phenomenological philosopher whose work focused on embodiment; and Martin Heidegger, focusing in particular on his work on hermeneutics, i.e. meaning making/interpretation. Additional reference was also made to the work of the ecological psychologist James Gibson and this theory of affordances, i.e. how we, as embodied humans, derive meaning from the world situationally, exploring and utilizing what the environment affords by way of possibilities, physical or otherwise. The outcome was a rich framework for rethinking the ways in which products, especially digital products, might be designed and interaction, generally, might be reimagined through a philosophic lens. The overall vision was referred to as the 'aesthetics of the impossible'.[36]

Since the 2010s, former DQI members have joined other research groups within Eindhoven, including the Transforming Practices[37] group and the Systematic Change group. Both broadly

---

[35] Kees Overbeeke, Steven S. Wensveen, Caroline Hummels, Joep Frens and Philip Ross, 2014, 'DQI Interaction Design Research'. In *Entwerfen-Wissen-Produzieren*, edited by Claudia Mareis, Gesche Joost and Kora Kimpel (Bielefeld, Germany: Transcript-Verlag, 2010), 193–206.

[36] Kees Overbeeke, *The Aesthetics of the Impossible*, TU Eindhoven, accessed 11 Feb 2020, research.tue.nl https://research.tue.nl/en/publications/the-aesthetics-of-the-impossible

[37] Caroline Hummels, Sander van der Zwan, Maarten Smith and Jelle Bruineberg. 'Non-discursive philosophy by imagining new practices through design.' *Adaptive Behavior* 30, no. 6 (2022): 537–40.

explore design in the context of socio-technical systems at the level of the community, herein investigating key societal challenges by designing 'technology-enabled interventions'. The Systematic Change group also aims to examine the effect of such work on ecosystems.[38] Following on in the tradition of the DQI, philosophy – in this case, *post*phenomenology – has come to thread through this work.[39] This postphenomenological alignment may have been based on familiarity: postphenomenology carries an obvious *phenomeno*logical pedigree, allowing for a continuity between DQI work and that of the present. However, it also enfolds a definite technological focus, something which classical phenomenology does not.[40] To date, this work has ranged from an exploration of such areas as internet of things work to social innovation contexts to more granular mapping techniques. More recently, however, a new line of investigation has opened up within the group's agenda: the scoping of the possibility of doing philosophy through a coupling of postphenomenology and design. This work is, at present, only in its early stage – a general position gradually taking shape, which has been expressed across a number of recent papers and presentations.

In such pieces, the group have labelled their efforts as an exploration of design–philosophy correspondence,[41] i.e. a looking at the ways in which design and philosophy can and do come together in the process of investigating joint concerns. Generally, philosophical concerns and concepts are explored, experimentally, in relation to design, allowing for the potential enrichment, it is claimed, of both fields. Projects have explored the notional divide between philosophy and design, linking a concern for ethics and

---

[38] Department of Industrial Design, TU Eindhoven, 'Systematic Change', 29 April 2023, https://www.tue.nl/en/research/research-groups/systemic-change

[39] Importantly, Peter Paul Verbeek is Rector of the nearby University of Amsterdam.

[40] Many would claim that Martin Heidegger's work does place an emphasis on technological concerns. This is true. Nonetheless, Heidegger was not explicitly seeking to develop a philosophy *of* technology, a label that postphenomenology very explicitly claims for itself.

[41] This term has come to the fore in the group's recent work.

values, the positioning of being-in-the-world, complexity and 'co-development'.

A number of potential strands open up within such work. At times, things are analysed via philosophy. In the postphenomenological vein, such analysis focuses on the role and impact of technology within the context of human–technology relations. Beyond analysis, the group have also trialled the use of postphenomenology as a means of framing the design of the made artefacts – in other words, as a *generative* tool. Intriguingly, this notion of philosophy being positioned as a generative tool is seen to open up the possibility of design informing philosophy itself.[42] In one specific example, the group explored how in designing a 'ritual' they might be guided by what they refer to as the 'dimensions' of technological mediation, which, following Asle Kiran,[43] are defined as practical, ontological, epistemological and ethical. The ritual process was supported by a printing device which produced cards that allowed for reflection on the dimensions.

Each dimension is seen to carry a two-sided quality or, to put it another way, be defined by contrasting/competing values, which one must reconcile in the context of design*ing*. For the practical, it is a matter of negotiating an enabling–constraining structure; for the ontological it is a matter of revealing–concealing; the epistemological is a matter of magnifying–reducing; and lastly, the ethical is framed in relation to involving–alienating. While the practical dimension was fully familiar to designers, the other dimensions were not. In explicitly positioning these dimensions within design process, designers are suddenly charged with 'co-shaping how humans experience and act in the world

---

[42] Sander van der Zwan, Maarten Smith, Jelle Bruineberg, Pierre Levy and Caroline Hummels 'Philosophy at work: Postphenomenology as a generative lens in design research and practice', In *Proceedings of DRS2020 International Conference, Vol. 4: Education*, edited by Stella Boess, Ming Cheung and Rebecca Cain (London: The Design Research Society, 2020), 1691–706.

[43] Asle Kiran, 'Four Dimensions of Technological Mediation', In *Postphenomenological Investigations: Essays on Human-Technology Relations*, edited by Robert Rosenburg and Peter-Paul Verbeek (Lanham, MD: Lexington Books, 2015), 123–40.

THE TECHNOLOGICAL HORIZON: DIGITAL ONTOLOGIZING

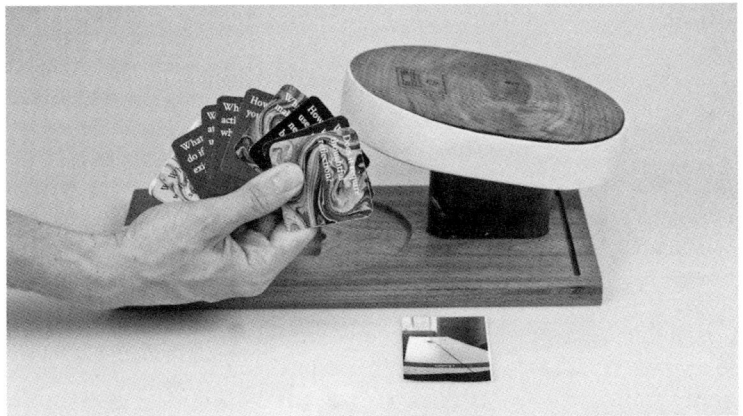

FIGURE 2.1 A printer that produced cards allowing for reflection on technological mediation as part of a ritual designed to explore the generative potential of philosophy at Eindhoven. Courtesy Sander van der Swan.

(human–technology–world relations)'.[44] The ethical responsibilities of design were also drawn to the fore, highlighting the inherent ethical character of all design decision making. In applying these dimensions within the design process and evaluating them in a live context, the team can claim to have framed a postphenomenological methodology, thus potentially contributing a 'design-informed philosophy'.[45]

Next to such approaches, the group have also proposed that project outcomes can be seen to function as a form of what they term 'non-discursive' philosophy (i.e. a non-textual or discourse-based philosophy). Here, it is proposed that made artefacts (e.g. artworks or design outcomes) can give form to a 'philosophical worldview'. In this framing, such artefacts are said to allow for reflection and imaginative engagement on what is being communicated.

---

[44] van der Zwan et al., 'Philosophy at work: Postphenomenology as a generative lens in design research and practice', 1704.
[45] Ibid, 1705.

Offering an example of such work, the group refer to a project undertaken with the Dutch Ministry of Infrastructure and Water Management, which explored cross-population scenarios for living in the Netherlands in 2050. In workshops, participants were offered an insight into emerging demographic, economic, political, socio-cultural and technological trends.[46] These were then coupled what was referred to as a 'playing field' or work area, which contained a series of physical artefacts, some of which were recognizable (e.g. as human figures) and others which were more abstract. The prototypic argument put forward by the group was that the process of discussion and associated imaginative action (in the form of framing scenarios) can be understood to amount to a means of philosophic form giving, a type of socio-material philosophizing that finds statement in the outcome.[47]

In all of such work, a philosophy through design is almost declared within the proposals, albeit with a distinctly technological focus. Indeed, as noted in the previous chapter, philosophy through design proposals have already been forthcoming from individuals associated with this group. Here, Jonne van Belle and colleagues also explored a form of philosophy through design that references 'research through design'.[48]

Aligning to the work of anthropologist Tim Ingold, their approach is grounded in the idea of a 'living philosophy', where the problems are experienced and dealt with directly as opposed to at a remove. In both cases, things are made, tested and presented. The distinction drawn between philosophy through design and design research through design is that while design research involving practice functions as a form of research that involves design, philosophy through design functions as a *philosophic* process that aims to produce philosophical statements through designing. Further distinction is noted in relation to the process

---

[46] Hummels et al., 'Non-discursive philosophy by imagining new practices through design', 538.
[47] Ibid, 539.
[48] van Belle et al., 'Towards a Tangible Philosophy through Design'

itself. In philosophy through design, it is recommended that philosophy act as a reference point when pressing practical challenges arise, allowing for a redirection when required. It is also claimed that working with philosophy in this manner allows for an explicit drawing out of the influences and references that have guided the design, enabling these influences/references to be 'philosophized about'.[49]

Looking beyond Eindhoven, a key, closely aligned partner is the Everyday Design Studio at Simon Fraser University in Vancouver, Canada, which is led by Ron Wakkary and William Odom. Like Eindhoven, the studio follows a postphenomenological programme linking, in particular, to the work of Verbeek. Their approach is termed 'material speculation'.[50] Projects have explored the role of speculative digital products in domestic environments, with the development and testing of peculiar artefacts such as 'tilting bowls' and 'morse things' (i.e. morse code-emitting kitchenware) in people's homes in Vancouver.[51] As with Eindhoven, attention is directed towards the meaning of particular forms of technological mediation, the values which such mediation gives rise to. For example, the morse things study allowed for reflection on how such objects elicit a search for humanness as well as a 'thing-centredness' and, linked to these, led to tensions in relation to the 'gap' between us (i.e. humans) and these things.[52]

The studio's programme diverges somewhat from Eindhoven in that their approach is positioned explicitly in 'posthuman' terms, meaning that the human is not centred within their

---

[49] Ibid.

[50] Ron Wakkary, William Odom, Sabrina Hauser, Garnet Hertz and Henry Lin, 'Material speculation: Actual artifacts for critical inquiry.' In *Proceedings of The Fifth Decennial Aarhus Conference on Critical Alternatives*, (New York: ACM, 2015), 97–108.

[51] Ron Wakkary, Doenja Oogjes, Henry W. J. Lin and Sabrina Hauser. 'Philosophers living with the tilting bowl.' In *Proceedings of the 2018 CHI Conference on Human Factors in Computing Systems*, 94, (New York: ACM, 2018) 1–12.

[52] Ron Wakkary, Doenja Oogjes, Sabrina Hauser, Henry WJ Lin, Cheng Cao, Leo Ma and Tijs Duel, 'Morse Things: A Design Inquiry into the Gap Between Things and Us.' In *Conference on Designing Interactive Systems* (New York: ACM, 2017), 508.

investigations. Rather, linking the postphenomenological to a range of perspectives, including, for example, the work of French philosophers Deleuze and Guattari, a vision for a networked more-than-human-centred design emerges.[53] This vision ultimately challenges or 'unbuilds' classic human-centred approaches to design. Here it is not just the designer that designs but an 'assembly of humans and non-humans'. Nor is it a matter of designing for, it is a matter of 'designing with'.[54] Emphasis is placed on relationality and what is referred to as 'nomad practices' – that is, practices that follows the needs of things to be designed.[55]

Reflecting on the above cases, it is clear that the firmament at Eindhoven and Simon Fraser is gradually instantiating a way of working that gives meaningful form to the idea of a philosophy through design (or something comparable) via design research involving practice or design research involving practice-like processes. In Eindhoven, we can see this in the idea of design philosophy correspondence – in particular, through the exploration of the use of postphenomenology as a generative tool or design outcomes as a form of non-discursive philosophy. Then of course, alongside this, there is Jonne van Belle and colleagues' explicit philosophy through design proposal, which begins to work through the potential of interweaving philosophy and design research involving practice. Further, at the Everyday Studio, the idea of material speculation can also be understood to act in generative terms, progressing our understanding of the potentialities of human–technology relations and how by designing and realizing novel technological situations we can discuss them philosophically, perhaps even challenging what design is, and can be, within the process.

Reviewing this work from a design perspective, it is possible to note that the approach taken across these examples can be seen to align with critical and speculative design of Antony Dunne, Fiona Raby and others, noted in the Introduction.[56] We see this

---

[53] Wakkary, *Things We Could Design*.
[54] Ibid, 234.
[55] Ibid, 233.
[56] Malpass, *Critical Design in Context;* Dunne and Raby, *Speculative Everything*.

in relation to both Eindhoven's 'non-discursive' work (as in the example of the Dutch Ministry of Infrastructure and Water Management 2050 project) and the material speculation of Simon Fraser. In both cases, futures are either envisaged and traced or unfamiliar possibilities (that may apply to the present) are explored. Viewed philosophically, this critical/speculative approach might be seen to enrich philosophical practice in so far as, leading off from a specific concern or point of intrigue (e.g. what might independently communicating objects mean in terms of human–object relations?), it allows for the imagining and then the direct investigation of potential meanings and values. Here, we can both notionally foresee possible technological relations (i.e. note what happens when objects *do* communicate) as well as reflect on current relations (e.g. consider thing-centredness in general).

In reviewing this work from a philosophic perspective, there are two further additional points. First, linking to the speculative/critical, it is worth highlighting the potential for a philosophical strengthening of this approach through reference to the philosophical method of 'thought experiments'. In philosophy, thought experiments are generally undertaken with a view to testing specific questions relating to ongoing disciplinary concerns, whether that be, for example, what it means to know something or the specifics of particular aspects of reality or an especially troublesome ethical quandary.[57] The outcomes will be short (or sometimes longer) written descriptions of a context or scenario which will include a note on the constraints (or not) of that context/scenario and the outcome and/or meaning of the context/scenario when related back to the specific questions that were to be answered. The point is that the ethical possibilities and consequences can be trialled with desirability or not of given outcomes appraised.

The potential of applying thought experiments as an ethical tool within design has been recently explored by Peter Buwert and Matt Sinclair.[58] Combining this with the 'non-discursive' or

---

[57] Nenad Miscevic, *Thought experiments* (Cham: Springer, 2022).
[58] Peter Buwert and Matt Sinclair, 'Thought Experiments In The Ethics Of Designing For Future People.' Paper presented at 'DRS2024: Boston' 23–28 June 2024, Boston, USA. https://doi.org/10.21606/drs.2024.518

'material speculation' approaches of Eindhoven and Everyday Design Studio might enhance our ability to anticipate the potential consequences of particular technological meanings and values, drawing in social and ecological or any number of additional thematics that were deemed to be relevant. The 'thought' of thought experiments might thus be rendered material within an ethical inquiry into things and their potential qualities.

Second, it important to attend to its special referencing of the postphenomenological perspective and the position this carries with respect to technology. As we noted in the opening section, Verbeek's postphenomenology explicitly rejects the abstract aspects of classical philosophies of technology (e.g. those of Heidegger, Jaspers), whereby particular values or qualities are ascribed to technology in general, and, instead, approaches technology in concrete terms, opening up an investigative space in which its real-terms moral dimensions can be explored. This is what is happening in this project work. Technology is being approached empirically, with its qualitative, material impacts being noted.

Had Eindhoven and the Everyday Design Studio referenced a different philosophy, their work would, of course, have taken a different direction. For example, a value-based perspective where potential of realizing a given technology possibility might be explored. In such cases, technology might be backgrounded, literally pushed back from the immediacy of interactions.[59]

Thus, should other designers be seeking to explore the philosophical aspects of technology, it would be desirable to hold some awareness of the existence of alternative positions. Other perspectives will offer other particular investigative affordances. Each will yield a philosophic outcome of a different tenor. It may be that, when compared to postphenomenology,

---

[59] An example of a philosophic perspective which might allow for such an investigation is Albert Borgmann's work. See e.g. Albert Borgmann, *Technology and the Character of Contemporary Life* (Chicago: University of Chicago Press, 1984).

such alternatives are judged to be unsuitable. Nonetheless, comparison will allow for surety here.

From the above, we will now move on to consider the wider implications of such work in relation to the possibility of progressing a philosophy through design.

THE DIGITAL SOURCE POINT: PROGRESSING A PHILOSOPHY THROUGH DESIGN FROM HERE

It would seem that, in its link to design and designing, the affordances of technology – in particular, digital technology – open up significant questions relating to the structure and meaning of human experience. It may be that the shift to a qualitative, experiential perspective within the field has led to such questions being askable. Either way, the importance of the issues has become evermore pronounced as technology, and its design, becomes increasingly embedded within our daily lives.

The examples from the last two sections demonstrate how some areas of design research have responded and mobilized in relation to these questions. This, as we have seen, has involved the referencing of philosophy, which has been drawn upon as *the* key means of working through the practical concerns that have arisen, whether relating to situatedness, embodiment or perception, feeling or morality. Supporting the development of new theoretical models – whether referred to as experience design, participatory design or postphenomenology – philosophy is helping to ground, frame and shape what is being surfaced in the entwining of design–technology within human experience.

The questions emerging here are both compelling and also very significant. Underlying the whole, we can detect a focus on what it means to be human in relation to the possibilities of technology. Equally, there is an unpicking of the broader sets of relations of the world, whether between humans and humans or humans and non-humans. In many cases, the ethical has come to the fore as a core concern. That some of these efforts seek to draw philosophy and design into close range or, indeed, seek to establish a philosophy through design, make this context all the more compelling.

Here, as a means of drawing the chapter to a close, I will seek to consider how we might move forward from this point, hoping to further tease out a philosophy through design from design's existing interrelating of technology and philosophy.

As I see it, this interrelating has surfaced a number of points of concern or value, which could be seen to function as a thematic grouping in the context of design–technology and its meaning for human experience and, more broadly, for our understanding of human and non-human relations. The key immediate opportunity here is to work outwards and position this grouping as a loose mapping, which, in turn, might guide and inform future work.

The question arises as to what has been surfaced. Though a final or even a comprehensive list would be beyond the scope of this text, surveying both the preceding literature and the cases, it is possible to note that the design–technology/design–research coupling has drawn out focused consideration of the following: the meaning of situatedness; the meaning of context; the meaning of embodiment; the moral agency of made-artefacts; and the extent to which humans and non-humans can be drawn into alignment in the context of designing. These points relate not only to the character of existence but also draw to the fore questions of how we should live, what is desirable and, to an extent, what is right in given situations. Of course, some of these points/questions are timeless in the sense that they have been asked many times before over the preceding millennia.[60] Arguably, however, design in concert with technology, particularly digital technology, can be seen as acting in a transformative capacity, changing reality as it changes.

This was already implied in our discussion of Verbeek's work on the morality of technology, where we noted his belief that design shapes 'the way people experience the world and organize their existence'. This points to the idea of design as a force capable

---

[60] Plato, for example, is famous for asking questions of 'the good life'. See Daniel Russell, *Pleasure and the Good Life* (Oxford: Oxford University Press, 2005).

of changing what is understood as real and what is not, a force for designing our very being. As alluded to in the discussion on design research involving practice (see the Introduction), such a possibility, though perhaps startling, has, in fact, long been registered by design theorists. Those who do tend to reference the term 'ontological design' to denote a way of seeing the discipline not only as a means of developing new 'things' (whether products or services) but also as an approach that shapes our existence.[61] Here, design itself is conferred with agency. New things modify our existing actions and interactions, both affording and limiting ways of experiencing and consuming. Humans and non-humans, indeed, the world is reshaped – designed – by those same outcomes. As Anne-Marie Willis puts it, when we design, 'our world acts back and designs us'.[62]

Dewey's work, too, offers a framing for this concept. Here, we have noted how, in his view, the meaning of things – as expressed in language, communication and action, i.e. what we think, say and do with things – shapes our understanding the world. This is particularly significant in relation to technology. New ideas, new meanings can bring about new technology and new technology, in turn, brings further new meanings and ideas. Our reality, as contained within our experience (and, as such, reality itself), is changed – the possibilities of the world are now different from before.

There are also new problems, of course, as exemplified in relation to Dewey's reflections on the perceived crisis of governance in the United States in the mid-1920s. For Dewey this required constant ongoing inquiry, allowing for exploration, understanding and the potential addressing of such problems.

Keeping account of both possibilities, as well as new problems and how they might be addressed via a philosophy through design,

---

[61] This view was first proposed in Terry Winograd and Ferando Flores, *Understanding Computers and Cognition: A New Foundation for Design* (Norwood, NJ: Albex, 1986).

[62] Willis, 'Ontological designing.'

would allow for a scoping of the potential meaning and value of the 'could be's' of the future. Extending from here, we will see in the next chapter how Dewey's perspective on ethical inquiry can build on this.

From Addams, we can additionally draw on the idea of those in power (in her case employers) being 'good with' – something we can see expressed via the democratic aspect of participatory design. Although designers may or may not be engaging in the workplace-based contexts where employer–employee relationships are at play, the principle of participatory practice still stands.

Combined, it is arguable that the Dewey–Addams notion of participatory inquiry is addressed within the work of Eindhoven and the Everyday Studio, but there is an opportunity for this to be progressed further. As intimated in the sketch at the beginning of the current chapter, the emergence of an open AI demands immediate and focused inquiry. Indeed, this is widely called for by leading figures within the field as well as within the media. It is ultimately a question of ethics of things as per the postphenomenology of Verbeek, with the meaning and possibilities of things – in this case, AI in particular – under scrutiny.

In closing, it is important to note that what is presented above, of course, is only the starting point, reflecting the current general positioning of design and technology with respect to philosophy and what might follow from this. There is further potential to reject or push past these present points of concern/value. For example, one might seek to progress a decolonial perspective, looking at alternative ways of relating to technology that trace distinct ontologies, allowing us to reflect on our own relationality to ourselves, to others, to the world. Progressed by active design-based experimentation, a philosophically bound programme investigating such perspectives might again offer fresh insight into the potentialities of human experience. Such a programme would aim to pick up and work through these perspectives, making and proposing in order to better understand their structure and scope. To help engender this, we would do well to maintain an openness to a plurality of voices as we seek to frame a philosophy through design study. As we will see, this applies whether the work is technologically focused or not.

Having covered the technological horizon up to here, we now will turn to the complementary area of the social. The social has, of course, threaded implicitly through our preceding discussions and, as we will see, allows us to extend on what has been set out. The time has come to address it explicitly.

3 The Social Horizon: Association in Experience

Though my wife and I live on the same island we each grew up on (Ireland), seeing our parents means an approximately three-hour drive or, alternatively, a five-hour train journey with two changes. As a result, neither of us have a direct support network to turn to when we need immediate help – a point of frustration when one has young children (3 and 5 years at the time of writing). This frustration is further exacerbated by the sense that we don't seem have much time to engage with those who live in direct proximity to us. I am friendly with those who live on my street but do not, for example, volunteer in the town I live in or engage in other community-level activities. The pace of my work as an academic is simply too intense; or so I tell myself. This is a point of regret, something I am aware of and seek to address from time to time but never quite manage to amend. At times, I wonder if it is a personal situation or something more endemic. Are we all as pressured?

Looking back, this was not the life my parents lived. They had their support networks. My father's mother, brothers and sisters all lived nearby when I was a child. I saw my grandmother on a near daily basis. Her house was just around the corner and my brother, sister and I visited often. My parents were involved in their community too. They had time to participate in voluntary groups and clubs. It appeared to me that they were able to find this time without a great deal of stress or any apparent worry.

The world was different then, of course. More people lived their whole lives in the towns they were born in than now. The people they grew up with were the people they would know for the rest of their lives. This is partly because economies were structured differently. Trade and distribution networks were smaller or, at least, less globalized than they are now. We generally consumed the goods we could buy locally. As a consequence, local employment was possible in ways that are simply no longer viable today. Technology was less complex too, of course. There was no social media, no video calling or text messages. Broadcast and print media functioned as the key information channels. Ultimately, this supported a different type of politics – one of greater cohesion, where other, diverging views were encountered if not, perhaps, always fully understood or accepted.

Such changes do raise a question regarding the meaning of community now and how people interact and come together in the present and beyond. With limitless opportunity for technological connection, where and in what forms should we seek out fellowship? Are local interactions to be prioritized as important in and of themselves? If so why and how might these be best facilitated? In relation to economic changes noted, how do we seek to preserve the valued aspects of local employment while also recognizing that circumstances are now different? Then there is the political layer. With the shifts in media consumption, how do we enable a more cohesive politics? One where others can better understand the views of those with whom they disagree.

The questions posed above are not wholly philosophical, but they do contain a philosophical angle and approaching them as such might conceivably yield novel answers relating to desirable values and how these are best attained. Equally, answering does not require that one design, but if we are to address what are understood to be problematic, the designing of alternatives will be important. Here, meaning and value can be better understood as we make and test, try things out.

Design, at this stage in its evolution, is also well equipped to take on such a challenge. The discipline, as we have noted, has made strident advances into the social and political arena. Here, through the proliferation of co-creative approaches such as participatory and codesign, a new and vibrant repertoire of designing with others has become established.

We have already encountered aspects of this in the last chapter. As noted there and earlier, the social implicitly threads through concerns relating to design–technology–philosophy and individually focused questions of human experience, as well as human and non-human relations. Considering questions of what it means to be situated, to be part of a context, to be embodied, to hold moral agency and to relate to non-humans all involves a social dimension. There are always other people to consider.

The social aspects of our lives were hugely significant to both Dewey and Addams, much more so than the technological, at least in terms how much of their writing was proportionally dedicated to the subject. For both, the social is entwined with the democratic, which in turn extends to the ethical. For Dewey, this also drew in the pedagogic. Here, education was to enable good citizenship, good citizenship was to enable healthy democracy, healthy democracy, in turn, was to enable positive life experiences and a vibrant culture of ethical inquiry. As we have seen, social concerns also drove Addams's and feminist pragmatists' impressive Hull House change-making programme. They literally centred themselves in real-world social and political concerns, working through how these could be addressed, sometimes failing and sometimes succeeding but always trying.[1]

In this chapter, we will link to these latter contributions but also look beyond them to consider the ways in which a philosophy through design might address the social horizon. While the course will be somewhat meandering, this meandering is undertaken with a purpose; we need to give some scope to the breadth of the social both as a field in and of itself, as well as in relation to the field of design.

---

[1] Addams, *Twenty Years at Hull House*, provides an evocative overview of both the context of Hull House as well as how a variety of strands of its programme progressed.

We begin by further exploring the social aspects of Dewey's and Addams's work. Then, beyond this, we will also turn to consider a series of related social perspectives that centre upon the areas of communication and culture. Consideration will also be given to decolonial stances. Next, we turn directly to design, examining the social as a broad concern within the field and briefly highlighting existing positions within this. Here, linking to the last chapter, particular attention will be directed to the distinct contribution of the late Bruno Latour, who, along with others, developed the now well-known actor network theory (ANT), a theoretical perspective that bridges philosophy–design–technology and the social. Broadly, the chapter will aim to give form to a strategy that provides for flexible ways of seeing, allowing a philosophy through design to move across social situations, noting general problems at the same time as mounting specific responses. To close, we will briefly look at how we can potentially aim to philosophize together, through design.

DEWEY AND ADDAMS AS SOCIAL PHILOSOPHERS

Pragmatism can be understood as a socially bound philosophy, with a commitment to the idea of community at its core.[2] For Dewey, the social forms a 'matrix' upon which other considerations, whatever they might be, can be contextualized and addressed. On his account, our thoughts, feelings, actions – indeed, our being – are social, so much so that rather than thinking of ourselves as individuals, Dewey proposed that we instead form 'an association' of other people and groups.[3] Similarly, Addams and her feminist pragmatist colleagues centred their understanding of human life within the social realm.

---

[2] James Campbell, 'A History of Pragmatism.' In *The Bloomsbury Handbook of Pragmatism*, edited by Sami Pihlström (London: Bloomsbury 2024 [2011]), 85–99.

[3] John Dewey, *The Later Works, 1925–1953, Volume 2: 1925–1927, Essays, Reviews, Miscellany, and The Pubic and Its Problems*, edited by Jo Ann Boydston (Carbondale: Southern Illinois University, 2008 [1984]), 353.

As has been noted, the work of the two can be seen as intimately related, particularly in regard to this specific thematic horizon, where Addams acted as a key source of inspiration for Dewey. Here, it is worth noting again that Dewey saw Addams as a primary source point for this democratic vision, attributing his concept of democracy as a way of life to her.[4]

In considering both here, we will quickly look to Dewey's work first. In doing so, it is important to remember that his call for reconstruction in philosophy was a plea for the discipline to take on a problem-solving role in the context of social and moral concerns, in particular. His broader programme of work in the twentieth century is ultimately focused on giving context to this. When it comes to identifying a common thread in his positions, it is possible to point to his commitment to democracy, what can be referred to as his 'democratic vision'. I have written elsewhere about the potential meaning of this vision for design.[5] In short, following Addams's theory of democracy as a way of life, the vision shifts the political centre of gravity away from any formal institutional concepts such as parliaments and voting rights and, instead, turns attention to the conduct of everyday, community-based interactions, the street corner processes that allow for local exchange and decision making. Here, it is citizens, as opposed to politicians, who become the central figures.

While the focus remains determinedly human, i.e. the vision centres on people and how they interact,[6] a new way of seeing

---

[4] Jane Dewey, 'Biography of John Dewey', 30; additionally, Marilyn Fischer has speculated that Dewey's ethics can be seen as deriving from Addams. Fischer, *Jane Addams's Evolutionary Theorizing*, 66.

[5] Brian Dixon, 'From making things public to the design of creative democracy: Dewey's democratic vision and participatory design.' *CoDesign*, 16, no. 2 (2020): 97–110.

[6] It is important to note that Marres sees Dewey's vision as deriving from a material or technological perspective. Her *Material Participation* thesis focuses on the materially bound aspect of the publics – that is, that technologies give rise to publics and the more technologies, the more publics. In this way, the publics concept is presented as particularly important for understanding our contemporary political situation. Noortje Marres, *Material Participation: Technology, the Environment and Everyday Publics* (London: Palgrave Macmiilan, 2012), 45–8.

politics is nonetheless still opened up. Later in the chapter, the perspective will act as a lead-in to the work of key object-orientated social theorists such as Bruno Latour and Noortje Marres.

More broadly, this simple but powerful proposal can be seen to connect with many other important areas of Dewey's work – particularly, as has been noted, education and ethics. For Dewey, schools were to be the heart of community, a site for modelling community interactions and processes and, in this, developing an able, active citizenry. The aim was to equip students with an ability to inquire and engage with findings of inquiry. Citizens who could inquire and understand the findings of inquiry could support an informed and balanced democratic life.[7]

In relation to ethics, Dewey took the view that most forms of morality were based on socially regulated customs and habit. This carries things forward most of the time; we know what we are to do and not to do based on convention. However, when a specific custom or habit breaks down and no longer aligns with the social context, then it is necessary to engage a process of reflection and, ultimately, inquiry. In this, the imagination was seen as a central force, allowing for exploration and trialling of possible consequences without having to act them out in direct terms. Here, democracy and ethics come together in an accompanying process of deliberation, where the desirability or not of foreseen consequences is discussed collectively and joint decisions made.[8] Over time, we can work progressively to trace and eventually realize a renewed custom or habit.[9]

Centred in context at Hull House, Addams and her feminist pragmatism colleagues were committed to working through social and political concerns by listening, coming to understand and shared problem solving in response. Ethics ran through the whole.

---

[7] John Dewey, *The Middle Works, 18991924, Volume 9: 1916, Democracy and Education*, edited by Jo Ann Boydston (Carbondale: Southern Illinois University Press, 2008 [1980]).

[8] John Dewey, *Ethics*.

[9] Frederic R. Kellogg, 'Moral Dilemmas, Ethical Particularism, and Dewey's Continuum of Normative Inquiry.' *European Journal of Pragmatism and American Philosophy* 13, no. XIII–2 (2021).

As noted earlier, for Addams, like Dewey, ethics was a socially bound concern directly related to democracy. However, her social ethics differed somewhat from his. So far as she was concerned, the problem with then-contemporary ethics was its singularly individualistic focus, i.e. being framed around individual-to-individual conduct. Instead, following a particular strain of German thought prevalent in the later nineteenth century termed 'evolutionary' theorizing,[10] she believed that ethics needed to 'evolve' to become a wholly social concern.[11]

On this framing, it would be founded upon the concerns of the wider community, considering how community need and community conduct link and jointly unfold. The role of the individual was to participate in the context in which they were based, understanding its constraints, working to find ways to make things better collectively and collaboratively in partnership with others. If one is to practise democracy as a way of life, as Addams did, there was no other choice; for her, no one 'can stand aside; our feet are mired in the same soil; our lungs breathe the same air'.[12]

This approach to ethics has been characterized by Maurice Hamington as being centred upon an 'embodied care'. The embodied aspect relates to being located in and working with the inner-city communities Addams and others served. In essence, it is about immediacy and the capacity to use one's faculties in direct, attuned terms (e.g. being able to listen on a one-to-one basis). Alongside this, the care-based aspect relates to 'the maintenance of right relationships in particular contexts'.[13] This relies on the active listening and participation already noted but also on the concepts of connected leadership and activism. The latter is about maintaining

---

[10] Fischer, *Jane Addams's Evolutionary Theorizing.*

[11] The evolutionary theory of the era offered a bio-social way of seeing based on the idea that humanity was and could progress towards more ideal forms. Ethically the ideal would have been a move from the person as centre to the group.

[12] Jane Addams, *Democracy and Social Ethics*, 112.

[13] Maurice Hamington, 'Jane Addams and a politics of embodied care.' *The Journal of Speculative Philosophy* 15, no. 2 (2001): 105.

constant, ongoing contact with those one is leading, meaning 'that participation becomes an ongoing element of . . . leadership'.[14] Next to this, activism is about ensuring that the group coheres around a common goal. Addams believed that 'social action, like the experience of caring, has a transformative quality whereby working together toward a goal may spread the democratic spirit, which in turn will have an impact on future actions'.[15]

Recent design scholarship has, in various ways, explored this latter positioning, as well as Addams's distinct mode of theorizing via practice. Key contributions come from Carl DiSalvo, Michael DelSesto and Danielle Lake and Judy Whipps. DiSalvo centres Addams's special approach to civic 'experimentation', which he positions as a form of 'democratic inquiry'.[16] DelSesto focuses on the social aspect of her contributions. In his view, Addams and her Hull House colleagues demonstrate a design-based, imaginative practice that connects 'aspirations of what *could be* with a spirt of hospitality, solidarity and care'.[17] Lake and Whipps honour her and the Hull House residents' general holism, whereby the *systematic* aspect of the situation was considered.[18]

Here, in the present text, with regard to forging a philosophy through design, it is important to highlight the potential value of Addams's ethics and, in doing so, tie it to Dewey's. A philosophy through design that positioned itself fully within the community would be able to attend to ethical concerns in direct terms, working through issues as Addams and Dewey both, in their own ways, sought to progress. To aid this, from Addams, we can pick up on the idea of the need for a non-individualistic perspective, a way of seeing and, more importantly practising, which focuses on the meaning of relating and relationships, honouring embodiment (being there) and care (based on listening, participating, and connecting while leading as an activist). From Dewey, we can

---

[14] Ibid, 118.
[15] Ibid, 120.
[16] DiSalvo, *Design as Democratic Inquiry*.
[17] DelSesto, *Design and the Social Imagination*, 137.
[18] Lake and Whipps, 'Feminist Pragmatist Design'.

draw on the idea of inquiry and not see ethics as a matter apart from our engagement with the world, but a constant ongoing process in which we must participate, either based on a referencing of social norms or, if these are in question, through a reflective, imaginative and deliberative process of questioning.

From here, we move to follow two further social threads of Dewey's which will allow for a further, productive widening of the discussion: communication and culture. Linking to these will open up an additional vista, from which other concerns for a philosophy through design may be considered and addressed.

SOCIAL PRAGMATISM THREADS TO FOLLOW: COMMUNICATION AND CULTURE

Communication and culture may, at first, appear to denote distinct and separate spheres without any clear overlap. The two are, however, closely related. Communication informs culture and culture informs communication. Social life is intimately shaped by this interdependency. In fields such as communication studies, cultural studies and anthropology, this joint shaping has long been recognized.[19] This is also true of classical pragmatism and the idea underpins Dewey's general philosophy. In relation to communication, in keeping with his contemporary and friend, George Herbert Mead, he saw communication as an essentially biological function, which allowed for a social binding in and around action. Positioned in this way it became a means, or grand 'tool', by which goals can be coordinated and achieved, as well as their achievement celebrated. Democracy as a way of life, as we have seen, relied on strong communal communication, with local dialogue and debate acting as the cornerstone of all political engagement.

Culture relates to this in so far as the practices that build up around activities of communicating come to define the social

---

[19] See e.g. Tony Schirato and Susan Yell, *Communication and Culture: An Introduction* (London: Sage, 2000).

group. For Dewey, the concept of culture was interchangeable with his broad understanding of experience, wherein experience was seen to relate not only to what happens but also to what is done, enacted, changed.[20] Adopting such a framing, culture helpfully draws together the full breadth of experiential possibility linking the social and historical, with felt-immediate, the reflective-intellectual and the emotional-aesthetic. Across these lines, all manner of human activity come together as one: not just as they impact or are enacted by the individual but also the group; not just how they are now but how they were.

Communication and, more especially, language, of course, occupied much of twentieth-century philosophy. From the semiotics of the post-war period, through to the linguistic turn of the 1960s,[21] through to the performative concerns of authors such as J. L. Austin, Michel Foucault and Judith Butler,[22] there has been a consistent thread of focus directed towards the meaning of signs and symbols, of creating shared meaning and how this affects actions and interactions. There has also been, within this, a concern with the theme of power. Here, the question is how power is acquired and maintained through a combination of text, speech, action and environment.[23]

Communication has been a central point of focus within design too. As one would expect, this is especially pronounced in the connection to the area of communication design where semiotics proved especially appealing through the latter half of

---

[20] For a time, he envisaged revising the title of the famous *Experience and Nature* to *Culture and Nature* in an effort to better position what he meant by experience. Sydney Hook, 'Introduction.' In John Dewey, *The Later Works, 1925–1953, Volume 1: 1925, Experience and Nature*, edited by Jo Ann Boydston (Carbondale, IL: Southern Illinois University Press, 2008 [1981]), viii.

[21] See Richard Rorty, *The Linguistic Turn: Essays in Philosophical Method, With Two Retrospective Essays* (Chicago: University of Chicago Press, 1992 [1967]).

[22] See Judith Butler, *Gender Trouble* (Abingdon, Oxon: Routledge, 1990).

[23] An introduction to these strands of work can be found in Jørgen Dines Johansen and Scend Erik Larsen, *Signs in Use: An introduction to semiotics*, translated by Dinda L. Gorlée and John Irons (London: Routledge, 2002).

the twentieth century.²⁴ This connection extends more generally too – for example, into the areas of industrial and product design, where the symbolic and meaning-based value of products has received significant attention over the years. Across this, there have been regular efforts to model the relationship between the designer, their designed artefacts and the audience or users who ultimately act as consumers of the process.²⁵ Power has not featured as prominently as it might within such discourse. This, however, is changing, with perspectives such as those of Sasha Costanza-Chock foregrounding justice as key concern.²⁶

Next to communication/language, the area of culture has not enjoyed the same attention in recent philosophy. As we have seen in the earlier part of this book, as the anglophone field turned towards logic and technical procedure through the twentieth century, interest in tackling the richness and variety of human experience fell away. Arguably, it has remained in certain areas, most notably in continental work – for example, in the contributions of the Frankfurt School through the studies of such individuals as Theodor Adorno, who explored the evolution of 'mass culture' through the impact of media such as film and television.²⁷ Equally, there is the broad register of the French philosophers Gilles Deleuze and Félix Guattari, who enfolded a breadth of cultural references as they gave gradual form to their rich re-envisioning of philosophy.²⁸ Then, the sociological work of Pierre Bourdieu traces the means by which power is gained and maintained through cultural processes and systems.²⁹

---

[24] Steven Skaggs, *FireSigns: A Semiotic Theory for Graphic Design* (Cambridge MA: The MIT Press, 2017).
[25] Klaus Krippendorff, *The Semantic Turn: A new foundation for design* (Boca Raton, FL: The CRC Press, 2004).
[26] Costanza-Chock, *Design Justice*.
[27] See Theodor Adorno, *The Culture Industry: Selected Essays on Mass Culture* (Abingdon, Oxon: Routledge, 2001).
[28] Gilles Deleuze and Félix Guattari, *One Thousand Plateaus: Capitalism and Schizophrenia*, translated by Brian Massumi (London: Continuum, 2004 [1980]).
[29] Bridget Fowler, *Pierre Bourdieu and Cultural Theory: Critical Investigations* (London: Sage, 1997).

Where individuals have made efforts to develop a generous cultural agenda within the field, they have tended to operate in relative isolation – in other words, by standing apart from their peers. One such bold attempt was made by one of Dewey's former students, Richard McKeon, who, following Dewey, interwove questions of communication and culture. For McKeon, culture was based on common understanding. If understanding was to be reached across distinct cultures or within plural cultural situations, it was necessary to explore the meaning of specific ideas guiding the thought and action of one or another group. Only within this productive interplay, this working through of difference such that degrees of understanding are reached, could humanity's true potential be realized.[30]

More recently, another broad-ranging pragmatist cultural agenda has been proposed by Morton White, who has suggested that rather than place the development of a philosophy of science at the centre of discipline, as proposed by Quine, a better aim would be to develop a much wider, more holistic philosophy of *culture*. Pragmatism, he believed – in particular, what he referred to as a holistic pragmatism – could support such a move. This culture-centred philosophy would function as a means of managing our understanding of key philosophic questions, with no limits being placed on the institutional or cultural context which was to be investigated (i.e. philosophy was not to be seen as a background to science).[31]

The question of culture has also impacted on another important emergent area of philosophy – what is referred to as the decolonial perspective. The term first emerged in sociological and political theory literature at the turn of the twenty-first century and points to an honouring of understandings of the world which seek to move beyond colonial or modernist conceptions of what is or is

---

[30] See Eugene Gaver and Richard Buchanan, *Pluralism in Theory and Practice: Richard McKeon and American Philosophy* (Nashville TN: Vanderbilt University Press, 2000).

[31] Morton White, *A Philosophy of Culture: The Case for Holistic Pragmatism* (Princeton, NJ: The Princeton University Press, 2002).

not real, what is or is not knowable, what does or does not hold value.[32] The call is that these other ways of being, knowing, valuing and, more broadly, thinking should be recognized as holding legitimacy in and of themselves.

Following on, the idea of decolonizing design has risen to prominence in recent years, with a series of ongoing calls for the field to critically reflect on and work through outmoded colonialist or modernist positionings, whereby non-Western ontologies (i.e. other ways of understanding being) and the place of design are disregarded and overlooked. A key early contribution to this discourse can be found in the work of Tony Fry and his concept of 'defuturing'.[33] On this account, design as it is presently practised within the capitalist paradigm is leading to an 'unsustainment' – a situation in which the future of our species and life more generally is negated, i.e. we have no future. To amend this, design and, more broadly, civilization must be remade. Fry's work, which is deeply philosophy, will be picked up on in the next chapter, where we focus on the ecological.

More direct decolonializing calls have followed. Perhaps most prominently, the establishment of a Decolonising Design Group in 2016 marked a watershed moment, wherein a general decolonizing agenda was introduced to the field at large. Here, the group called for a reorientation of the field, with an opening up to non-Western perspectives – ontological and epistemological – and greater awareness of design's political and social impact.[34]

Alongside the establishment of the decolonizing design group, there have been significant theoretical decolonizing contributions in the field. Perhaps most impactful is the work of Arturo Escobar, through a vision that he terms the 'pluriverse' – that is, a world in which many worlds or many ways of being can coexist.[35] Culture

---

[32] See e.g. Anibal Quijano, 'Coloniality of Power and Eurocentrism in Latin America'. *International Sociology*, 15, no. 2 (2000): 215–32.

[33] Fry, *A Design Philosophy*.

[34] Decolonising Design, 'Editorial Statement', 18 December 2021, https://www.decolonisingdesign.com/statements/2016/editorial/

[35] Escobar, *Designs for the Pluriverse*.

is integral to this vision. Escobar links, in particular, to the decolonial perspective of the 'epistemologies of the [global] south'. Drawing a link between these and contemporary design, he traces a path outwards from our contemporary social, political and creative situations to envisage a future approach to designing wherein plurality, perhaps pluriversality, is not only possible but seen as desirable and valued. This notional approach is referred to as 'autonomous design', a form of design that, though involving designers, would nonetheless be embedded both within and led by communities. Such communities are seen as being intimately connected not only to each other as a group but also to their environments and special, local ecologies.

For Escobar, an autonomous design process would commit to the principles that a community designs itself, its practices are in constant state of being designed; when designing, a community will practise 'their own knowledge'; communities first design learning systems about themselves; and problems and possibilities must be stated so that a response may be decided upon. The framing of a response would involve 'the design of a series of tasks, organizational practices, and criteria by which to assess the performance of the inquiry and design task'.[36]

Though this work is not explicitly pragmatist in orientation, it is possible to draw links to pragmatist themes. Directly, the idea of a pluriverse mirrors an early twentieth-century metaphysical proposal of William James's that we live in a pluralistic universe (i.e. one of many realities).[37] There is also a connection to be made with Dewey in relation to his integral bringing together of the environmental, social and cultural, as well as commitment to problem-based inquiry (see Chapter 3). Equally, Richard McKeon's work on plural cultural situations and communication was framed on the basis of richness in distinction and the need to accommodate many perspectives democratically. Then, in

---

[36] Ibid, 184–5.
[37] William James, *The Collected Works of William James: A Pluralistic Universe*, edited by Fredson Bowers, Ignas K Skrupkelis, Frederick Burkhardt (Cambridge MA: Harvard University Press, 1977 [1909]).

reference to the present section, we might also suggest that communication, how we collectively create meaning together, forms a bedrock upon which such cultural concerns can be explored.

These connections, though loose, allow us to note an alignment between this way of seeing and pragmatist values. Escobar's proposal may also be positioned as pragmatist and, more broadly, philosophical, in so far as it seeks to ground a new way of seeing – a grand vision for how we might negotiate our collective sharing (and contesting) of reality – in and through practical action. There is an immediate opportunity to be noted in relation to the framing of the type of philosophy through design that is gradually being shaped here: we are being offered a strategy for working with communities, which acknowledges and honours their unique positioning and special qualities at the same time as allowing us, in this, to ask emerging questions in relation to meaning and value. This is important and a point we shall return to at the end of the chapter.

For now, however, having considered the threads of communication and culture and, within this, decolonizing design, we will look to a recent example of design research that aligns with the latter agenda. This is the work of two specific designer researchers – Nicola St John and Yoko Akama – which, as we will see, carries definite philosophic concern.

RETHINKING RELATIONS IN 'DESIGNING WITH'

Recent research undertaken by Nicola St John and Yoko Akama[38] – both of whom are design academics based in Australia – can be found to offer an insight into how indigenous experience might approached within design research when one is not indigenous oneself.[39] Here, the pair start from the position that to respectfully

---

[38] What follows describes work that was delivered by St John; its contextualization, however, is the outcome of a joint authorship and as such can be seen to give insight into Akama's general approach.
[39] Nicola St John and Yoko Akama, 'Reimagining co-design on Country as a relational and transformational practice.' *CoDesign* 18, no. 1 (2022): 16–31.

engage with indigenous communities, one must work to appreciate their worldviews and specific ways of being and knowing. Within their own context – that of Nataria in the Central Desert of Australia, which is part of the Western Arrarnta traditional lands – these are seen as bound up in a powerful culture–place relationship, captured in the term 'Country'.

We are told that to co-design 'on Country' or, to put it another way, to co-design within the framework of place-based worldviews/ ways of being and knowing, requires that one seek to reshape one's own ways of being or ontology through process of 'a relational, collaborative learning'.[40] In the case described, where design workshops were collaboratively developed with Nataria youth, this was to be achieved by cultivating a distinct form of situational attentiveness referred to as '*anma*'. *Anma*, an Arrarnta term, refers to a patient way of relating, based on responsively giving space and taking time as and when required. One waits and is attuned to 'when to engage, when to ask questions, when to remain silent, when to leave and come back'.[41] This is framed as a an ethical, humble and reflexive stance. The researchers' ability to work in this way resulted in a more meaningful engagement for all. In the end, they were able to shape a joint creative process in which the Nataria youth explored their own distinct approach to design, producing a series of rich visual outcomes across a range of formats (e.g. t-shirts and postcards). Ultimately, through a prolonged process of trust building, they were able to tell their stories, express themselves and the meaning of their Country in new ways, facilitated by design.

In considering the above example, it is important to note that although the pair refer to philosophy and philosophic terms, they do not at claim to be practising a philosophy through design. Rather, they are striving to imbue their work with a deep relationality that not only repositions the process of engagement but also calls up an onto-epistemic stance, how they seek to understand being-knowing. This becomes as much a part of the inquiry as

---

[40] Ibid, 16.
[41] Ibid, 27.

the direct design subject matter itself. We are told, for example, that the work 'reimagines co-design as co-ontological ways of becoming'.[42]

Given the important of this onto-epistemic angle with work, I take the view that what is undertaken and reported on does point to a nascent approach to philosophy through design, even if tacit and unarticulated. We have questions being asked of relationality within design, the meaning of given practices and the value of particular ways of being and knowing with respect to the creative process. While there is no absolute method demonstrated, we see that these questions can be asked and answered through design on the basis of argument, an argument that develops in relation to a situational concern and works outwards to a point where it can be reported on and presented as such.

From this example, we will now move to widen the discussion and turn to consider the broader contours of the social within the field of design.

THE SOCIAL IN DESIGN

The social aspects of design may appear straightforward at first. Designers design for people, for society. They also design as part of teams, ideas are shared, decisions are jointly made. However, things get more nuanced when one begins to consider the social in direct terms within the design process. First, there is the methodological angle. This opens up when 'non-designers', i.e. members of the public or groups such as the Nataria youth, who are not themselves design professionals, become involved in design activities. This has been the focus of much discussion and debate over the last four to five decades in the field, with questions emerging around how such a process is best conducted, what the various steps are or should be, and what one should aim to achieve, as per the above example's concern within engagement and reflexivity.

---

[42] Ibid, 16.

Alongside this, a second, further line of questioning exists in relation to design for social contexts. Here, focus might be directed towards particular visions for how specific social concerns – whether related to areas such as justice or disability – might be addressed, or, alternatively, looking at how social experience itself might designed, i.e. whether or not designers can contribute to a process of giving form to how people come together, act and interact within specific situations.

To understand the social within any prospective philosophy through design, we must consider both of these strands.

Of the two, it is certainly the first, the idea of designing with others, that has drawn the most attention over the last number of decades. Here, a group of more or less distinct approaches have emerged, including co-design, human-centred design, participatory-design, user-centred design, empathic design, to name but a few.[43] Across this work, one can identify a spectrum of alignments, with some approaches, such as the St John–Akama co-design example, offering a means of supporting design practice proper (e.g. through generative ideation) and other approaches, such as ethnography, aiming more towards the gathering of research data. There is also a scale of involvement at play; some approaches restrict the involvement of non-designers to particular points within the design process, others encourage full participation throughout, from beginning to end.

Projects that draw on these approaches have, over the last two decades, gradually shifted understandings of the design process. It is now almost illegitimate to not involve others and design alone.[44] The role of the designer has been reconsidered. They have, to varying degrees, moved from being a central agent to just another contributor among many, someone who supports efforts to progress an activity or plan but not the one who conceptualizes and realizes those activities and plans. We see

---

[43] For a landmark article providing an overview of the subject, see Elizabeth Sanders and Pieter Jan Stappers, 'Co-creation and the new landscapes of design.' *Co-Design* 4, no. 1 (2008): 5–18.

[44] This new approach is perhaps most broadly captured in Ezio Manzini, *Design When Everyone Designs* (Cambridge, MA: The MIT Press, 2015).

this with St John and Akama, where a 'co-ontological becoming' of the designer is seen as necessary.

Turning to the second strand of social questioning within design noted above – i.e. looking at the possibility of designing for specific social concerns and social experience more broadly – we can observe a particular trajectory of development of over the last fifty years, with two distinct phases emerging.[45] In the opening phase, stretching from approximately the early 1970s through to the late 1990s, designing for social contexts was conceived as designing for social responsibility. This is the era in which individuals such as Victor Papanek and Buckminster Fuller called for a reconstruction of the relationship between designers and society.[46] For Papanek and others, this translated into a call for designers to offer their skills in service to society, apportioning a percentage of their time to pro-bono work. Proposed areas of work, at the time, included design for the 'Third World'; teaching and training those with disabilities; medical needs and contexts; the support of experimental research; sustaining life in marginal conditions; and breakthrough concepts (such as non-wasteful products).[47] For Fuller, the question was how one might achieve a better world by design, with the view being taken that if we did not envisage and plan for a utopia we were destined for 'oblivion'.[48]

The legacy of this work extends into the present, with an ever-expanding group of contributors scoping dynamic and diverse social agendas for the field. By way of quick examples, there is work on: design and disability, where design's role in shaping

---

[45] Ilpo Koskinen, 'Agonistic, convivial, and conceptual aesthetics in new social design.' Design Issues 32, no. 3 (2016): 18–29.

[46] Although published later, it is also worth mentioning Nigel Whitely, *Design for Society* (London: Reaktion Books, 1993). We see a consolidating social agenda emerging here, which like Papanek blends a focus on social and environmental responsibilities, within a general ethical positioning.

[47] See Papanek, *Design for the Real World*, 3rd Edition, 234–47.

[48] For an overview see Jonathan Keats, *You Belong to the Universe: Buckminster Fuller and the Future* (Oxford: Oxford University Press, 2016).

perceptions of disability is explored;[49] feminism, where taking a feminist stance is positioned not simply as a matter of designing, but also being;[50] and race, where the discipline's role in the construction of race is examined and challenged.[51]

Perhaps one of the most impactful recent perspectives has come from Sasha Constanza-Chock through their design justice work.[52] As noted in the Introduction, Constanza-Chock here argues that design must position itself as a liberating force for the marginalized and oppressed. Their work is ultimately about the relationship between design and power, calling for a critical reflection on who and what[53] makes/informs design decisions, who/what these decisions serve and who/what they do not. To achieve design justice, difference and diversity must be supported by design, not erased. A number of important areas for further investigation open up beyond this, relating to values, collaborations, narratives and pedagogy. Design is challenged to become more aware and more active.[54]

Alongside and aligning to this social agenda work, we can detect the emergence of a further, distinct phase of social design development from the 1990s onwards based on an initially subtle but definite shift in practice. Here, design began to become more generally 'socially focused' in its practice and its methods. Product design and industrial design came to enfold what were initially referred to as user-centred ways of working.[55] This gradually

---

[49] Bess Williamson and Elizabeth Guffey (eds), *Making Disability Modern: Design Histories* (London: Bloomsbury, 2020).

[50] Feminist design has a long history and is not to be viewed as a newly emerging agenda. Nonetheless, the consolidation of texts such as Alison Place (ed.), *Feminist Designer: On the Personal and the Political in Design* (Cambridge, MA: The MIT Press, 2023), points to a healthy growth.

[51] Peter Claver Fine, *The Design of Race How Visual Culture Shapes America* (London: Bloomsbury, 2021).

[52] Constanza-Chock, *Design Justice*.

[53] 'What' is meant to denote non-human entities that carry agency beyond human input (for example, algorithms).

[54] Ibid, 223–36.

[55] While this developed in multiple directions, a landmark text is Norman, *The Design of Everyday Things*.

evolved into service design (covered in the Introduction) where the intangible aspects of an organization's customer experience were drawn to the fore. Through new techniques such as journey mapping, all the social processes of organizational structures were suddenly rendered visible and as such designable. This work has extended into the political arena, where particular government services are now designed to meet particular citizens' needs. Policy too is now presented as something that can be prototyped, designed with people.[56]

In another important line of work, designers began to engage directly with communities in their contexts to help realize shared goals, often taking an activist stance. While this work progressed across multiple disciplinary paths, a key series of developments occurred in relation to the area of the participatory design, in particular. As noted in the last chapter, participatory design arose in Scandinavian industrial settings in the 1960s and 1970s, aligning with a generalist Marxist agenda. Here, supported by trade unions, researchers and workers came together to explore how various workplace technologies could be designed in such a way as to preserve workers' agency and autonomy.[57] This translated into a democratic practice, a prototyping process founded upon dialogue and progressive development.

Through the 1980s and 1990s, however, this general positioning underwent a radical reconfiguration. In line with the economic and political upheavals of the period, there was a decline in union-based partnerships.[58] Practitioners and researchers gradually shifted their focus from workplace settings to the civic arena, with community as opposed to workers' concerns coming to the fore here. The aim was to establish new ways of designing wherein designers would embed themselves within existing social networks

---

[56] Lucy Kimbell and Jocelyn Bailey, 'Prototyping and the new spirit of policy-making', *CoDesign* 13, no. 3 (2017): 214–26.

[57] Pelle Ehn, 'Work-oriented design of computer artifacts.' PhD diss. (Arbetslivscentrum: Stockholm, 1988).

[58] Morten Kyng, 'Bridging the Gap Between Politics and Techniques: On the next practices of participatory design.' *Scandinavian Journal of Information Systems* 22, no. 1 (2010): 49–68.

and work with these networks to frame and shape immediate change as well as build longer-term capacity among the group. Within this, the Deweyan concept of 'publics' – referring to politically motivated groups that cohere around a given problem – was mobilized as a means of contextualizing these more open-ended forms of participation.[59] Additionally, in North America, this line of activity gave rise to the areas of agonistic and adversarial design, which, in opening up spaces for democratic debate, focus on the productive potential of disagreement and contestation as opposed to consensus. This work has been linked explicitly to the pragmatism of Dewey and Addams through its honouring of small-scale experimentation at a community level.[60]

Concurrently, another area of development occurred in relation to social innovation. Led by individuals such as Ezio Manzini, here again attention was directed to how design could support efforts to progress community-led processes of regeneration. Designers are here positioned as facilitators, individuals who are contributing but were not necessarily leading. The underlying agenda focuses on the progression of sustainability as a general society-wide project, based on the incremental capacity building over time.[61]

Though these latter examples would appear to point to a formal, delineated 'social design', the idea that there might be an area of practice that functions specifically as social design proper is a much-contested question. Some suggest that there is no such thing and nor should there be.[62] Others take the view that while there is no one cohesive social design approach, there are general principles, which can be traced through certain areas of design, that stand as a set of commitments to a social design

---

[59] Carl DiSalvo, 'Design and the Construction of Publics.' *Design Issues* 25, no. 1 (2009): 48–63.
[60] DiSalvo, *Design as Democratic Inquiry*.
[61] Manzini, *Design when Everyone Designs*.
[62] This position has been attributed to Ezio Manzini, see Cameron Tonkinwise, 'Is Social Design a Thing?' In *The Social Design Reader*, edited by Elizabeth E. Resnick (London: Bloomsbury, 2015), 9–16.

positioning.⁶³ Others still register a latent practice containing a typology of forms – undefined yet already practised existent ways of doing 'social design' – that range from the grand and 'utopian' to the more humble 'molecular' scale where change is explored at ground level directly with communities.⁶⁴ The field has found it challenging to push beyond this plurality, though recent discourse has seen proposals that suggest a wider means of grouping such work around concepts such as the 'social imagination'.⁶⁵

Surveying the above positions, it is possible to note at the outset that each approach – whether a matter of designing with others or designing for social contexts – points, in its own way, to an implicit philosophical commitment, a way of seeing the world, which underpins its techniques and drives forward its own particular agenda. As scholars such as Ron Wakkary have recently noted, there is a fundamentally humanist orientation running through such work; that is, they focus upon human need and agency, with little if any attention being directed towards the needs and possible agency of other non-human constituent groups, whether animals or ecosystems, plants or objects.

As noted in the last chapter, scholars and practitioners are beginning to attend to this concern, with philosophy providing paths by which responses can be shaped. Here, we explored how Peter-Paul Verbeek talks about 'things', objects, as being part of the moral community. Equally, we noted how Wakkary's 'designing with' proposal offers an approach that moves beyond human-centred design. These were, of course, technologically orientated positions, as they allow for distinct framings of technology and what it means. Nonetheless, the concerns they point to are bound up in our imaginaries – that is, our understanding — of the social;

---

[63] Christian Nold, Patrycja Kaszynska, Jocelyn Bailey and Lucy Kimbell, 'Twelve potluck principles for social design.' *DISCERN: International Journal of Design for Social Change, Sustainable Innovation and Entrepreneurship* 3, no. 1 (2022): 31–43.

[64] Ilpo Koskinen and Gordon Hush, 'Utopian, molecular and sociological social design' *International Journal of Design* 10, no. 1 (2016): 65–71.

[65] DelSesto, *Design and the Social Imagination*.

of what it includes and does not include, what is social and what is not. While this remains an ongoing concern, design has historically addressed this direct question of social meanings by turning to the work of the French sociologist Bruno Latour, who offers a vision of the social that moves away from people, humans, alone and instead looks to how every*thing* connects. This does not dissolve or remove the sorts of concerns noted above. It is still a matter of coming together and, in this, debating. Now however, the complexity increases.

ACTOR NETWORK THEORY: DESIGN IN THE SOCIO-MATERIAL NETWORK

The exact meaning of actor network theory can be difficult to grasp when first encountered. In simple terms, it offers a theory that presents social life as not only involving interpersonal and group interactions but also taking complex networks of interactions that link humans and non-humans together in their doings. This notion of the non-human, as has been alluded to, includes forms of technology and general everyday objects, as well as other lifeforms.[66] This is all underpinned by a commitment to what is referred to as a 'flat ontology', a view of reality that resists divisions between the natural, social and artificial.[67]

The central idea is that one seeks to trace the networks of interactions and thereby detail the relationships that emerge. In envisaging interactions and relationships, the point is not to think only in terms of linking but also of mediation, of change. In their relationships, or to be more precise, *through* the network, humans and non-humans are transformed.

The establishment of actor network theory is commonly attributed to the French sociologist Bruno Latour.[68] As we have

---

[66] Latour, *Reassembling the Social*.
[67] Levi R. Bryant, *The Democracy of Objects* (Ann Arbor: Open Humanities Press, 2011).
[68] Other founding contributors include Michel Callon and John Law, see Ignacio Farías, Anders Blok and Celia Roberts, 'Actor network theory as a companion:

seen, Latour's theories have been enthusiastically received in design, especially participatory design, where, since the mid-2000s, various authors have picked up on his concept of 'Thing politics' or 'Dingpolitik'.[69] The proposal here is that rather than considering issues or 'matters of concern' as isolated problems relating to humans alone (i.e. just to publics), the complexities of the contemporary world demand a wider frame of reference involving non-human constituents. In this view, if matters of concern are to be properly addressed, these non-humans need to be acknowledged, represented and given a place within a collective forum of dialogue and exchange. Political discourse becomes a hybrid socio-material assembly.

Enfolding this theory within participatory design, ideas of democratic practice are reconceived in relation to these much-expanded networks of actors and actions.[70] Projects become 'design Things' and participation a much richer concept than before. It is now not only people who participate but also non-humans, whether directly or indirectly. This positioning ultimately supported participatory design's general move from the workplace to the civic arena, with the unbound space of Things providing a limitless horizon upon which understandings of the social and, indeed, democracy itself can grow and expand.[71]

Beyond this, the last ten years has also seen dedicated explorations of how ANT can be mobilized elsewhere in design, with the more general areas of co-design and speculative or critical

---

an inquiry into intellectual practices.' In *The Routledge Companion to Actor-Network Theory*, edited by Ignacio Farías, Anders Blok and Celia Roberts (Abingdon, Oxon: Routledge. 2019), xx–xxxv.

[69] Bruno Latour, 'From Realpolitik to Dingpolitik or How to Make Things Public.' In *Making Things Public: Atmospheres of Democracy*, edited by Bruno Latour and Peter Weibel (Cambridge, MA: The MIT Press, ZKM/Center for Art and Media in Karlsruhe, 2005), 14–41.

[70] Thomas Binder, Giorgio De Michelis, Pelle Ehn, Giulio Jacucci and Per Linde, *Design Things* (Cambridge MA, The MIT Press. 2011).

[71] Erling Bjögvinsson, Pelle Ehn and Per-Anders Hillgren, 'Design things and design thinking: Contemporary participatory design challenges.' *Design Issues* 28, no. 3 (2012): 101–16.

design being explored via an ANT lens. These explorations have been broad-ranging, with scholars testing ANT's general applicability and adaptability. For example, Karl Pålmas and Otto Van Busch have investigated the role of power in the context of collaboration through an ANT approach.[72] In another pertinent example, Alex Wilkie has explored the productive potential of ANT, examining the extent to which it might be applied as a means of supporting a speculative design process. Here, alongside looking back over socio-material actions and interactions through visualizations – a process Wilkie terms 'retroscription' – there is also a seeking to look beyond this via a process called 'procomposition'.[73] In procomposition, the visualization is approached with a view to mobilizing and re-patterning what is described.[74] One aims to adjust the existing collective via an engagement with the representation of that collective. Wilkie's example centres on a smart meter. In the retroscription phase of this work, people's lived, situated experiences of such devices informs the development of a visualization of a socio-material collective. Once developed, this, in turn, allows for the procomposition of a novel interactive device, termed the Energy Babble, which shares live, general energy use data from the internet.

Such examples point to a flexibility in ANT that might not be apparent at first. As Wilkie notes, there is a need to devise approaches that enable a reflexive 'becoming-together of ANT and design'.[75] Explorations such as Wilkie's further this from within the context of design, providing a useful reference point for those who wish to follow.

Elsewhere, in related work, sociologists themselves are focusing on the idea that 'objects' and 'devices' and even environments can

---

[72] Karl Palmås and Otto Von Busch, 'Quasi-Quisling: co-design and the assembly of collaborateurs.' *CoDesign* 11, no. 3–4 (2015): 236–49.

[73] Alex Wilkie, 'How well does ANT equip designers for socio-material speculations?' In *The Routledge Companion to Actor-Network Theory*, edited by Ignacio Farías, Anders Blok and Celia Roberts (Abingdon, Oxon: Routledge, 2019), 389–99.

[74] Ibid, 389.

[75] Ibid, 390.

THE SOCIAL HORIZON: ASSOCIATION IN EXPERIENCE

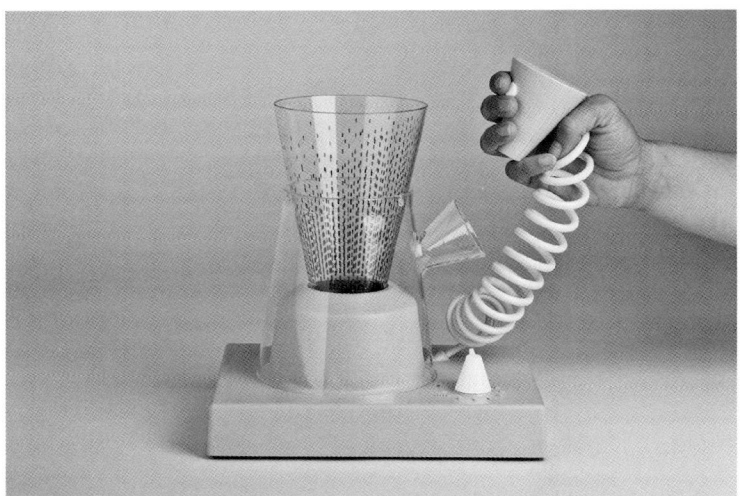

FIGURE 3.1 A novel interactive device termed the 'Energy Babble' produced through an ANT-inspired 'procomposition' process. Courtesy Alex Wilkie.

carry out a central productive role in social and political contexts. Here, Dutch sociologist Noortje Marres has advocated for a more-than-descriptive approach to the empirical investigation of what she terms 'material participation'. Her argument is that rather than simply treating philosophical problems in critical terms – that is, as matters to be argued or analysed away – they should, in line with the pragmatist agenda, be addressed in practical terms.[76] The point is to explore how objects, devices and environments – technologies in the widest sense – open up particular forms of engagement and, as such, can and do reframe democratic participation in what is, in the end, materially bound terms.

From the point of view of a philosophy through design, work such as the above offers a means of conceiving of social and political relations in ways that extend beyond 'just' the human alone. Politics is no longer simply about person-to-person debate or, more fundamentally, language, but, rather, draws in the manifold

[76] Marres, *Material Participation*.

and unyieldingly complex world of the non-human too. Ultimately, in this coming together of non-human agency and design, we have a robust starting point for a consideration of the 'more-than-human' world and, within this, the contribution of design. In the last chapter, we saw how this latter idea has now entered the mainstream in design. It is something that we will consider directly in the next chapter.

We will now move to draw the present chapter to a close by seeking to link its various threads at the same time as briefly scope a forward path relating to method.

MANY WAYS OF SEEING: THE SOCIAL IN PHILOSOPHY THROUGH DESIGN

The opening (personal) vignette noted how social and political shifts (driven by recent economic and technology changes) have led to particular patterns of social experience emerging for some living in the Global North (in my case Ireland) and elsewhere. Questions were raised regarding community, inter-relationality, of being and acting together in the tangle of economics and technologies. Obviously, these do not mark the limits of contemporary social concerns but nonetheless point to potential starting points for philosophical inquiries that might involve design (as a means of working through them).

As will be apparent by now, it is not just a matter of identifying specific concerns. Just as was highlighted with technology, one must also consider the perspective with which one aligns, the way of thinking and working through our sociality that should be prioritized.

Adopting a pragmatist stance, we have a starting point in the situation at hand; this will determine the specifics of the particular approach that is required. It may be a live social or political issue, which is general or else particular to a specific community. It may arise through personal reflections that carry a philosophical bent, as with the vignette.

Regardless of the particular angle taken, in a philosophy through design this situational measure will require attentive care as, depending on the undertaking, the social is likely to be both a subject of concern as well as a part of the overall approach (e.g. by designing *with* a community). This relates to the underlying commitment to democracy as a way of life, based on communication and deliberation. Here, we might also draw on Addams's concept of a social ethics: situating ourselves with a community, relating at a group level while working to design with others.

This complicates matters, as concern and approach will likely overlap. To manage this will require a flexibility of movement, as insights emerge in context at the same time as in and through the socially bound ways of working that will likely be necessary. It is worth briefly considering how this might unfold.

If questions relate to issues concerning the group or community itself – for example, following my own reflections on how life has evolved in recent years – a guided philosophy through design could function similarly to Escobar's autonomous design, whereby the group is supported in their efforts to understand themselves as well as the problems they might face. We might take on a lens of communication or culture, but focus would need to centre on sense making, trying to grasp questions of who they are and what they do such that problems could be properly defined and addressed. In this, there would also be an opportunity to explore group ideals, to understand that which is most valued and appraise the extent to which such values are or are not appropriate, do or do not lead to positive outcomes. There might also be ethical concerns. Following Dewey, we might be examining the breakdown of a specific custom or habit, moving to progressively identify how a new norm might gradually be scoped out. Making might form a part of this process – whether in the form of tools or artefacts – allowing communities to share perspectives both among themselves and with others.

Questions of power, of where it lies and what its manifestations and impact might be, could also arise at any stage within the approaches/processes described above. Such questions may be peripheral in that they form part of a wider set of questions. However, there is every chance they will form a central concern within a philosophy through design inquiry. In such cases, a valid strategy will need to be mapped, one which takes register of forms of design seeking to challenge power structures and equally, from a philosophic perspective, perspectives that can structure this work.

Linking to this area of concern, through decolonizing design, we have seen how issues of cultural dominance can be drawn out and explored. Here, it may be that sense making and developing a greater sense of communal being and doing will surface issues of oppression or legacy traumas. As with the pattern of autonomous design, these would need to be challenged and addressed. In this, philosophy becomes an active matter. We are doing-thinking and thinking-doing at the same time, as per the example of St John and Akama's work. In finding ways of righting the situation, we are not only contributing to a response to the challenge of an immediately identified problem, but also gradually, progressing a renewed ethical position with respect to the issue at hand, helping to establish a new norm over time.

Within all of this, there will also likely be questions of the meaning of human and non-human relationships, as we have seen with ANT. Here, it may be appropriate or, indeed, necessary that a socially focused philosophy through design may explore the broader networks that are being drawn into given situations, blending the human and non-human, complicating and transforming what is happening and how. These wider mappings of actions and consequences, interactions and influences would of course allow us to strike outwards to readily enfold the technological and ecological and so change the centre of gravity within our way of seeing. Doing so will inevitably change how a situation is understood, what holds meaning and what does not, what is valuable and what is not.

The above outline can be seen to demonstrate how a flexibility of movement in a social philosophy through design might operate in practice. Emerging concerns and interests would link one to a particular perspective, which in turn suggests an approach. Altogether, in ideal terms, the designer(s) would work with a group/groups, a community/communities, or, more broadly, a network of stakeholders to jointly frame problems, questions and potential strategies of response. Within this, design would support a registering of the situation, as well as the means of responding: one which is, by definition, situational.

As has been noted, philosophical insights might derive from method itself; how we work with others to achieve something together might itself allow for a broader statement to be made. As such, these insights might have general import beyond the context, saying something broadly about the meaning and value of collaborative practices while also referencing the 'how' of the approach discussed. Equally, our process might lead to an outcome that offers insights relating to, for example, inter-relationality, ethics, communal concerns, issues of power, decolonizing or more-than-human concerns. Better still, both might be achieved; we could potentially progress insights in relation to ways of working together at the same time as progressing outcomes that, in turn, progress understanding.

In all of the above, the question of how the design process unfolds is of course key. As will likely be apparent, in some instances, our focus or model of the social can act as a useful guide, framing the type of design work we might undertake. For example, if our aim is to provide a more-than-human account, we might well apply an ANT approach. If this is the case, we will endeavour to map actions, interactions and relationships, identifying how a collective of actors, both human and non-human, are implicated in given issues. Design can then evolve within and beyond this, as in Wilkie's proscription exemplar. In other instances, where there is no ready focus or model, design may be the route to understanding a doubtful situation and, as such, acquiring a focus or aligning to a model. There is no one way to proceed here. As has been noted, early observations might enfold design techniques such as visual mapping, allowing for a gradual identification of a point of focus and, next to this, a model of the social. Alternatively, one might foreground these techniques as the way into a community setting, relying on the technique to progress the definition of any problems. More broadly, such work could potentially have a bearing on philosophical practice itself, which, conventionally at least, does not foreground ideas of collaboration within its methods. We will pick up on this as an area for further methodological consideration in the final chapter.

For now, having reached this chapter's end, we will move on to consider our final thematic horizon: the ecological.

4 The Ecological Horizon: Connecting Everything

I grew up in a place called County Wicklow, an area to the south of Dublin, in the Republic of Ireland. It's known the 'Garden County'. Dotted throughout, there are rolling green hills, sylvian valleys and wooded lakes. In many respects it is, in a very obvious sense, a romantic landscape, conforming to a type of Wordsworthian ideal – the sort of space that has been exalted by Western European culture since the early nineteenth century. As a child, I gradually learned to appreciate this prescribed sense of beauty, little by little becoming increasingly fluent in reading its particular aesthetic markers.

In the last number of years, however, I have come to see things differently. I am no longer reading the landscape on the basis of a culturally bound appraisal system or, at least, I am not only doing that. Rather, what was 'nature' has been opened up. I now try to see and, in this, understand the special unique ecology that Wicklow and other similar places present. This has taken much time and some effort. Reading texts that surface recent natural history, as well as contemporary flora field guides, I have slowly trained myself in the identification of particular plant types as well as learned the markers of particular types of ecosystems.

What I have come to understand is that all is not as it should be. Beyond the managed Wordsworthian ideal, this landscape, like all landscapes, has own inherent processes, its own systems of organic relationships that make it what it is.

Ultimately, it harbours a desired way of being. Once the land I grew up in was likely a temperate rainforest – a rare ecosystem in global terms – made up of densely packed ancient trees covered in rich green mosses and dripping ferns. Fragments of this original ecology remain here and there. I have found small abundant pockets in my wanderings where the world has been left alone. Entering such spaces, the air carries a certain primordial magic, full of secrets and lost promise.

There is an incredible gulf between this vision and contemporary design. We lack a way of seeing that can draw a relationship to this notion of ecological integrity and, next to it, allow us, as citizens, as members of a community, to frame plans of action that can lead to a better, more accommodating future.

A philosophy through design would or, at least, should allow a questioning here, a tracing of unseen practical pathways that somehow draw connections between local meaning and value, the global challenges we face and, equally, the possibilities we may take advantage of. The point is we – designers, the design community and more generally society – need to do so.

Concerns such as these are urgent. Daily, we are reminded of the long list of unfolding environmental crises we face, from biodiversity loss to the ever-worsening climate emergency. Disasters are not something that are going to happen but rather have already begun. At present, without any meaningful register of the depth of the catastrophe, we are living through what has been termed the sixth great extinction.[1] When we look to the future, there are warnings of an uninhabitable earth.[2]

Ultimately, simply taking register of these problems is no longer enough. It has become clear there is now a need to act and act fast. Unfortunately, we appear to lack an ability to do so. Action, although necessary, is not forthcoming. We have neither understanding of the depth of the challenges we face nor a clear

---

[1] Ron Wagler, 'The sixth great mass extinction.' *Science Scope* 35, no. 7 (2012): 48–55.

[2] David Wallace-Wells, *The Uninhabitable Earth* (London: Penguin, 2020).

sense of the scale of the response that is required in order to properly address them.

In such a set of circumstances, a turn to philosophy may seem meaningless. What can it, an essentially abstract discipline, offer when immediate, practical change is needed now?

There is no clear answer here other than that a philosophy through design could be responsive, that it could allow for a framing of action in relation to the contexts at hand. As I see it, this would potentially carry a dual aspect.

First, a philosophy through design might allow us to better understand and, ultimately, accept our absolute interdependence with the wider biosphere as we are designing. This is where the type of perspective traced out above in the opening vignette might come into play. Here, designers might adopt a philosophic stance as a means of developing new modes of ecological being. In some contexts, such as my own Western European example, this would be a matter of relearning historic practices (e.g. pursuing locally bound construction techniques) at the same time as seeking to unlearn present patterns of unsustainable behaviours (e.g. relying on globally sourced sustainable materials).

Second, and leading on from this, in being action-orientated, a philosophy through design could also allow for the gradual mapping of paths by which we can act; as with ethics in the last chapter, inductively scoping a way forward as we investigate the problem. This would be a matter of doing and thinking with increasing ecological insight, seeking all the time to experiment and adapt to do better, to be better.

When it comes to design proper, as we shall see, environmental or ecological issues have grown in prominence in the last number of decades and are increasingly entering conventional practice. There is more to do, however. Designers, after all, have as much, if not more, responsibility to face up to such issues as everyone else.

Taking up the ecological as thematic horizon, this chapter will focus on how a philosophy through design might support efforts to progress on all of the above. We open by briefly considering the ecological in pragmatism and, from this, will quickly sketch out design's expanding ecological agenda. Next, we consider the work of Åsa Ståhl and Kristina Linström, who explore design in the context of the climate crisis. Then in the following section, we return to philosophy. Here we consider key perspectives that centre the ecological, ranging across both conventional and other lesser-known concepts such as ecophenomenology, for example. Within these sections, an exploration of the area of ecofeminist design is also offered. Following on, we briefly consider the ecological aspects of pragmatism. To close, the strands of design and philosophy are drawn together with the aim of tracing a more robust ecological positioning for design based on a philosophy through design. Here we will consider how an ecologically orientated philosophy through design might support the engendering of an ecological way of seeing and being. If humanity and, indeed, life on earth is to survive, this is a fundamental concern.

THE ECOLOGICAL IN PRAGMATISM

While classic pragmatism's definite emphasis on the human may suggest an anthropocentric orientation, this has been countered on the basis that human-held values need not in themselves be human-centred.[3] One can be human and value the environment on an intrinsic, non-instrumental level.

Taking a broad view, it is arguable that classical pragmatism in the round can be understood as a strongly ecologically orientated philosophy and that this was the case from the outset. It emerged at the mid-point of the nineteenth century, referencing Darwin's work on evolutionary theory. Linking to this, early pragmatists mapped a pragmatist worldview conceived on the basis of a naturalized understanding of life. Here, importantly, Charles Sanders Peirce offered an early ecological psychology, based on his theory of signs, where human social and environmental interactions are seen to rely on signification and interpretation.[4]

---

[3] Anthony Weston, 'Beyond intrinsic value: Pragmatism in environmental ethics.' *Environmental Ethics* 7, no. 4 (1985): 321–39.

[4] Alex Kirlik and Peter Storkerson, 'Naturalizing Peirce's semiotics: Ecological psychology's solution to the problem of creative abduction.' In *Model-Based*

How we act, too, was a matter of *relating* to the world. For Peirce, we form patterns of behaviour – habits – by progressively moving from of states of doubt to states of belief as we act. Alongside Peirce, William James's radical empiricism, too, drew the areas of thought, experience and the environment together. For James, our mind was part of the environment, not apart from it.[5]

Later, as a second-generation pragmatist, Dewey carried forward such perspectives by proposing a continuity between person and world, creature and environment. For him, the two formed an inseparable coupling with one linking into the other. This, in effect, was his baseline ontology – an underpinning position for all his philosophy. There is no inquiry or theory of experience without this key link. We are who we are because of our environmental immersion.

In line with this account, Hugh McDonald positions Dewey's ethics as a means by which environmental ethics might proceed.[6] The proposal here is that Dewey's approach to ethical inquiry, positioned within his general ecological baseline ontology, can function as an approach to environmental ethics that allows for a non-human-centred appraising of value.

Recent Dewey scholarship has also surfaced a direct, if peripheral, environmental commitment in his work. Here, Larry Hickman picks up on a 1909 Dewey text, titled 'Nature and its Good: A Conversation',[7] wherein Dewey compares the pragmatist philosophic perspective on the environment to two other perspectives

Reasoning in Science and Technology: Abduction, Logic, and Computational Discovery, edited by Lorenzo Magnani, Walter Carnielli and Claudio Pizzi (Berlin: Springer, 2010), 31–50.

[5] Harry Heft, 'William James' psychology, radical empiricism, and field theory: Recent developments.' *Philosophical Inquiries* 5, no. 2 (2017): 111–30.

[6] Hugh P. McDonald, *John Dewey and Environmental Philosophy* (Albany, NY: State of New York University Press, 2004).

[7] This was originally written as an introduction to a fiftieth anniversary edition of Darwin's *The Origin of the Species*. John Dewey, 'Nature and its Good: A Conversation.' In John Dewey, *The Dewey, John, The Middle Works, 1899–1924, Volume 4: 1907–1909, Essays on Pragmatism and Truth*, edited by Jo Ann *Boydston* (Carbondale, IL: Southern Illinois University Press, 1977), 15–30.

dominant at the time, namely rationalism (i.e. a position that foregrounds reason) and idealism (i.e. a position that foregrounds abstract values). For Hickman, in this essay, these latter two perspectives are shown to locate environmental/ecological value away from the person, whether to reason or a concept of a wider being.[8] A pragmatist environmental ethic emerges through the social morality, knowledge base and sense of meaning within which one is encultured. The task of the pragmatist is to ask questions of how this morality, knowledge and sense of meaning impacts on one's environmental relationship and decision making.[9] One might add it can also support a process of asking how it might be otherwise.

Addams, for her part, focused on the late nineteenth- and early twentieth-century environmental conditions of Chicago, most especially those of the immigrant-dominated slums adjacent to Hull House. Working with others such as Florence Kelley and Julia Lathrop, she took up an 'environmental justice' agenda based on empirical inquiry into the impact of these conditions on the communities who lived there.[10] This involved projects that mapped and documented 'housing and sanitation status', alongside issues such as instances of disease. Addams and the others used the evidence gathered to lobby city authorities for environmental reform, resulting in marked changes in building and fire safety regulations and, ultimately, transforming the lives of those who lived in Chicago's poorest neighbourhoods.[11]

Feminist pragmatist environmental contributions do not end there, though. As we will see below, other feminist pragmatists also engaged in environmental advocacy, aligning with a particular philosophic perspective we would today call ecofeminism.

---

[8] Larry A. Hickman, *Pragmatism as Post-Postmodernism: Lessons from John Dewey* (New York: Fordham University Press, 2007), 168–9.

[9] Ibid, 175–6.

[10] Harold L. Platt, 'Jane Addams and the Ward Boss Revisited: Class, politics, and public health in Chicago, 1890–1930.' *Environmental History* 5, no. 2 (2000): 194–222.

[11] Ibid, 202.

Broadly, in recent decades, positions and examples such as those outlined have allowed for the articulation of specific presentations of a wide-ranging *environmental* pragmatism.[12] The claims made here are that, when related to contemporary environmental positions, pragmatism can be found to offer compelling strategies for asking and answering environmental and ecological questions. The positions put forth have explored general environmental perspectives as well as a series of reflections on the area of animal rights in particular.[13]

At a general level, contributors note how, through the pattern of inquiry, pragmatism offers an approach for engaging with context, asking questions in relation to the problems faced, allowing for an examination of value as well as the desirability of specific situational decisions/actions. In this way, much like McDonald's argument with Dewey's work, it has been claimed that it can stand as an environmental ethic in and of itself.[14]

Next to this, pragmatist animal rights work is more limited but does point to the potential for a robust pragmatist consideration of the relationships between human and non-humans. Here, it is noted that though individuals such as Dewey can be seen to have drawn a dividing line between humans and animals, the flexibility of Deweyan ethics allows for an opening up of the ethical domain such that, through adaption, animals' suffering may be carefully and sensitively explored as a genuine and valid concern.[15]

---

[12] Andrew Light and Eric Kratz (eds), *Environmental Pragmatism* (Abingdon, Oxon: Routledge, 1996); Hugh P. McDonald (ed.), *Environmental Pragmatism* (New York: Rodopi, 2012).

[13] Erin McKenna and Andrew Light (eds), *Animal Pragmatism: Rethinking Human-Nonhuman Relationships* (Bloomington, IN: Indiana University Press, 2004).

[14] Sandra B. Rosenthal and Rogene A. Buchholz, 'How Pragmatism *is* an Environmental Ethic', In *Environmental Pragmatism*, edited by Andrew Light and Eric Kratz (Abingdon, Oxon: Routledge, 1996), 38–49.

[15] Steven Fesmire, 'Dewey and Animal Ethics.' In *Animal Pragmatism: Rethinking Human-Nonhuman Relationships*, edited by Erin McKenna and Andrew Light (Bloomington, IN: Indiana University Press, 2004), 43–62.

Broadly, a key point that can be drawn out from the above is that an environmental pragmatism, whether focused on ethics or not, enables ongoing appraisal and reappraisal of how we see/understand our environmental situation, what holds value or raises concern within it and, potentially, how we (like Addams) can address concerns through concerted action. As always, what is valued and what needs addressing is to be identified in imaginative dialogue – i.e. through democratic engagement – with the situation. Following a pragmatist orientation, a philosophy through design might capture this appraising, becoming the means of taking register of our deeply held environmental valuations, as well as how we need to mobilize in relation to concerns. We will pick up on this below.

DESIGN'S EXPANDING ECOLOGICAL AGENDA

It is possible to take the view that design is moving in a broadly sustainable direction. Over at least the last three decades, the concept of sustainability has emerged as a central concern within the discipline. There is now near constant talk of sustainable materials, sustainable processes and sustainable futures. Taking a lead, the materially bound areas of fashion, textiles and product design can be seen to actively map the possibilities of an adapted practice through a constant scoping of new materials, processes and scenarios. All of this aligns with a clear consumer demand. Contemporary brands often compete on the basis of their green credentials and the depth of their commitment to an ecologically sound business model.

Running alongside these developments, design theorists have sought to establish robust intellectual and practical frameworks that can further progress a wider sustainability agenda. In the early years, theorists and commentators tended to focus on exploring design's potential as a creative means of responding to the emerging environmental crisis. We can see this in Victor Papanek's *Design for the Real World* where, in environmental terms, it is suggested that design might be capable of contributing solutions to problems such as large-scale industrial pollution, the need to redesign our transport systems, and food insecurity. This is presented in programmatic terms; new visions are sketched for how design might address such problems, with the underlying assumption being that solutions were/are possible.

As the decades have passed, more granular presentations of strategies and tactics have been set out, with the emergence of detailed handbooks profiling specific sustainability agendas across a vast range of design contexts.[16] Alastair Fuad-Luke's *EcoDesign*, for example, sets out what is termed 'eco-pluralistic approach to design', through overviews of products, buildings and materials that seek to 'improve the status quo in small or large increments'.[17]

Alongside this expansion in strategies and tactics, later theoretical contributions shifted in tone somewhat. We see this in the positions set out by design academic Stuart Walker in the early 2000s, where he works through the issue of sustainability not only from the perspective of materials and consumption patterns but also from the perspective of how we value or not particular functions and qualities.[18] It is proposed that new conceptions of value are required such that we can appreciate the sustainable qualities of products. Following on, special value would attach to products that use minimal new resources and locally sourced materials, allow for easy reuse and are able to be repaired or repurposed locally.[19]

Here, in the work of Walker and others,[20] we may often note a growing tension between the level of response required and the level of response that is possible via a particular strategy.[21] Ultimately, it is becoming ever more apparent that sustainable

---

[16] Ibid, 191.
[17] Alastair Fuad-Luke, *EcoDesign: The Sourcebook*, 3rd Edition (San Francisco: Chronicle Books, 2010), 5.
[18] Stuart Walker, *Sustainable by Design: Explorations in Theory and Practice* (London: Earthscan, 2006).
[19] Ibid, 191.
[20] Further, more radical contributions are covered below.
[21] Seeram Ramakrishna and Rajan Jose, 'Addressing sustainability gaps.' *Science of The Total Environment* 806 (2022): 151–208.

fashion, textiles and product interventions are often only sustainable by degree rather than in absolute terms.[22] The wider economic and cultural paradigm in which they sit – with its promotion of conspicuous consumption through rapid production cycles and the planned obsolescence of products – renders such efforts tokenistic at best and deceptive at worst. This has been accompanied by the deep and entrenched problem of 'greenwashing', whereby products are sold on the basis of false or misleading claims regarding their environmental impact.[23] Treated in this way, sustainability becomes nothing more than empty rhetoric, a marketing tool that encourages further consumption and, as such, only exacerbates the problem.

Such tactics have been called out by an increasingly vocal group of campaigners and theorists (like Walker) who now agitate for a much bolder programme of society-level reform. Fundamental questions are being asked about how business and wider economic models might be transformed in order to properly respond to the unfolding crisis we, humanity and wider planetary life, now face.

The depth of such proposals varies. At one end of the scale, commentators promote relatively accessible ideas relating to the repairability of products. In such cases, grassroots organizations encourage the development of practical repair skills, introducing specialist techniques and helpful hacks to the wider public. More broadly, a 'right to repair' movement has made impressive headway at a policy level, achieving legislative success in the European Union, which will set a wider global precedent for other jurisdictions to follow.[24] At the other end of the scale, some advocate for the

---

[22] Kate Fletcher and Mathilda Tham (eds), *Routledge Handbook of Sustainability and Fashion* (Abingdon, Oxon: Routledge, 2015).

[23] Netto de Freitas, Sebastião Vieira, Marcos Felipe Falcão Sobral, Ana Regina Bezerra Ribeiro and Gleibson Robert da Luz Soares, 'Concepts and forms of greenwashing: A systematic review,' Environmental Sciences Europe 32, no. 1 (2020), 1–12.

[24] Miriam Imarhiagbe, 'The Right to Repair in EU Competition Law.' *Nordic Journal of European Law* 5, no. 1 (2022): 166–72.

more radical concept of degrowth, i.e. pursuing the progressive reduction of economic activity (including the production and consumption of goods).[25]

While highly compelling in many ways, these proposals still require further articulation and working through. Part of the problem is that, if properly pursued, each requires a profound (and, in the case of degrowth, near total) transformation of the paradigms (economic and cultural) underpinning our existence. It is not simply a matter of sourcing and integrating new materials or adopting one or another new process but, rather, upending the patterns of how we live day to day, generation to generation.[26]

If a product is repairable then there will not be a need to replace it and, as such, the obsolescence cycle, which underpins corporate profits, is undone. Equally, degrowth stands as an absolute challenge to the contemporary economic order, where growth is taken as the norm. To begin to determine a different future, which explicitly requires a targeted reduction in material consumption, would inevitably be met with deep resistance.[27] Accordingly, these areas stand as not yet realized possibilities, developments that could happen and could bring change if we were able to map a path towards implementation.

A growing number of design theorists have begun to work through this complexity in direct terms, seeking to draw out possible implications for both design and society more broadly. These perspectives tend to take a radical slant, proposing that nothing less than a deep and full-scale reconstruction of the discipline is required if humanity is going to mount anything approaching an adequate response to the challenges we face.

Recent work from Walker reflects this shift. Rather than talking of sustainability alone, he now speaks of the wider idea

---

[25] Giacomo D'Alisa, Frederico Demaria and Giorgos Kallis, *Degrowth: A vocabulary for a new era* (Abingdon, Oxon: Routledge, 2015).
[26] Arguably with degrowth, it is a return to the not too distant, once-stable models of the past.
[27] Milena Büchs and Max Koch, 'Challenges for the degrowth transition: The debate about wellbeing' *Futures* 105 (2019): 155–65.

of design for resilience.[28] While this enfolds sustainability, it also extends beyond it, calling for a 'deeper' approach, one that contributes towards an economic remodelling, whereby a 'postconsumerist' society – i.e. one that does not centre upon material value – might be realized. This would rely on design becoming 'far more reflective and self-critical', working to confront the 'serious issues' we face today and establishing a dedicated programme of design criticism, which would allow for a more rigorous 'discernment, discussion and debate' within the field.[29] As has been noted, the perspective is couched in deeply philosophical terms, with Walker ultimately aligning his proposals with the broad-based human concern of 'how should we live?'.

Perhaps the most philosophical and certainly most radical general offering has come from Tony Fry, whose concepts of defuturing and unsustainment were noted in the last chapter. Through his defuturing argument, Fry makes clear that our current economic system, along with the politics that underpins it, is utterly unsustainable. Humanity is seen to be entering into an age of 'unsettlement', following on from earlier ages of nomadism and settlement, where our 'being and being-in-place become perpetually insecure'. We are, in short, tilting towards collapse.

Design is seen as fully culpable within this, complicit within our present unsustainable economic systems. Be that as it may, it is also seen as capable of enabling a meaningful response to this crisis. For this to occur, however, design must be remade. Fry argues for a reimagining of the discipline in 'futural' terms, whereby it contributes to the futuring as opposed to defuturing of life.

Design would here become a 'redirective' practice, one that moves away from what is as it aims towards true 'sustain-ability'.[30] In application, redirective practice would carry two key strands. The first is guided by the concept of elimination, where what is

---

[28] Walker, *Design for Resilience*.
[29] Ibid, 87.
[30] The hyphenation of sustainability is meant to underscore the *ability* of sustaining. Fry, *Design Futuring*, 55–6.

deemed unnecessary is not designed in the first place or, alternatively, crucial aspects are removed. This would involve a reappraisal of needs, materials, functions, values. Norms and expectations would change. We would have and use fewer things.[31]

The second strand is the concept of recoding where design aims at 'the transformation of the sign value of objects, images, structures, spaces, services and organizations'.[32] This relies on the idea that meanings can be redesigned. Here, global events such as the Olympic Games, which are perceived to carry immense cultural value, would be repositioned in negative terms on the basis that they contribute to a process of defuturing.

Broadly, such practices would not only 'redirect' design and what is designed but also the global economic, political and social systems in which we operate. In short, our world would be remade too. This leads to a further bold proposal. If we, as a species, are to have a future, Fry argues that it is not just a matter of redesigning of economic, political and social systems, but also redesigning ourselves and our fundamental human *being*. Here, he picks up on what he sees as design's essential evolutionary role. Design and designing, he proposes, has made us who we are as a species and, equally, can be positioned as a means by which we can define who and what we need to become in the future, in order that we have a future.[33]

Combined, all of this would allow for what Fry terms the 'Sustainment', a fresh 'epoch'[34] centred on the 'common good'.[35] At the core, we would have an economic paradigm that disavows ideas of 'continual quantitative growth', makes a commitment to working with our existing material base, and carries a recognition that unsustainability is an ontology, i.e. a way of being for humanity (with the implication that it must be overcome).[36]

---

[31] Ibid, 76–80.
[32] Ibid, 81.
[33] Tony Fry, *Becoming Human by Design* (London: Berg, 2012).
[34] Fry, *Design as Politics*, 22.
[35] Fry, *Design Futuring*, 47.
[36] Fry, *Design as Politics*, 23.

As highlighted in the Introduction, in setting out these arguments, Fry draws on the work of European philosophers,[37] most especially the German phenomenologist Martin Heidegger and his work on being (i.e. how it relates to presence and temporality) and technology (i.e. how technology can be seen to frame and restrict our understanding of the world).[38] This interrelating of philosophy with contemporary design in order to shape a twenty-first-century disciplinary agenda can be understood as a demonstration of how philosophical insights might be positioned so as to potentially inform design practice. Indeed, Fry's working through of what design can become is also very much linked to philosophy. At one point in his writing, in presenting design 'as politics' he positions it as a means by which philosophy might be reinvigorated with a specific goal and purpose: the attainment of the age of sustainment.[39]

Another deeply critical, if not quite as radical, agenda has recently been put forward by Joanna Boehnert.[40] Reflecting on contemporary ecological positionings within design, Boehnert argues that a problematic entanglement of capitalism, harmful political agendas and various erroneous philosophical worldviews has given rise to design in its present, problematic (i.e. unsustainable) form.

In her view, through its complicity in the furtherance of consumer culture (e.g. via advertising, branding, driving the cycles of fast fashion and the wastefulness of product design), design directly contributes to wider patterns of environmental degradation. As with the above proposals, the only solution is a programme of reform. For Boehnert, for this to be successful, it must be underpinned by the development of a whole new literacy in design

---

[37] Alongside Heidegger, there is regular reference to Nietzsche, Bourdieu and Latour. Dewey receives significant reference in *Design as Politics*.
[38] Fry, *Design as Politics*, 22. This vision was crucial to Heidegger's later understandings of technology where the environment was positioned in terms of Gestalt.
[39] Ibid, 80.
[40] Joanna Boehnert, *Design, Ecology and Politics: Towards the Ecocene* (London: Bloomsbury, 2018).

– what she terms *ecological* literacy. Running deeper than conventional sustainability strategies where design practice is only adjusted marginally (e.g. in terms of material or process), this would allow for a direct and careful attending to the ecological impact of design throughout the process, based on a more holistic appreciation of the discipline's wider role in maintaining healthy, functioning ecosystems.

Beyond the above positions, we may note other proposals for change more directly aligned to practice. In recent years, the key example here has been the emergence of transition design, a movement that explores how the practice of designing for societal transitions leads towards a more sustainable future.[41] Intriguingly, transition design takes its lead, at least in part, from philosophy. Specifically, it draws on the research of one of its founders, Gideon Kossoff, who, through his doctoral work, developed a holistic framework for 'reconstituting everyday life'.[42] The framework draws together social psychology, social practice theory, the phenomenological scientific approach of the German philosopher Johann Wolfgang von Goethe and alternative economic theory.[43] From Kossoff's perspective, while these reference points give transition orientation and direction, they do not define it in absolute terms.

This, in turn, means that there are no absolutes in transition design. Rather, the movement is based on a framework of four key mutually reinforcing areas of 'knowledge, action and self-reflection' in order to shape the new approach. At a base level, there is 'posture' and mindset, i.e. how one approaches transitional situations of the present moment. From here, there are two outward branches, one connecting to new ways of designing and another to theories of change. The first relates to the 'how' of

---

[41] Terry Irwin, 'Transition design: A proposal for a new area of design practice, study, and research.' *Design and Culture* 7, no. 2 (2015): 229–46.
[42] Gideon Kossoff, 'Holism and the Reconstitution of Everyday Life: A Framework for Transition to a Sustainable Society' PhD diss. (Dundee: University of Dundee, 2011).
[43] Terry Irwin, Gideon Kossoff and Peter Scupelli, *Transition Design 2015* (Pittsburgh, PA: Carnegie Mellon University, 2015).

practice. Reference is made to place-based and context-based approaches, transdisciplinarity and collaborative approaches such as co-design. The second connects to interdisciplinary perspectives on change. Here, the various fields noted above in relation to Kossoff's work come to the fore, allowing for rich multilayered ways of seeing in relation to what might need to change, whether scientific, social, environmental or otherwise. Both of these areas – design and theories of change – connect to the area of 'visions of transition', i.e. the type of sustainable transition one hopes to bring about.

The whole is to be seen as co-evolving and interconnecting. One does not start at the bottom and move to the top. Instead, the areas connect into each other, back and forth, up and down. The reference points of one area can allow for special reference to be made in another area. All can change.

In reflecting on the above threads of design's sustainability arguments – from repairability, to degrowth, to futuring, to ecological literacy, to transition design – we may note the broadness of possibilities, as well as the distinction in the scale and areas of focus in all of this. As with so many aspects of design, there is no one way into the ecological. The crisis we face requires that we address the need for a strategy.

To gain a sense of how some designer researchers have approached such questions, we now turn to consider the work of Kristina Lindström and Åsa Ståhl.

KRISTINA LINDSTRÖM AND ÅSA STÅHL: DESIGNING AN UNDESIGNING

Based in Sweden, design researchers Kristina Lindström and Åsa Ståhl have, over the last two decades, worked to trace a series of relationships between making, ideas of community and matters of concern. In this, their research practice has tended to centre upon the activities of sewing and patchworking, with technology sometimes providing a platform of connection and communication within this. Here, in making, groups who do not know each other are brought together and invited to share concerns, creating what Lindström and Ståhl term a 'temporary assembly'.[44] Concerns might relate to the past or, equally, new concerns might arise within the context of the assembly. The long-term benefits of sharing these concerns cannot be known, nor are they necessarily traceable. Nonetheless, for Lindström and Ståhl, the assemblies can be seen to provide an opportunity for reflection and conversation that would not otherwise exist.[45] Such opportunities open other possibilities, for the participants, for those they connect with and beyond through the things that are made.[46]

More recently, the pair have turned their attention to environmental concerns, through the concept of what they refer to as 'un/making'.[47] Un/making takes its reference from Cameron Tonkinwise's 'deprogressive design' proposal,[48] which advocates for a disciplinary redirection from the unsustainable towards the sustainable – an adjusting of that which is deemed preferable.[49] Next to this, Lindström and Ståhl present un/making as the coming together of 'the creative and destructive aspects of design'[50] – a foregrounding of making within a wider process of unmaking, where the unsustainable is being unmade through new makings.

Illustrating un/making in the context of a public exhibition within a museum, the pair take the much-maligned plastic straw and its problematic disposability as their focus. The potential

---

[44] Kristina Lindström and Åsa Ståhl, 'Making private matters public in temporary assemblies,' *CoDesign* 8, no. 2–3 (2012): 145–61.

[45] Ibid, 159.

[46] The temporary assemblies are positioned as Things – as per Latour's reanimation of Heidegger's 'Things'-as-parliaments (see Chapter 5). Ibid.

[47] Kristina Lindström and Åsa Ståhl, 'Un/Making the Plastic Straw: Designerly Inquiries into Disposability,' *Design and Culture*, 15, no. 3 (2023): 393–415.

[48] Cameron Tonkinwise, ''I Prefer Not To': Anti-Progressive Designing.' In *Undesign: A Critical Practice at the Intersection of Art and Design*, edited by Gretchen Coombs, Andrew McNamara and Gavin Sade, (London: Routledge, 2019), 74–84.

[49] Tonkinwise calls for an exploration of past – but still persistent – practices or ways of living that did not insist on progress. Examples given are slow food, walking to school and the use of a push mower. See ibid, 81.

[50] Lindström and Ståhl, 'Un/Making the Plastic Straw', 393.

for un/making the plastic straw was explored through four predetermined thematic trajectories defined by short texts: temporality, caring relationships, microbiological co-living and aftermath. These each allow for different ways of approaching the problems presented by the straw as it is, in its present form. In un/making, a series of four speculative design artefacts was produced in response, one per theme. These 'draw on past and emerging alternatives' to the straw.[51] In other words, in the process of responding, there is both a looking back and looking forward.

For example, for the theme of temporality, concern is directed to the mismatch between the longevity of the object and its use in the context of drinking. Reference is made to historic straw designs (e.g. the use of reeds). By way of speculative response, the pair produce a frozen cordial straw which melts while drinking, quickly dissolving into a liquid itself and thus perfectly aligning to the temporality of the object as and when it is used. As a further example, in relation to the theme of microbiological co-living, concern is directed towards the way in which ever-stricter public health requirements have, over time, led to what can be conceived of as an overly sterile human environment. It is arguable that this, in turn, has reduced our general microbiological health (i.e. alongside reducing the spread of dangerous pathogens there is, equally, less opportunity for us to acquire beneficial microbes as we interact in daily life). In this instance, a shared drinking glass vessel with multiple individual (metal) straws is produced. This is positioned as a compromise between absolute sterility (as symbolized by existing single-use plastics) and allowance for a degree of microbiological 'co-living', i.e. a group will be drinking from the same drink and as such sharing microbial life.[52] It is also durable as opposed to disposable. As a final noteworthy collaborative initiative undertaken in response to the theme of aftermath, a plogging (picking up waste while jogging)

---

[51] Ibid.

[52] The authors note that in the context of the COVID-19 pandemic – when they were writing about their research – such a proposal carried very different connotations from when it was initially developed.

FIGURE 4.1 A shared drinking glass vessel produced as part of the Un/Making project. The vessel has multiple individual (metal) straws to support microbiological 'co-living'. Courtesy Åsa Ståhl.

activity was undertake with members of the public, drawing attention to the unresolved life cycle of single use plastics.

Generally, these artefacts and activities are seen to both provide a contingent answer to an initial concern (e.g. the possibility of richer microbiological co-living) at the same time as opening up other, related concerns (e.g. the extent to which microbiological co-living can be managed). Ultimately, they each function as meditations on the concept of un/making that Lindström and Ståhl are seeking to give form to. Reflecting on the artefacts individually and collectively, the pair are able to comment on what is possible through a designerly un/making and what is not, what it could mean, what its limitations are and what would be required to progress beyond what has been achieved within this context. Indeed, they conclude by arguing that in order to respond to the challenges of disposability, wholly new economic arrangements are called for; design alone cannot meet the challenges posed.

For our present purposes, it is important to note that Lindström and Ståhl do not discuss their work in philosophical terms. The above projects – both Threads and Un/Making – are very much positioned as research through design, with speculative design sitting at the core. However, within this work, we may draw out philosophic concerns relating to areas such as, for example, time and health. Broadly, un/making itself can be seen as very much a philosophical question of what it means to deconstruct at the same time as construct within the status quo, working to remake the frameworks of our living. Underpinning the whole, there are questions regarding the meaning of objects, their use, as well as the value they represent. For example, the meaning of disposability is being explored repeatedly throughout, with multiple alternative variations of this being produced (from the dissolvable to the more durable). Equally, the value of given artefacts (e.g. the straw itself) and processes (e.g. how we can come together in new ways microbiological) is picked up on in the un/making activities. Within a philosophy through design, these aspects could be drawn out further, with more refined statements being possible in relation to the potential parameters of un/making and the meanings and values they call up. We will consider how this might function more generally within an ecological context at the chapter's end.

From Lindström and Ståhl, we will now, through the following sections, turn to consider how the ecological concerns are directly addressed within philosophy itself.

ECOLOGY IN ENVIRONMENTAL PHILOSOPHIES

Like the social, the meaning of the ecological is difficult to grasp in a single sentence or definition. Ecology is perhaps best thought of as a process, a coming together of many things in productive interaction, which, as a dynamic whole, constitutes a lifeforce, a driving energy without clear boundary.

The relationship between the ecological or environmental and the philosophical is a complicated matter. The complexity of the issues we are dealing with, especially the profound existential consequences of the climate change, demands nothing less than our total attention. Within this, a philosophic working through of the issues might help us to begin to better understand the current situation. Yet, strangely, ecological and environmental concerns remain largely absent from contemporary philosophy, forming a largely peripheral discourse when compared to other more popular disciplinary agendas, whether relating to technology or the mind or some other area.

How did this situation come about? Arguably, one of the key challenges in developing a stronger ecological perspective in Western culture is likely to relate, at least in part, to the traditional humanist emphasis of this discourse. Historically, ecology or 'nature', to use a more traditional term, was only an implicit philosophic concern, forming a background against which other, more significant issues might be considered and ultimately dealt with. We see this, for example, in relation to Newton's framing of a mechanical universe and, within this, a mechanical world. Equally in Descartes's exploration of reason and method, the metaphysics of life and bodies are all considered but only as an offshoot of questioning the capacities of the human mind.[53]

Such positions can be seen as the out-workings of a tradition stretching back at least to ancient philosophy, which placed humanity at the centre point of metaphysical proposals or theories of existence. Animals, plants, the world and all that is in it have followed on as lesser beings and entities in this hierarchy. It has been difficult to escape this way of understanding ourselves and how we relate to the other living and non-living entities – life and non-life. Nonetheless, we have begun to try.

---

[53] For a history of this see Edward Grant, *A History of Natural Philosophy: From The Ancient World To The Nineteenth Century* (Cambridge: Cambridge University Press, 2007).

We have already encountered a key example of such work in the technological and social contexts of the preceding two chapters, where the more-than-human perspective of actor network theory was discussed. Here, as we have seen, the world is recast as networks of relating entities which draw together in the interactions of action. As with the political work discussed in the last chapter, ANT tends to approach ecological questions through the prism of matter of concern, where 'things', collectives, are seen to assemble around issues. This translates into a way of negotiating existential questions that allows for a reaching beyond the human, recognizing how actors, whether human or non-human, living or not, all have agency in the situations in which they are implicated.

More particularly, beyond ANT, when it comes to drawing in the non-human, we may also look to environmental philosophy proper. While this discourse has not yet achieved a significant status within the field and currently lacks a wide scholarly following, its popularity has begun to increase. At present, focus is directed towards the area of ethics, wherein the environment becomes a context in which the rights and wrongs, duties and responsibilities of human action are considered and given bearing. Here, as will be discussed, questions such as how do we recognize the rights of future generations and to what extent do entities such as rivers have rights are asked and sometimes answered. Alongside this, we may observe the emergence of focused strands of work such as ecofeminism and ecophenomenology, which we will also briefly consider below. Further, a range of environmental philosophical themes have begun to develop around the subject. Predominately ethically focused, these reference considerations such as the intrinsic meaning and value of nature and natural things, nature-based aesthetics, and human–nature relationships.[54]

Given this layering and wide scope, the work varies greatly in orientation, emphasis and form. Accordingly, it is a broad and somewhat disconnected discourse but still provides an axis around which ecology and philosophy can meaningfully interact.

---

[54] Andrew Brennan and Yeuk-Sze Lo, *Understanding Environmental Philosophy* (Abingdon, Oxon: Routledge, 2014).

A key early contribution to environmental philosophy emerged through Arne Naess's pioneering deep ecology proposals.[55] We begin with it.

Deep Ecology

In contrast to what Naess terms shallow ecology – a perspective which seeks to maintain the socio-economic status quo with subtle adjustment and amendment – deep ecology holds that humanity and nature are integrally intertwined and, as such, our current socio-economic situation requires complete transformation/transition.

For Naess, understanding this relationship to the environment is ultimately an ontological concern, a question of how to conceive of our being. Thus, for two parties to come to a shared view on the environment, it is necessary for them to jointly explore how their ontological understandings connect to the ecological. Without this, mutual understanding may be limited or, alternatively, both might clash. It is not only a matter of interpersonal meaning, however. Naess recommends that we reflect on our own environmental position. Here, he envisages that individuals and groups will be able to develop their own ecological philosophy – an 'ecosophy' – which would function as a declaration of our being in relation to the wider being of the ecological world.

As a means of supporting this, he and American philosopher George Sessions developed what they referred to as a deep ecology platform, a set of eight commitments which outline essential deep ecological values or aspirations.[56] The underpinning principle is that ecology is primary and humanity must understand its needs in relation to this wider ecology. The expectation is that by working through their alignment with the platform, individuals

---

[55] Arne Naess, *Ecology, Community and Lifestyle: Outline of an* Ecosophy (Cambridge: Cambridge University Press, 1990).
[56] Arne Naess and George Sessions, 'The Deep Ecology Platform' In *Clearcut: The Tragedy of Industrial Forestry*, edited by Bill Devall (San Francisco: Sierra Club Books and Earth Island Press, 1993).

and groups would have a framework to live by – a deep ecological strategy.[57]

Other environmental philosophies have also emerged alongside Naess's work. Key here is ecofeminism.

Ecofeminism

First emerging in the 1970s,[58] ecofeminism explores the problematic aspects of humanity's relationship to the environment (e.g. the extraction and despoiling of natural resources) from the perspective of gender.[59] Linking domains such as social and political theory, economics and the arts, the essential argument is that the oppression of women and the environment, inclusive of the planet's manifold species and ethnic groups, may be understood as intertwined and intertwining – patriarchal domination ultimately maps across all.

In this, varying focal concerns have garnered attention over the years. These have included science and technology, embodiment, reproduction, animal ethics, colonialism and spirituality.[60] While early voices were concerned with addressing existential threats such as nuclear weapons,[61] contemporary theorists tend to align

---

[57] This self-led approach has been criticized in a number of quarters as being too individually focused. See for example Luís Homem and Bruno Rego, 'Deep Ecology and Utopia: Eco-centric Nowhere.' *International Journal of Critical Cultural Studies* 13, no. 1 (2015): 9–19.

[58] Françoise d'Eaubonne's 'Le Feminisme ou la mort' is seen as the source text. See Françoise d'Eaubonne, 'Le Féminisme ou la mort' In *New French Feminisms: An Anthology*, edited by Elaine Marks and Isabelle de Courtivron (Amherst, MA: University of Massachusetts Press, 1980).

[59] Mary Phillips and Nick Rumens (eds), *Contemporary Perspectives on Ecofeminism* (London: Routledge, 2015).

[60] See e.g. Maria Mies and Vandana Shiva, *Ecofeminism* (London: Zed Books, 1993); Greta Gaard (ed.), *Ecofeminism* (Philadelphia: Temple University Press, 1993).

[61] Benedikte Zitouni, 'Planetary destruction, ecofeminists and transformative politics in the early 1980s.' *Interface* 6, no. 2 (2014): 244–70.

with a broader agenda centring on climate change.[62] Perspectives have also become more complex. For example, taking a transdisciplinary approach, Ariel Salleh argues for an examination of the ecological within the economic.[63] Across all contributions, regardless of the focus taken, one can identify a unifying thread in the consistent advocacy for feminist alternatives.

Intriguingly in the context of the present book, alignments have also been drawn between ecofeminism and feminist pragmatism generally, on the basis that the feminist pragmatists were among the first to draw attention to the need to relate social and environmental considerations. On this front, the work of both Caroline Bartlett Crane and Charlotte Perkins Gilman,[64] in particular, has been highlighted as offering distinct examples of what has been termed 'ecofeminist pragmatism'.[65]

Caroline Bartlett Crane is seen to have connected the devaluation of both women and the environment. Taking a sociological approach, her work focused on the need for access to a clean physical environment, as well as opportunities for recreation and play.[66] She was also alert to the damage of industrial pollution and acted as an early advocate for the conservation movement.[67]

Charlotte Perkins Gilman was an early feminist social reform advocate and writer who pursued an agenda not only of women's rights but also animal rights. Her work explored relationships

---

[62] See e.g. Greta Gaard, 'From 'cli-fi' to critical ecofeminism: narratives of climate change and climate justice.' In *Contemporary Perspectives on Ecofeminism*, edited by Mary Phillips and Nick Rumens (London: Routledge, 2015), 169–92.

[63] Ariel Salleh, *Ecofeminism as Politics: Nature, Marx and the Postmodern*, 2nd Edition (London: Bloomsbury, 2017).

[64] Mary Jo Deegan and Christopher W. Podeschi, 'The Ecofeminist Pragmatism of Charlotte Perkins Gilman.' *Environmental Ethics* 23, no. 1 (2001): 19–36.

[65] Linda J. Rynbrandt and Mary Jo Deegan. 'The ecofeminist pragmatism of Caroline Bartlett Crane, 1896–1935.' *The American Sociologist* 33, no. 3 (2002): 58–68.

[66] Rynbrandt and Deegan. 'The ecofeminist pragmatism of Caroline Bartlett Crane, 1896–1935', 62.

[67] Ibid, 64.

between humans and the environment and humans and animals at a time when such relationships were not widely discussed. What is compelling from a design perspective is her use of what we might now call speculative narratives or design fiction. Here, through the early twentieth century, Perkins Gilman produced a series of texts that envisaged worlds distinctly different from our own. In *Herland*, in particular, she sketches out an alternative society where women enjoy a fully equal status next to men. Labour is shared and rights and responsibilities evenly and fairly distributed. Not only this, but the relationship between humans and animals is also fairer, with animals no longer involved in domestic labour.[68]

These connections, of course, link to the other ecological/environmental-pragmatist connections, highlighted above. Before moving on from ecofeminism, it important to note that it already has a small but widening following within design.

Ecofeminist Designing

The last decade has seen a number of ecofeminist contributions emerge in both design studies and the related area of architecture. These range from wholly theoretical proposals through to design research involving practice. With regard to the theoretical, authors generally link to an ecofeminist perspective in seeking to address a wide-ranging societal concern. As an example, Eeva Houtbeckers and Idil Gaziulusoy relate an ecofeminist understanding of care to a sustainable transitions agenda and, in doing so, explore how this could inform a degrowth framework.[69]

---

[68] Charlotte Perkins Gilman, *Herland* (New York: Dover Publications, 1998 [1915]).

[69] Eeva Houtbeckers and Idil Gaziulusoy, 'Ecofeminist Understandings of Care and Design for Sustainability Transitions: Towards a theoretical framework of work for the degrowth movement.' *Proceedings of Bi-Annual Nordic Design Research Society Conference, Nordes, Who Cares?, 2–4 June, 2019.* Alto: Alto University,

In terms of design research work, a recent example is found in Tara Falconer and Marcos Mortensen Steagall's *Grounded* project.[70] The project explores how ecofeminism might inform the design of graphic outcomes to support young women to develop a 'dialogical relationship with nature'. This, it is proposed, would incorporate 'wellbeing and ecological consciousness'.[71] The process involved the techniques of mind mapping, printmaking, scrapbooking and collage.[72] Taking a 'reflective inquiry' approach, ecofeminist thinking guided these making practices, allowing the designer to ask questions of their relationship with the environment via philosophical stance. Additional insights were also drawn from a questionnaire sent to young women. The result was a 'graphic set' comprising forty cards relating to the five senses. In centring a particular sensory possibility, each card points to the always-present potential for growth and flourishing through environmental interaction. It is proposed that the set might act as meditational prompts, supporting a natural dialogue for those who encounter it.

In examining the above, we must first note that *Grounded* is limited in scope. The survey work aside, it relies largely on the personal perspective of the designer and the outcome (the cards) is untested in that we have no sense of what its use might look like in empirical terms or, equally, how effective this might be. Nonetheless, in saying this, we must also note that *Grounded* does point to the possibility of applying approaches such as ecofeminism as a perspective within a philosophy through design. In the project, we may observe philosophy operating as a guiding source point. It allows for a selection of subject matter (feminine environmental relations) and informs the framing of an outcome. Use of the cards might allow for reflection on our relationship with the environment, opening up questions of meaning and value

---

[70] Tara Falconer and Marcos Mortensen Steagall, 'Grounding: A Practice–led Graphic Exploration of Ecofeminism, Wellbeing and Ecological Consciousness for Young Women', *DAT Journal*, 8 no. 1 (2023): 101–34. https://doi.org/10.29147/datjournal.v8i1.689
[71] Ibid, 118.
[72] Ibid, 123.

FIGURE 4.2 The material used in developing the *Grounded* project outcome. Courtesy Tara Falconer.

on an individual level – an activity that could, over time, support the engendering of an ecofeminist perspective for individuals and potentially groups. Unlike Lindström and Ståhl's Un/Making work discussed above, the aim is not to explore the possibilities of a novel shaping of a concept or process (i.e. un/making) but, rather, to explore the possibilities of designing with respect to an existing philosophical perspective. *Grounded*, then, can ultimately be seen as a testing of ecofeminism in practice, for practice.[73]

Looking beyond ecofeminism and ecofeminist designing, we will now turn to the complementary area of ecophenomenology.

Ecophenomenology

As David Woods puts it, ecophenomenology functions as both an ecological phenomenology and phenomenological ecology,

---

[73] In terms of addressing any limitations here, to progress beyond this point, it is required that others take up the same task – that they also design within an ecofeminist framework, investigating the impact on their practice and the potential to derive insights. The same goes for designing with reference to other perspectives, whether environmentally bound or not. It is something we must do and, in doing, evaluate.

allowing for a thinking through of 'Nature and the natural', which cuts across domains.[74] Here, following classical phenomenology's focus on our perceptive and interpretative capacities, we are invited to restore a 'participatory engagement (bodily, imaginative, etc.) with things'[75] and, as such, with the world more generally. This process of restoration is about articulation and description, noting relations and constraints and, through this process, activating that which was not previously activated.

Recently, the idea of what is termed the 'more-than-human' has come to the fore in such work. This perspective is not just about drawing alignments between human and non-human, living and non-living, but also understanding how, in coming together, something greater is formed. Here, ultimately, we are asked to think beyond ourselves, as we relate to ourselves. In exploring this idea, David Abrams seeks to draw our attention back to our embedded animality.[76] We are reminded of the often-forgotten agency of our body, the deep physicality of our situatedness and, within this, the expansive interrelationality of existence.

Following a similar vein, James Brindle proposes a reconsideration of how we understand intelligence.[77] His plea is that intelligence not be approached as the singular preserve of humans alone but, rather, as an indeterminate capability expressed in the actions and processes of living (e.g. plants and animals) and non-living (i.e. machines). In this, we are asked to imagine the manifold forms that intelligence might take across a spectrum firmly grounded within ecology – that is, in the end, all links backs to ecology. Working outwards from this, he proposes that machine intelligence, in particular, might be positioned in cooperative as opposed to instrumentalist terms. It could, he argues, support

---

[74] David Wood, 'What is ecophenomenology?.' *Research in Phenomenology* 31, no. 1 (2001): 78–95.

[75] Ibid, 82.

[76] David Abrams, *Becoming Animal: An Earthly Cosmology* (New York: Vintage, 2010).

[77] James Bridle, *Ways of Being, Animals, Plants and Machines: The Search for a Planetary Intelligence* (London: Penguin Books, 2023).

ways of seeing and ways of coming together with other beings and things. The choice is a matter of perspective.

Designers are yet to fully embrace a phenomenological perspective. While the Designing for Quality Interactions (DQI) group at the University of Eindhoven aligned with the work of Heidegger and Maurice Merleau-Ponty through the 2000s and into the 2010s,[78] their impact remained limited and was eventually superseded by the postphenomenological work of today. Subsequent work has been isolated to individual researchers.[79] Ecophenomenology presents an opportunity to reimagine the way in which phenomenology can play a role in design: first, by offering a novel method for engaging in ecological contexts; second, by offering an additional method, beyond actor network theory (for example), which allows for a surfacing of relationality, of coming together, as suggested in the Brindle work noted above.

Tracking back through the work of this and the prior sections – Naess, the ecofeminists, the above ecophenomenology – we may identify a progressive decentring of the human or anthropocentric worldview and a movement towards a more environmentally or ecologically orientated vision – what is commonly termed a biocentric worldview. This brings us at last to the area of environmental ethics, briefly noted above.[80]

ENVIRONMENTAL ETHICS

Environmental ethics is an evolving discourse. Over the last number of decades, the ever-greater urgency of the climate crisis and biodiversity loss, coupled with the increased awareness of

---

[78] Caroline Hummels and Pierre Lévy. 'Matter of transformation: Designing an alternative tomorrow inspired by phenomenology.' *Interactions* 20, no. 6 (2013): 42–9.

[79] Camilla Groth has made sustained contributions to phenomenological work in design, examining the area of embodied knowing in particular. See Camilla Groth, *Making Sense through Hands* (Helsinki: Aalto University, 2017).

[80] David R. Keller (ed.), *Environmental Ethics* (Chichester: Wiley Blackwell, 2010).

our entangled relationship with the living world, has helped guide a shift in emphasis from anthropocentric perspectives (i.e. human-centred viewpoints) to biocentric perspectives (i.e. ecologically holistic viewpoints).[81] In some ways it is arguable that a similar pattern has been followed in design itself. Ultimately, it has become increasingly difficult to sustain anthropocentric positions, whether implicit or explicit. With biocentric or holistic positions, the challenge lies with building a framework that extends beyond the human. As with all ethical frameworks, this is a problem of justification, of building out the rationale that allows for claims to be made.

One of the earliest such positions put forward came from American ecologist Aldo Leopold, who set out what he termed a land ethic. For Leopold, land, or more accurately the biosphere, needs to be understood from the perspective of the food chain – of how species and entities relate and depend on each other. At a base level there are soil and plants. Thereafter it is a matter of ever greater specificity rising up from invertebrates, to rodents, to smaller carnivores and omnivores (including humans), to apex predators such as canines and felines. On this account, humans were not only to be seen as a community unto themselves but as members of wider ecological communities. The ethical principle across this community is one of maintaining balance across these levels. As Leopold put it, something is 'right when it tends to preserve the integrity, stability and beauty of the biotic community' and wrong when 'it tends otherwise'.[82]

---

[81] If we were to approach things anthropocentrically (i.e. by centring the human), one might focus on our place in nature or the extent to which animals have rights as living creatures. If we were to take a biocentric perspective, one might seek to forge a *holistic* worldview, drawing ecologies together as moral communities. On both fronts, however, it is a question of responsibility and value. Who and what is responsible to whom and what? Who and what hold value and in what ways; for example, is a tree intrinsically valuable in and of itself beyond the use-value of its timber?

[82] Aldo Leopold, *A Sand Country Almanac* (Oxford: Oxford University Press, 1966 [1949]), 224–5.

Leading on from Leopold's early twentieth-century work, others have sought to further contextualize and give form to the biocentric, holistic outlook. One of the key dividers to emerge within this work lies in whether the biocentrism is hierarchical, meaning that certain species are given higher status based on perceived characteristics; or whether, like Leopold's land ethic, it is egalitarian, meaning that all are seen as equally deserving of moral consideration.

With the hierarchical positions, the key challenge lies in assigning status, defining the thresholds at which higher or lower status is assigned. Some draw distinctions on the basis of sentience – that is, the perceived level of awareness held by particular lifeforms – others on the basis of whether or not a lifeform is capable of suffering.[83] Any such distinctions are, of course, problematic, as one cannot be certain of levels of sentience or another entity's mode of experiencing being.

With egalitarian positions, by contrast, all life is seen as *intrinsically* valuable, something which has worth in and of itself and as such a right to being and existence. This, of course, brings complications of its own: if there is no distinction to be drawn between lifeforms, how does one approach the problem of those that hold competing interests (e.g. a parasite and its host)? The only possible response is to aim to strike a careful balance. Here, in the parasite–host example, the host can be seen to have a right to self-defence.[84]

Regardless of the specific position adopted, we can draw out the general principle that the role of the human in environmental ethics requires a much more nuanced approach than is often taken. Much like Leopold's land ethic, our lives must be understood within a much wider network of value.

---

[83] Mikel Torres Aldave, 'Who owns nature? Sentience, environmental ethics and intervention in nature.' *Estudios de Filosofía* 65 (2022), 7–29.

[84] Holmes Rolston III, 'Challenges in Environmental Ethics.' In *The Environment in Question*, 2nd edn, edited by David E. Cooper and Joy A. Palmer (Abingdon, Oxon: Routledge, 2005), 144–54.

From this brief surfacing of environmental philosophy across the preceding sections, we now turn at last to consider how we might give initial form to an ecologically orientated philosophy through design.

AN ECOLOGICAL PHILOSOPHY THROUGH DESIGN

What might an ecologically orientated philosophy through design look like? How might a philosophy through design support the engendering of ecological ways of seeing that can secure a future for humanity and planetary life? In seeking to address these questions, the present chapter has explored a number of distinct strands of work that relate to this context.

We explored pragmatism from an ecological standpoint. Then there was contemporary design with its degrees of critique of and responses to our present crises. From this, we turned to philosophy with its still-developing ecological/environmental perspectives, enfolding areas such as deep ecology, ecofeminism, ecophenomenology, as well as the distinct domain of environmental ethics.

This has surfaced positions relating to design's response to the climate emergency, including practical strategies and theoretical reflections. In relation to philosophy, it has also opened up questions regarding the relating of the human to the environmental, the environment and gender, the human and more-than-human, as well as whether, morally, we are attending to the human over the environment (anthropocentric) or the human alongside and/ or within the environment (i.e. biocentric positions).

Tracing back through this material, we may turn first to the present situation in design itself and, here, following a pragmatist tack, seek to note what is problematic. Taking register of the whole, what stands out is a lack of cohesion in the discipline's response to the current crisis. There are possibilities, but there is no one clear approach that can claim to offer a definite solution to the challenges we face.

Arguably this plurality may be seen to work in design's favour. It is quite probable there is no one solution to our present situation. Success is more likely to emerge in different forms at different times via these different strategies. In such a situation, a multipronged approach is no doubt sensible.

Be that as it may, it would still appear that a stronger disciplinary understanding is called for, one that offers a clearer sense of direction and a deeper understanding of what may or may not work. This, in turn, demands a working through of the interrelationship between strategies, of their value (or not) next to one another.

For this to happen, however, designers as well as society more broadly must work to better understand the challenges faced – that is, the scale of the crises and what is at stake. We are beginning to undertake this work – at a faster rate than ever before perhaps – but we are not yet close to a point where there is agreement or, indeed, anything approaching clarity on the challenges faced.

I take the view that, not unlike the guide provided by Fry's futuring principle, this is where a philosophy through design can begin to contribute in an ecological context, supporting a gradual shift towards truly ecological ways of seeing (and ultimately being).

What would this look like?

In the first instance, activity would need to foreground programmes of deliberative debate of the sort discussed in the last chapter. Through such programmes, be they small-scale or large, key issues could be progressively explored and worked through. We could begin to ask questions about what is happening and why. As problems and possibilities are identified – ones which do or could involve design – we can also consider what an appropriate design *and* societal response can and should look like, what these responses can and should achieve, and why they are worth pursuing (e.g. because of the intrinsic ecological good they can preserve or progress). Further, and finally, in designing in and around problems/possibilities we have the opportunity to work to see ourselves and our situation anew and, from this, decide how to design anew. To give this latter aspect some context, with Lindströn and Ståhl's Un/Making project we saw how the artefacts functioned as mediations on their concept of un/making. This allowed for reflection on the possibilities and limitations of un/making as a proposal, with further trajectories and concerns (ecological and otherwise) opening up within the process.

Returning to environmental philosophy, it is proposed that the perspectives set out here can act as a key touchstone within such a process, material from which we are able to draw reference as we seek to understand the challenges faced as well as the role design could/should play within the process. Additionally, in doing so, it then becomes possible for a philosophy through design to ask questions of the meaning and value of the ecological – i.e. what matters and what is good (intrinsically or otherwise) – through the lens of what has already been argued for and reasoned through.

Naess's deep ecology proposals provide us with a useful example here. In picking this up, we are called upon to understand the challenges we face as we work through our own environmental philosophy, specifically, our environmental ontology or sense of our environmental being. As we have seen, this can happen at a group level and, indeed, should, if the necessary progress is to be made.

Here, communities and stakeholders can come together around issues and work through their understanding of both the challenges faced and the meaning of their environment to them, of what it is and what it enables. As a group, it would be possible to note convergences and distinctions and over time establish an agreement of sorts. Within a philosophy through design approach, not only would it be possible to cultivate a comprehensive understanding of the challenges faced but also a working through of possible solutions in an open-ended manner. This would mean looking beyond the purely instrumental or meeting of an immediate need and require a more strategic outlook, such as the work highlighted by Eindhoven's Dutch Ministry of Infrastructure and Water Management 2050 project in Chapter 2. Here, we touch on what might be termed specifically 'futures' work. The possibility of exploring this further methodologically in philosophy through design will be addressed in the next chapter.

Questions of meaning and value could be dealt with as they emerge – for example, the mattering of this river, the intrinsic value of that forest, what makes a landscape special and what the characteristics of that relationship are. Equally, creativity could open up unexpected trajectories and insights extend beyond an ecological context, such as what occurred in Linström and Ståhl's Un/Making project, where artefacts were seen to function as contingent answers to questions which, in turn, opened up further concerns within the process. All such questions and concerns could be accommodated within the wider process (even if only partially) one by one, with some trajectories/insights taking focus and others falling away.

In envisaging such possibilities, it is important to remember environmental philosophy is much broader than deep ecology on its own. As we have seen, areas such as ecophenomenology and ecofeminism stand as examples of further, additional perspectives through which an ecologically orientated philosophy through design might progress.

The important point to draw out here is that in adopting a philosophical frame of reference as designers there is the potential to ask questions that derive from that framework. With the examples of ecophenomenology and ecofeminism, we are invited to explore the role of the body, the character and quality of specific forms of intelligence and modes of being, as well as the role of gender in our environmental interactions. Further, there is the potential opportunity to trace new methods of designing which link to the body, other forms of intelligences and modes of being, and the environmental role of gender. Next to this, ecofeminist pragmatism could take reference from the work of such individuals and Caroline Bartlett Crane and Charlotte Gilman Perkins and explore how the environment and gender would fold together with an active inquiry, where transformation and advocacy for change form a central goal. This was nascent at the turn of the twentieth century; a philosophy through design that draws reference from pragmatism could carry it forward.

Returning to the general possibilities of environmental philosophy, regardless of one's alignments, it is vital not to lose sight of the offer of environmental ethics as a broad orientational framework. Given the urgency of our environmental situation, an ethical stance might well form a starting point within philosophy through design. Here, for example, it would be possible to explore the ways in which design will have to reform itself if we are to adopt a truly biocentric agenda.

Alternatively, mirroring pragmatism's specific embedded ethics, environmental ethics might thread through such work, allowing for the constant consideration of what is being centred and what is not, what is granted significance and what is not and, most importantly, why. To offer an example that extends beyond pragmatism, if one were following a deep ecology approach, one might work to shape a set of ethical commitments for one's practice, e.g. a biocentric egalitarianism, which decentres the human.

The above proposals allow us to consider what an ecologically orientated philosophy through design *could* look like. Within this, as has been intimated, the engendering of ecological ways of seeing would ultimately be the purpose of such work – the wider managing of our broader environmental relationship through design. Though the broad arc of what has been traced – i.e. working outwards from where people are in their understanding and ontology, moving gradually towards solutions based on new ways of seeing – may seem an unlikely path to salvation, it is the only route available; there is no other way to *collectively* transition except through understanding.

5 Philosophy through Design: A Starting Point

We have now covered our three thematic horizons or areas of focus as they were referred to at the outset of this book – the technological, the social and the ecological. As we have progressed through each there have been continual pointings to the potential of a philosophy through design, looking and the form it might take and at the role it could play.

This chapter will draw the book to a close by looking back on the progressive arc that was shaped through these discussions and, from this, will put forward a final proposal for how a philosophy through design might function as a process. We will also consider its similarities and dissimilarities with design research involving practice. Then, following on, the characteristics of a potential new figure – the designer philosopher – will be profiled as an emergent archetype, a practitioner that *could* be.

From this, we will look forward to a series of areas for future methodological consideration including how connections might be drawn to perspectives which extend beyond the Euro-American, Global North starting point of this text. Finally, to close, a general case will be made for the overarching value of a philosophy through design, looking not only at its potential impact for the field philosophy directly, but also for society and the wider global community more broadly.

TRACING A PHILOSOPHY THROUGH DESIGN: LOOKING BACK

This book found its starting point in design. Specifically, in the idea that as the discipline expands into novel contexts (e.g. service and policy design) and comes to be positioned as a means by which we can respond to the grand challenges we face (e.g. climate change), its associated burden of responsibility has grown exponentially. This is not to say that design has not previously held significant responsibility. It has. What is different now is that in expanding and in being positioned as means by which grand challenges can be addressed, the level of responsibility assigned to design has grown wider and deeper than ever before. It has become a central problem-solving tool for our culture. This was explored across the above areas of the technological, where our sense of self and the interpersonal is being redrawn; the social, where design works to attend to lived experiences, working through all manner of concerns and opportunities that fit within this; and the ecological, where the sustainment of planetary life is at stake.

In order to begin to answer the question of how design might start to respond to these (relatively) new-found responsibilities, a turn to philosophy was proposed. Specifically, the proposal was that a philosophy *through design* would allow for problem identification and the exploration of solutions/answers in practice where these responsibilities take shape.

While there are several existing points of connection between design and philosophy (e.g. the area of design philosophy), focus was directed to the nascent link that exists through the methodological approach of design research involving practice. Philosophy is embedded within design research involving practice through the selection of methodological reference points, which will, by necessity, link to a specific philosophic reference point, whether explicit or not. The openness of design research involving practice means that a degree of philosophical understanding – often a greater degree than in other fields such as the natural sciences – is required in selecting one's approach. Equally, given the general focus on quality of experience, which is often present in such studies, in certain instances such work also appears to lead to investigations and insights that extend beyond mere contextual understanding and instead point to philosophical reflections relating to meaning and value, as well as ethical questions regarding the desirability of particular proposals or possibilities. We have seen this emerge in some of the examples of design research discussed through this text (e.g. the Everyday Studio work exploring the meaning and value of speculative technologies in domestic settings).

Taking this general position into account, it was proposed that that design research involving practice might provide a template for an approach to undertaking philosophy through design work. Within this, it was envisaged that design might function as the outcome or end of such a process – i.e. an artefact or artefacts, plan or system proposal might be the result of the philosophic process. The point was also made that whether something is designed or not, the process and outcome would be seen to act as a form of argument, which would stand as a philosophic contribution.

To progress the discussion, a particular philosophic entry point was identified in classical pragmatism or, specifically, the work of John Dewey and Jane Addams and the feminist pragmatists more generally. Here, we referenced Dewey's reconstruction proposals and Addams's programme of social transformation in late nineteenth- and early twentieth-century Chicago, which together point to the idea that philosophy might be reconceived a means of social and moral problem solving. Next to this, we also considered Dewey's denotative method, which held that philosophic questions would be directly addressed in active, real-world inquiry. Inquiry in this regard would still be a matter of reflection, of working through in thought, problems and possibilities but also involve an active experiment. From Addams and feminist pragmatists, this was given form with reference to their absolute commitment to social transformation; we saw how they literally *placed* themselves *in* the social context, inquiring and reflecting.

From this point on, we turned to consider the thematic horizons mapped by the areas of focus. As we progressed through these chapters, a number of potential philosophy through design positions and strategies were gradually identified. In the context of technology, these were framed in relation to the way in which the design of technology can be seen to enable reflection on what it means or could mean to be human. In relation to the social, it was noted that, following a general Dewey–Addams approach, the designer(s) would work with a group, a community, a network of stakeholders to jointly frame problems, questions and potential strategies. Within this, design would support a registering of the situation, as well as a means of mapping out a specific response. Finally, in relation to the ecological, focus was directed towards the need to develop a stronger disciplinary understanding of what an adequate response to the crises of climate emergency and biodiversity loss might look like. In working towards this, a society-wide programme of deliberative debate was proposed. The aim would be to cultivate a comprehensive understanding of the challenges faced, but also a working through of possible solutions in an open-ended manner, to design in and through seeking to understand. Questions of meaning and value could be dealt with as they emerge. Philosophy would weave in and around discussions, supporting ontological and ethical framings. The aim would be to engender ecological ways of seeing, such that a future for all life, human and non-human, might be secured.

Having set out our trajectory, we may now consider where we have arrived at, looking first to how a philosophy through design might function in general.

PHILOSOPHY THROUGH DESIGN: THE PROCESS AND ITS OUTCOMES

Philosophy, whether technical or not, relies on arguments. Such arguments do not appear fully realized but, rather, are gradually shaped over time. A final argument will have a form, loosely based around a beginning, middle and end. Arguments flow into one another and productively overlap. A philosopher registers the arguments of others and then sets out to develop their own in response. Each talk, paper, article and book is ultimately supposed to set out an argument, a set of claims which are justified. Discourse emerges through the layered, back-and-forth exchange that results in and across positions where contributors agree or disagree, extend or refute what has been said.

While design is not often conceived of in terms of argument, it has been claimed that design and, indeed, designs in and of themselves can be understood in this way. Such a view has long been the proposal of Richard Buchanan. Over the last forty years, he worked to highlight how the contributions of philosopher Richard McKeon, who, as we have seen, was a former student of Dewey's, might afford special insights for our understanding of design. Here, focus is directed towards what is referred to as McKeon's 'new rhetoric', which, taking a historical view, examines how the structure and structuring of argument can be seen to hinge on the principles of creativity and invention, fact and judgement, sequence and consequence, objectivity and intersubjectivity. If framed in this way, McKeon proposes that arguments can enable discovery.

Drawing on this material, Buchanan positions design as a form of argumentation aimed at persuasion, a way of bringing things together via technological reasoning, emotional appeal and expressive character.[1] In this positioning, it becomes the portal by which we make collective decisions, whether consciously or unconsciously, as to how to live our lives.[2] Such a positioning is not too dissimilar to a philosophy through design but, as we shall see, there is an important difference. To unpick this, we must first return to our methodological template in design research involving practice.

As has been noted repeatedly, in design research involving practice, projects design can be positioned as an outcome or end. This may take the form of a made artefact or artefacts, plans or system proposals. We saw this in the case of Lindström and

---

[1] Richard Buchanan, 'Declaration by design: Rhetoric, argument, and demonstration in design practice' *Design Issues* (1985), 4–22.

[2] There are alignments to be drawn here – to my knowledge, as yet unarticulated – with the idea of ontological design, which sees scholars argue that design is central in the shaping of our reality, e.g. to Willis, 'Ontological designing.'

Ståhl's Un/Making project where a series of speculative design artefacts was produced as a means of giving form to ideas relating to the un/making of the plastic straw.

As happened in Un/Making, artefactual outcomes will generally be accompanied by a text in order to contextualize what is referred to as an 'argument'.[3] The two can be read/viewed side by side with one interacting with the other. How this dialogue is framed is, of course, an important consideration. Recently, the concept of what is referred to as an 'annotated portfolio'[4] has gained traction within the field. Ultimately, one is here expected to curate one's project, presenting any made artefacts but also giving these context.

It is also worth noting that Un/Making was part of a museum exhibition. This opened it up to a visiting public, where its speculative explorations might be viewed and considered. It was also possible to involve the public within this process. In this, they had the opportunity to contribute to the shaping of any final argument. As I will note below, this is an opportunity to reprise public philosophy by not reconstituting what was but shaping something new, a way of communicating and co-creating visions of meaning and value that reflects/responds to the needs of the present/future.

It will be helpful here to recall the denotative method. This, in the end, is a useful way of thinking through the potential role of design in a philosophy through design along the lines of the design research involving practice model. As outlined in Chapter 1, Dewey here suggested that philosophy apply itself directly to broad plane of experience and, within this, things in the broadest sense of the word: facts, dreams, events, acts, desires, fancies

---

[3] This artefact–text–argument relationship was a point of contention in the early days of practice-based creative research, with the question of whether or not an accompanying text was necessary triggering significant debate. See Michael Biggs, 'The role of the artefact in art and design research.' *International Journal of Design Sciences and Technology*, 10 no. 2 (2002); 19–24.

[4] Bill Gaver and John Bowers, 'Annotated portfolios.' *Interactions* 19, no. 4 (2012): 40–9.

or meanings, to follow his suggestions. These *things* are pointed at, marked out as the beginning of inquiry and thereafter the material by which inquiry proceeds. Any conclusion must be tested in experience and, again, the result is to be pointed at. This is not about truth, about ensuring a faithful representation of reality as it were. Rather, denotation, as Dewey had it, comes first and last.[5] The value of this approach to is allow the argument to be retraced and followed back to source so others can observe the logic and see the outcome for themselves.

The denotative method can be seen to capture the essence of the above research involving practice model in a number of ways, as well as link back to the opening design-as-argument idea. There is a starting point or inspirational source in the world; we work through ideas and then test these, again, in the world. If we draw design into this process, things will be made. This is potentially a difference which is not evident in Dewey's denotative outline as covered in Chapter 1. We do not step back once inquiry begins. Rather we lean in. We speculate, propose, imagine, reimagine, make, remake. This will potentially lead to further material to point to. Equally, if we are called upon to retrace an argument, such a process can be supported by design itself, whether directly in the case of artefacts or, alternatively, through a contextualization of these in such formats as an annotated portfolio or exhibition. The world will be remade philosophically (as in there will be a meaning or value-based argument attached). Here we could potentially encounter – that is, see, feel, respond, make, and situationally experience and reexperience – the argument, as per Buchanan's framing and, in doing so, change what is (i.e. design something that was not there before).

A difference to be noted in the above, which diverges from Buchanan, is that, as hinted, the argument is no longer an implicit background element but instead would come to the fore as an outcome in and of itself – a product as opposed to a *by*-product.

It should also be noted that the arguments presented would not necessarily be aimed at persuading in relation to how we are

---

[5] Dewey, *Experience and Nature*, 372.

to live our lives in specific aspects (as per Buchanan) – at least not exclusively so. Alongside persuasion in relation to a specific possibility (e.g. the viability of a particular approach to sustainability) there is also the potential to prompt questions in relation to wider meaning and value, what matters and what doesn't, what is good or bad, better or worse. These questions might be technological or social in focus, ecological or other, but their ultimate positioning is to be understood as philosophical.

Here we link back to Dewey's *Experience and Nature* proposals (see Chapter 1), specifically his positioning of philosophy as the cultivation of wisdom. This is a form of wisdom which – interweaving with the pointings of the denotative method or, in our case, philosophy through design – is guided by interdisciplinary evidence brought together in concert, looking at what is known and what this means through *criticism*. This, in turn, is seen to allow for a tracing of how and in what ways 'goods' could be created and sustained. Following Thomas Alexander, philosophy is thus positioned as a means of considering the quality of life-world relations (see Chapter 1). Our technological, social, ecological or any other questions are pursued and thus become philosophical on this basis.

As an important side point, while philosophy through design could not, in and of itself, bring the full range of evidence from all disciplines together in criticism, it could contribute to such a process. Its project-based inquiries might draw on specific disciplinary knowledge bases and allow questions to be asked (as we have seen in some of the examples in the prior chapters, such as Un/Making) and thereafter meaning and value to be traced such that the creation and sustainment of goods could be better understood and appreciated.

In offering the above, it is acknowledged that there is work to do in order that the above outline can be realized concretely in practice in experience. Linking the concepts of arguments, design research involving practice, the denotative method and philosophy-as-wisdom only gets us so far. What might this look like in practice?

To aid the above process of concrete realization, the following staged protocol for how philosophy through design projects might proceed is offered. This follows a start, middle and end sequencing.

It is intended to frame a possible structure but is not seen as an absolutist model for how one might proceed.

The Start

Following Dewey's outline of the denotative method, it is envisaged that philosophy through design would commence with a concern or point of intrigue arising in experience. This where the actual pointing occurs. Here, the germ of a question would likely emerge in something specific that is troubling or compelling, perhaps an observation or moment of insight that was unexpected, that encourages (and potentially demands) further investigation. This could relate to something directly observed – for example, noting the value of a particular social experience (e.g. how local communities come together in celebration). Or alternatively it might be something conceptually bound but which nonetheless references the real world. By way of example here, it might be about the meaning of a particular technology in our lives (e.g. a type of generative AI) or the possibility of framing of a particular set of ecological relationships and how these might be sustained (e.g. how we build a design philosophy that requires that one draws immediate contextual connections as a matter of course).

There would be two envisaged starting points thereafter. In the first, one might be motivated to undertake such a project in and of itself. The troubling or intriguing situation would come about and one would be driven by a desire to explore this from a philosophy through design approach. In such a scenario it is likely that a view would be taken that design might open up a given issue in a way that reflection or abstract argumentation alone could not. This might relate to the possibilities of given ways of acting or being – for example, what is the meaning of technologically enabled cooperative action? Or can we enhance our relationship with specific ecological systems?

A second starting point for philosophy through design might emerge from within an ongoing design research project or, indeed, a standard design project. In such cases, it is likely that something especially significant would emerge within the research or practice: a troubling insight, a sense of something that extends beyond a question of what design can do or enable.

A designer would have a choice of engaging with existing philosophy early on or with literature from other disciplines (e.g. psychology), or waiting until a later point. At the onset, this might support the framing of a question and an initial positioning of what is troublesome but, again, the situation and what it is should initially guide the process. It is also important to note that to do so in a structured way would of course require training or, at very least, some familiarity with certain literatures. Recommendations for how a philosophy through design might be taught follow in the next section.

The Middle

Following on from the noting of a concern arising in experience and the framing of a question, the process of engaging in the actual project would begin. This would take place in a context or set of contexts that relate to, or at least mirror, those that gave rise to the original question. One would be designing or potentially researching through design and reflecting. The question would act as an orientating reference point within this. One's efforts would be guided by a search for an answer. Designing would be positioned as a process of experimentation. One would be trialling the situational conditions of a response.

There are seen to be two potential routes by which this might advance. In the first instance one might focus on present issues, things that are concerning or intriguing in the here and now, and then move to work through them in the here and now. Here, we might imagine a project in which designers work with a given community who are experiencing particular social problems, whether relating to a crisis in loneliness or a lack of economic opportunities in a post-industrial context. The aim, in such a scenario, would to be work directly with the community and to reflect on the *meanings* and *values* that have led to the present situation, defining where the community would like to get to and, through participative experimentation, exploring ways in which this could be achieved and what the meanings and value of realizing this might be. This would not be a matter of instrumentally 'solving' a problem but rather beginning to work through a problem's definition and mapping a path to resolution. One would seek to demonstrate or test a possible response in practice, seeing if it works. As with the above example, we might again be dealing with an ethical matter, asking whether or not particular outcomes are desirable or not.

As a second route, one might ask questions of possibilities, exploring concerns (that arise situationally) that point to or suggest something which is not yet the case but the potential for it to be is identified. By way of example, if the situational concern is technological, it might be a matter of exploring how particular forms of novel technology such as generative AI (noted at the opening of Chapter 2) could result in particular forms of personal and interpersonal experiences. Within this, one might examine what meanings and values were/could be possible. Could something be perceived in this way? Does this feeling or quality emerge in relation to this presentation or function? One might also examine whether the possibilities and their consequences were to be judged as positive or negative, taking register of the meanings and values that emerge within this. Such judgements might be ethical, as in a particular technological capability might be deemed desirable or not for particular groups, whether humans or non-humans. This points to the potential for the enfolding of a prospective or speculative approach, as highlighted in relation to design research involving practice. This might be positioned in a 'futures' context, where one imagines conditions that are not yet the case but could be within a temporal frame (i.e. a point in time) that extends beyond the present. As per this latter example, there would likely be a strong emphasis on co-creation. Working in groups, one could map, trace, identify, imagine, propose, experiment and test. The working through of the meaning and value of things would be collaborative. While there are not many examples of collaborative philosophy, there is the potential for this to be explored here, as will be discussed below.

The End

From the above, as a final stage one would be expected to present a clear, communicable argument. This argument would derive from the process of experimentation pursued as per the above examples. As such, it would be demonstrated or tested and verified in the 'coarseness and crudity' of ordinary experience.[6] Here it would be possible to speak of the particular possibilities regarding types of situational concerns, and the meanings and values that attach to these: whether particular meanings and values are possible and by what means, as well as whether or not these are deemed to be desirable or not, notionally right or wrong. It is not expected that any argument would be fully general, i.e. hold in all contexts. Rather it would offer situated, contextual perspectives – possibly relating to the technological, the social or the ecological, but possibly not (e.g. one might hold economic, political, aesthetic, spiritual concerns). It might provide insights for others considering specific meanings and values, or the desirability or non-desirability of these meanings and values. It might not. The point would be that the insights are shared and sharable.

This brings us to the question of just how this argument would be presented. This is important if we are required to be able to trace our way back to the original pointing, that is to the things that were originally noticed and identified – whether facts, dreams, events, acts, desires, fancies,

---

[6] Dewey, *Experience and Nature*, 39.

meanings or something else. This will ultimately require a text. As we have highlighted above, this might also involve artefacts or alternative contextualization in formats such as an annotated portfolio or exhibition. Whatever form is taken, it is here proposed that the key criteria of quality of the argument would be: communicability (i.e. it can be understood); retraceability (i.e. one can understand as well as reconstruct the process and logic underpinning the project); and finally, from this that it is also transferable (i.e. others could reference the material if they sought to pursue a similar process in a similar situation).

Following the example offered by Addams, it is important to note that the development of a philosophical argument could be a long-term process, something that takes place over an extended period of time. There might be several iterations, several positions, generally building, generally progressing as more evidence emerges, more insights are garnered.

We may here also briefly turn back to the discussion of audiences for philosophy through design and the potential opportunity to reprise the role of the public philosophy noted above. Philosophy through design would likely function best as an avowedly public philosophy, whereby the core audience is not philosophers as such (though they may well be interested in the outcomes) but rather publics, groups that are interested in the issues at hand.

In this, efforts could be made to be more experiential than past philosophers; to engage in a creative conversation with an audience and jointly examine what it is that is being said. Here, over time, there could be a further adaption of an argument, a further untangling of meaning and value, what matters and what is right, discussion by discussion, exhibition by exhibition, workshop by workshop. This would allow for the public to very explicitly play a role in the shaping of what is finally said.

It is important to note that, in the end, there may not be one generic approach to philosophy through design. In fact, it is unlikely this will be the case. As our consideration of the areas of focus (thematic horizons) have indicated, different things matter in different cases and different responses are required. This is the promise and potential of a philosophy through design. It too can be designed.

Before moving on, it will be useful to set out a number of qualifiers regarding the similarities and distinctions that can be drawn between the above outline of philosophy through design and design research involving practice. These are aligned to the points made in relation to the characteristics of design research involving practice set out in the Introduction.

Similarities

- In terms of similarities, as per Point 1 in the Introduction, it is expected there will be a motivational context relating either to something observed in the real world or, alternatively, a conceptual concern that references the real world.
- As per Point 2, both will hold focus on experimentation; that is, trying things out in experience to explore whether or not the particular possibilities can be realized *in* experience.
- As per Point 3, there could be a collaborative process, whereby partners are involved in the creative activities through co-design or participatory design or, simply, the application of co-creative techniques.
- As per Point 4, there is a similar opportunity to be prospective and speculative in one's work, i.e. one can investigate future possibilities.
- As per Point 5, the possibility of artefactual and other design-based outcomes would still hold. As before, the need to ensure textual explication will remain.
- As per Point 6, one would aim to offer transferable as opposed to generalizable conclusions (i.e. philosophic propositions that would notionally hold regardless of context).
- As per Point 7, communicability, retraceability and transferability – highlighted as possible evaluation

criteria for design research involving practice in the Introduction – remain.
- As per Point 8, the possibility of ontological transformation, of changing what is/was via the process – in this case, a philosophical as opposed to a research-orientated process – remains.

Distinctions

- In relation to what is distinct, first and most importantly, as has already been stated, philosophy through design would not be concerned with knowledge production. It would not be seeking to extend disciplinary understanding in areas such as particular design approaches or how specific outcomes might be achieved. Concern, as noted, would be directed to understanding meanings and values in the here and now or, possibly in future temporalities, how these can/could be attained and sustained and how desirable or not specific meanings and values might be.
- There would not be a focus on conventional data collection as exemplified by social or natural sciences. This is not to debar data collection. There might be 'data' in philosophy through design, for example in the form of notes, recordings or annotated observations. However, this would not be a requirement. The key steps would be designing, reflecting and, potentially, referencing interdisciplinary knowledge as well as other philosophically bound theoretical resources, ways of seeing or insights, as one sets about developing an argument regarding meaning and/or value. Any data, whether notes, recordings, observations and so on, would be drawn upon to support these steps. The steps, however, would remain integral and primary.
- Unlike design research involving practice, which must deliver conclusions within a constrained timeline of a given project or set of projects (i.e. have a prescribed beginning, middle and end in which data collection and

analysis takes place), there is the potential for philosophy through design to take place over an extended time period. Here, insights might be garnered over the longer term, gradually substantiating into a philosophical position. One might work across a number of projects and situations and, through all, work to develop an argument.
- The audiences for such work would no longer, in the main, be particular knowledge communities, whether in design or beyond (though these parties may still be interested in the work), but would now also involve philosophers as well as members of the public.
- The above qualifiers do not preclude the possibility of a philosophy through design approach emerging in a research or practice context. As suggested above, such work could layer in but at the same time stand apart, with the outcomes that emerge being positioned beyond this latter activity and its outcomes.

Having offered the above outline of a philosophy through design process, it is also possible to note a number of areas for further exploration in the context of potential design–philosophy methodological connections.

AREAS FOR FURTHER METHODOLOGICAL CONSIDERATION

As we progressed through the text, there were a number of areas that were noted as pointing to the potential for further methodological consideration. We will now briefly review the potential of these.

Design–Philosophy Methodological Connection 1: Thought Experiments

As noted in Chapter 3 in our exploration of the work of Eindhoven and the Everyday Design Studio at Simon Fraser, philosophical thought experiments have not received much attention in design, though this has recently been picked up on from an ethical perspective.[7] Arguably, as highlighted in the Introduction, thought experiments share much in common with the now established areas of critical and speculative design, as well as design fiction, at least in terms of their basic structuring. One frames scenarios and, in this, tests what the outcome of specific events and actions might be. The point in both cases is to ask 'what if' and from there see what can be explored imaginatively, looking, in particular, to identify likely consequences of particular actions. However, the two – thought experiments and critical design, speculative design and design fiction – often diverge in relation to subject matter and most times in relation to outcomes.[8] In critical, speculative design and design fiction, scenarios tend to be broad-ranging – for example, examining how we might live in the future, as in Eindhoven's Dutch Ministry of Infrastructure and Water Management 2050 project. The outcomes are often presented through rich imagery, whether illustrated or photographic. There will likely also be prototypes of possible design artefacts.

With regard to our present discussion, thought experiments are important because, within this work, we can identify a dedicated line of experiments focusing on the area of ethics.[9] The most famous of these experiments is what is referred to as the 'trolley experiment', where individuals are asked to consider how they might react in a situation where a runaway tramcar is likely to cause the death of one or another group of individuals. Though such thought experiments are often criticized on the basis that they are abstract and lack meaningful context, it is possible to envisage their use in the context of design whereby they might be applied as a means of scoping out the possible consequences of pursuing a particular course of action, exploring the good and

---

[7] An ethical exploration of design experiments is available in Buwert and Sinclair, 'Thought Experiments In The Ethics of Designing for Future People.'

[8] Fry's *Writing Design Fiction* could be seen as conforming with thought experiments, at least in so far as it is text-based. See Fry, *Writing Design Fiction*.

[9] We see this in Buwert and Sinclair's proposals.

the bad, the better and worse of the potential outcomes. In this, through further work, they could be positioned as a method for underpinning a speculative philosophy through design process.

Design–Philosophy Methodological Collaborative Philosophy 2: Collaborative Philosophizing

Within an emergent philosophy through design there is an important opportunity to explore how concerns and insights could be jointly framed and *philosophic* practice might be undertaken as a group exercise. Intriguingly, it would appear little attention has been being directed to the possibility of establishing collaborative philosophy – that is, a philosophy that seeks to draw together multiple perspectives jointly in the process of framing a position as a core aspect of the method. On the face of it, this is perhaps unsurprising. After all, Western philosophy has predominantly centred around the individual (mostly white male) contributions and, within this, honouring conceptual provenience, i.e. noting where concepts and proposals have emerged and lining up one's own insights next to these established trajectories. This has resulted in a situation where there are philosophies of collaboration but not collaborative philosophies. Here, even the idea that philosophy could be interdisciplinary has been met with resistance.[10]

Be this as it may, when we give thought to the possibility of a collaborative philosophy, its absence as an explicit method becomes perplexing. Coming together to discuss and debate is a core disciplinary practice, allowing for the testing and refinement of arguments, the progression of theory and the framing of wider agendas. Equally, as with any other disciplines, co-authorship is widely practised from journal articles to books. Philosophy, then, can be characterized as collaborative (at least to a degree), even if it is not represented and articulated as such at present.

---

[10] Andrew Higgins and Alexis Dyschkant, 'Interdisciplinary collaboration in philosophy.' *Metaphilosophy* 45, no. 3 (2014): 372–98.

A philosophy through design that sought to trace social concerns would do well to draw this aspect to the fore, especially in the absence of a specific collaborative method within philosophy proper (beyond discussion and debate). In doing so, reference might be drawn from design's pre-existing interdisciplinarity. It is possible that such an approach might allow for a productive blending of the two disciplinary perspectives, supporting a coming together of ideas and arguments via a creative process. What form this takes is, of course, something that requires definition through experimentation, a designing in and of itself.

Design–Philosophy Methodological Connection 3: Futures Work

Distinct from the design futuring of Fry[11] set out in the last chapter, we can also look to futures work in design as a potential area of methodological connection between design and philosophy that might merit further attention. In many ways, like thought experiments, futures work can be seen to relate to the areas of critical design, speculative design and design fiction in so far as alternatives are envisaged and the potential of as yet unrealized possibilities explored.[12] Nonetheless, unlike critical and speculative design, futures work, by necessity, insists on a beyond the present endpoint for the design process.

Futures work is perhaps best understood as an emergent area of design practice that lacks a pre-specified methodology.[13]

---

[11] Fry, *Design Futuring*.

[12] Here a current problematic was examined with a view to developing alternatives that trace other possibilities. This, in turn, links to the area of critical design, developed by Antony Dunne and Fiona Raby and discussed in Chapter 1. Futures work, on the other hand, seeks to explore what could be at a point in time that extends beyond the present, assuming that particular conditions were met.

[13] Recent texts tend towards offering a spectrum of perspectives as opposed to a definitive account. See for example Rachel Charlotte Smith, Kasper Tang Vangkilde, and Mette Gislev Kjaersgaard, *Design Anthropological Futures* (Abingdon, Oxon: Routledge, 2020).

In relation to our present concern, it must be underscored that this is an approach that originates in design as opposed to philosophy. Arguably, however, it carries a philosophical aspect. Here, working within this space in the context of both social and policy design, design researcher Lucy Kimbell has, in recent years, honed in on the idea of an 'anticipatory logic'.[14] Drawing a contrast between conventional approaches to innovation and deliberation, she maps anticipatory logic to design practice. There is no specific sequence to follow. Through speculative practices such as creating objects or proposals, the strategy is to act as a 'visionary' outside of 'norms/frames' with attention being directed to 'reimagining' and 'exceeding'.[15] It is a logic that looks towards 'what could be', rather than a matter of developing new solutions for society (innovation) or understanding what matters to people (deliberation).

To present this as logic as opposed to simply a practice or set of practices is in line with a Deweyan pragmatist perspective, i.e. whereby logic is seen to function as a theorization of successful action (see Chapter 1).[16] Following this understanding, a futures approach within the context of a philosophy through design would aim to consolidate a pattern or patterns for successful speculative work, noting how specific ways of looking ahead might have yielded useful foresight and allowed particular things to happen. Indeed, approached in this way, a more general anticipatory logic could form a bridge between philosophy and philosophy through design. In simple terms, there is opportunity to open up a dialogue between conventional logic, scoping the affordances of this alternative pragmatic framing.[17]

---

[14] See e.g. Lucy Kimbell 'Logics of social design.' Paper presented at *Design as Common Good*, Online, March 25–16, 2021.

[15] Ibid, 5–6.

[16] John Dewey, *The Later Works, 1925–1953, Volume 12 1938, Logic: The Theory of Inquiry*.

[17] I have already explored the relationship between Deweyan logic and general design research involving practice methodologies, noting how seeing logic in this way allows for a strengthening of epistemological position. See Dixon and French, 'Processing the method'.

Having traced out the above, we will now move to consider how, from the emergence of a philosophy through design, we might well see the emergence of a designer who is, at least in certain aspects, also a philosopher.

THE DESIGNER PHILOSOPHER: THE PRACTITIONER WHO COULD BE

Up until this point, we have explored the potential of the *practice* of philosophy through design. However, apart from the prototypic exemplars of Dewey and Addams, there has not been much discussion of *who* might do this work, of who will be or become the 'designer philosopher' mentioned earlier.

Perhaps it is best to consider a point of origin. How might these individuals emerge?

Through a regular referencing of design research involving practice, it has been implied that, as a first stage possibility, designer philosophers would likely also be designer researchers. As has arguably been demonstrated within the cases set out through the chapters, the line between researching, theorizing and philosophizing is vague at times. It may be that designer researchers, such as those profiled, could cultivate an ability to see the philosophy that is often already implicit in their work and come to declare it as such. In such a scenario it is possible that the title may begin to appeal. In its oddness, it could capture the coming together of two previously distinct modalities and, in that, allow for a new understanding to emerge. In this scenario, the title might allow an individual to better represent their position to others, in design and beyond, in philosophy and beyond.

Another potential route is through education. As a longer-term possibility, it is foreseeable that designer philosophers could be instructed in philosophy through design at postgraduate or even undergraduate level. While this could take many forms and would no doubt require much testing and iteration, two possible models are seen as viable here. The first would follow an interdisciplinary agenda, with philosophy and design being brought together in a curriculum that would aim, as far as would be possible, to integrate both. This could scale in various ways. At a large scale – in, say, a master's programme – a series of modules might each instruct in specific areas progressively across a twelve-month (or longer) cycle. By way of example, within a first semester there might be an introductory module relating design theory to existing strands within philosophy. Sitting alongside this, a practical, studio-based module could allow students to explore how philosophy can progressively take form in the context of a design project, guiding them through the process as they design. Successive semesters would follow the same pattern, building on the initial theoretical and practical integrations until a final 'capstone' philosophy through design project would be delivered at the programme's end. At a smaller scale, at the level of micro-credentials, a single standalone module might aim to cover the principles of the philosophy through design process through a combination of theoretical and practical instruction. The content might initially focus on offering an insight the into key theoretical resources that underpin these and require that students seek to apply this to a project of their own. As a second model, philosophy and design might be brought together but initially remain distinct. Here, assuming a high degree of design literacy among a notional cohort, there could be initial intensive modular instruction in specific, relevant philosophical principles, methods and approaches (e.g. in modes of argumentation or particular areas of ethics). Following on, students would then gradually apply their learning in a series of practice modules, which allows them to personally integrate both disciplines. The benefit here would be that the integration – the coming into being of a philosophy through design – becomes a learning task for the cohort.

Leaving aside questions of emergence and learning, there remains a question of purpose. We have already outlined what such individuals might 'do' as practitioners in the last section's protocol. In following this in their work, a designer philosopher would be an individual who designs with view to attending directly to questions of responsibility and/or concern – whether technological, social, ecological or other – through a designing. Within their process, they would work through problems and opportunities, as any designer does, following a specific disciplinary approach or not. In this, they would, as a given, need to demonstrate a level of design proficiency, a certain expertise. The challenge would be to ensure that at the same time they are also working to consciously pick through the wider issues at stake, following the threads of meaning and value from start to end as required. This is because, in applying the denotative method outlined above, designing would here be understood as a process of practical reasoning and, ultimately, as above, *argumentation*. Their central concern then would be not losing sight of the argument and the need to engage in argumentation while design*ing*.

In this, they might well work alone. As discussed, philosophy generally progresses through the presentation of individual arguments, which are responded to by other individuals, over time. However, given the collaborative agenda of design and the need for an interdisciplinary perspective in the forms of activity traced out through this book, it is equally possible that a designer philosopher would be collaborative and interdisciplinary, working within teams to provide a perspective that would not otherwise be available. In such a scenario, philosophy through design would not sit as a standalone method or practice, but rather as a practice within a wider community of practice.

Before drawing to a close, it will be useful to offer a final sketch for how non-Western perspectives extending beyond those presented in this text might be better mobilized in the practice of philosophy through design.

MORE FUTURE WORK: A FIRST STEP IN EXPLORING PHILOSOPHICAL PLURALISM FROM PRAGMATISM

It is (and has been) acknowledged that the vision of philosophy through design set out here aligns predominately to a Euro-American, Global North perspective. Crucially, the link between philosophy and design was drawn, in the initial phase at least, by the twentieth-century American figures of Dewey and Addams. We are dealing with a particular way of seeing the world here. Both were of European descent. Both, in their own way, held privileged positions within the historical era they lived through.

Be this as it may, there are important counter points to offer here at the end. First, as was noted at the opening, this does involve a feminist perspective via Addams and her feminist pragmatist colleagues. Through the text I have sought to demonstrate how this is not only a matter of referencing feminism but also contributes to the repositioning of Dewey's work in design.[18] Here, by drawing Dewey into greater proximity with Addams, his work is recontextualized and, accordingly, rebalanced. For example, we can greater understand how his democratic vision is grounded in Addams's concept of democracy as a way of life and, in turn, see how this is grounded in notions of embodiment and care (see Chapter 3). Equally, his notion of experimentation in philosophy – a practice Addams and feminist pragmatists directly modelled – is given a context it would otherwise lack.

Beyond feminism, in relation to the social thematic and ecological horizons in design, there was also consideration of the emergence of decolonizing design movement, Tony Fry's futuring work and pluriversal design. In each, we see a looking beyond modernist convention and the entrenched power structures of the Global North. In this, there is an exploration of the potential to reposition design's disciplinary orientation and practices, all of which could inform a philosophy through design in direct terms. For example, designer philosophers might seek to centre indigenous knowledge working through the contextual meaning of particular ways of seeing.

In addition to the above, there is the further, crucially important point that pragmatism embraces diversity, difference and alternative perspectives. It is, as will now be clear, democratic in spirit. Accordingly, if one is of the Global North (e.g. European) and seeking to properly move beyond such perspectives, one is permitted to do so while still maintaining an authentic cultural starting point. This would be a matter of inquiry, of taking up a problem and aiming for resolution.

Such work should, however, always, by necessity, be contextual – i.e. be related to the concerns or points of intrigue of the situation

---

[18] Danielle Lake and Carl DiSalvo can be seen as key figures who are already driving this work.

at hand. We will pick up on this point below. For now, it is important to note that opening up to the possibilities of perspectives beyond one's own requires care and sensitivity. Some perspectives will be meaningful and allow for integration and others will not. The world is, nonetheless, philosophically rich beyond measure. The regions of Asia, Africa, the Middle East, Latin America, not to mention some areas of Europe, each offer manifold ways of seeing that have not yet been properly explored nor are understood by Euro-American scholars. Confucianism, Taoism, Hinduism and Ubuntu are but some of these. Beyond such possibilities, when it comes to pragmatism in general – i.e. the philosophy as a perspective in its own right – there is another ready alignment to be drawn beyond the Global North. Specifically, pragmatist insights have been shown to connect to insights found in strands of Buddhism.[19]

This is, at present, an emergent discourse within comparative philosophy and one which, as yet, has not reached a set of definite conclusive positions. In so far as conclusions exist, literature tends to highlight aspects of the work of figures such as William James, Charles Sanders Peirce, alongside Dewey,[20] as well as,

---

[19] This positions Buddhism as a philosophy and such a view is somewhat controversial, in that it is predominantly defined as a religion. However as a religion it can also be approached as a value system, which, in turn, can be understood as a philosophic framework. See David J. Kalupahana, *A History of Buddhist Philosophy: Continuities and Discontinuities* (Honolulu, HI: University of Hawaii Press. 1992).

[20] There are also alignments which draw reference to others beyond pragmatism. For example, the Anglo-American philosopher Alfred North Whitehead's work in process philosophy has been identified as a potential bridge between Western and Eastern perspectives. It is important to note that Whitehead was not a classical pragmatist. Nonetheless, he did respect their work and drew reference from it. As such, it is possible to draw alignments on certain points. See, for example, William T. Myers, 'Is Whitehead a Pragmatist? On the Pragmatic Elements in Whitehead's Metaphysics.' In *Thinking with Whitehead and the American Pragmatists: Experience and Reality*, edited by Brian G Henning, William T Myers and Joseph D. John (London: Lexington Books, 2015): 3–24. In terms of Whitehead–Buddhist connections see e.g. Ryusei Takeda, 'Mahayana Buddhism and Whitehead's Philosophy.' *Process Studies* 23, no. 2 (1994): 72–86.

more recently, Addams and, in this, note the similarities such as they are. For example, James's ideas of self have been related to perspectives found in Buddhism.[21]

Limited though such work is, it is beyond the scope of the present text to systematically summarize existing claims. Nonetheless, with a view to supporting efforts to progress a philosophy through design, we can trace some initial key points of connection here, all of which link to one another.

The first relates to understandings of reality. In one early presentation on pragmatism–Buddhism relations, Nolan Jacobson[22] argued that pragmatism and Buddhism sit within a discrete grouping of philosophies that can be understood to share a special, complementary understanding of how reality and our place within it is best apprehended. Here, rather than focus on what is fixed and solid,[23] as is the case in classical philosophy, both pragmatism, Buddhism and a specific strand of Greek philosophy coming from Heraclitus[24] can be seen to direct their focus instead towards *process*, that is, to what *happens*. On this account, reality, as a broad-based framing of all-encompassing existence, is seen to be dynamic and always-changing. Things are not to be understood as things in and of themselves but, rather, as temporal becomings. The world is thus a place of events as opposed to things. There are actions and interactions. Relationships form, fall away and

---

[21] Dinesh Chandra Mathur, 'The historical Buddha (Gotama), Hume, and James on the self: Comparisons and evaluations.' *Philosophy East and West* 28, no. 3 (1978): 253–69.

[22] Nolan Pliny Jacobson, *The Heart of Buddhist Philosophy* (Carbondale, IL: Southern Illinois University Press, 1988).

[23] The technical term applied here is 'substance'. An early history of the concept of substance is found in Henrik Lagerlund, 'Material Substance'. In *The Oxford Handbook of Medieval Philosophy*, edited by John Marenbon (Oxford: Oxford University Press, 2012), 468–85.

[24] Heraclitus was a Greek philosopher in the sixth century bce. Almost nothing of his work remains save for fragments. Nonetheless, what has survived suggests a highly original perspective that foregrounds transformation and change. This diverges markedly from the fixed concepts of being found contemporaneously across the Greek world. See Charles H. Kahn, *The Art and Thought of Heraclitus: An edition of fragments with translation and commentary* (Cambridge: Cambridge University Press, 1979).

end, on and on in overlap.²⁵ If accepted, this presents a transformative view of what is, with potential implications for how we apprehend the idea of designing itself, as well as its impacts and outcomes. For example, if we were to view design as a process of temporal becoming rather than the realization of fixed and final objects and systems, we would be required to look ahead and aim to 'see' the likely impacts of our decisions, of where they might lead and what the consequences might be, whether positive or negative.

Linked to this view of reality, the next point relates to *experience*. Here, we can note the shared commitment in both pragmatism and Buddhism to honouring *direct* experience for what it is, in the way illustrated through the discussion of the denotative method set out in Chapter 1. Here, experience was not only positioned in passive terms but also considered actively, looking at the role of the person within the wider environment, as well as the intricacies of the social and cultural realities that people reference and relate to. We *do* experience as well as perceive, act alongside thinking. Experience, from this perspective, is varied and multifold,²⁶ and knowing is just one form of experienc*ing*.²⁷ This aligns with Buddhism's general commitment to qualitative immediacy over abstraction, whether conceptual or textual.²⁸ We are called upon

---

²⁵ For an introduction see Nicholas Rescher, *Process Metaphysics: An Introduction to Process Philosophy* (Albany, NJ: State University of New York Press, 1996).

²⁶ While it has not been the focus of the present text, Dewey's treatment of experience and situational value has been discussed in *Dewey and Design* (see Chapters 2 and 7). McCarthy and Wright also link their vision of experience-centred design to the experiential commitments within Dewey's writing, see John McCarthy and Peter Wright, *Technology as Experience* (Cambridge, MA: The MIT Press, 2004).

²⁷ John Dewey, The Middle Works, 1899–1924, Volume 3: 1907–1909, Essays on Pragmatism and Truth, edited by Jo Ann Boydston (Carbondale, IL: Southern Illinois University Press. 1976).

²⁸ Mario Poceski draws a link here between Mahāyāna Buddhism and William James's idea that the usefulness of an idea or concept underpins its ultimate value. Mario Poceski, 'Philosophical Reflections, Identity formations, Buddhist Responses to Religious Diversity'. In *Buddhism in Dialogue with Contemporary Societies*, edited by Carola Roloff, Michael Zimmermann, Wolfram Weiße (München, Bayern: Waxmann, 2020), 95.

to attend consciously to what is, as it is, there and then, not name it or seek to contain it conceptually in explanation.[29] The point is to honour this 'what is, as it is' on its own terms by attending to its situational integrity with awareness and openness. In a design context, it has been argued that this honouring-integrity-with-awareness could lead to greater attunement to situational needs and how one makes decisions in relation to these.[30]

Leading on from the above, the final point relates to ideas of truth. Recent comparative work here has noted the relatability of pragmatist notions of truth and belief with those of Buddhism.[31] We have already seen how the pragmatist approach to inquiry eschews ideas of fixed and final truths in favour of ideas of evidence and persuasion. Similarly, Buddhism – with its appreciation that knowing and understanding arise in varied, multifold experience, where sensation, perception and cognition are at play – rejects the idea of singular truth.[32] For Buddhists, as for pragmatists, to assess the validity of ideas and concepts, we must test them in experience and assess the extent to which they stand. This aligns well with design, which requires practical demonstrations of value as a means of confirming the worth of specific proposals. We see this same underpinning in the denotative method, when Dewey insists that philosophical conclusions be returned to 'ordinary experience' to test and secure their value.

Beyond these broad links to Buddhism, it is also possible to note the personal, cultural links that existed for Dewey in relation to Asia. Through his 1919–21 trip to Japan and China, he can be seen to have maintained an openness to the perspectives he

---

[29] Christian Coseru, *Perceiving Reality: Consciousness, Intentionality and Cognition in Buddhist Philosophy* (Oxford: Oxford University Press, 2012).

[30] Meredith James, 'Advancing design thinking towards a better understanding of self and others: A theoretical framework on how Buddhism can offer alternate models for design thinking.' *Form Akademisk* 10, no. 2 (2017): 1–14.

[31] Shurendra Ghimire, 'Buddhist Pragmatism or Pragmatic Buddhism: What is the relationship between Buddhism and Pragmatism?' *BMC Journal of Scientific Research* 4, no. 1 (2021): 49–64.

[32] Ibid, 56.

encountered while travelling, describing his visit as akin to a 'a renewal of youth'.[33] The reconstruction proposals that underpin this general text were, as I have outlined, the outworkings of his China lectures (see Chapter 1). Further, I suggested that one can detect a change in register in the work that follows through the 1920s. This links in with 1925's *Experience and Nature*, which presents the denotative method.

It is also worth noting that Dewey had considerable influence in China extending beyond his 1919–21 visit. Here, we may note the many Chinese students who had attended Columbia University where he taught and sought to apply their learnings on their return to China. For example, his approach to teaching was explored in direct terms by Tao Zingzhi, who established various China-wide associations and movements aimed at educational reform.[34] Equally, his theory of inquiry and democratic vision was championed by another former student, Hu Shih,[35] a Chinese academic and diplomat who worked to draw connections between pragmatism and Chinese philosophy.[36]

Further, this Dewey–China influence has extended to the present-day context of design, where Asian design scholars have actively embraced his ideas. A key example here is Xin Xiangyang, a Carnegie Mellon graduate in China, who focuses on the idea of the 'experience economy',[37] and Miso Kim in

---

[33] Dykhuizen, *The Life and Mind of John Dewey*, 205

[34] Yusheng Yao, 'Rediscovering Tao Xingzhi as an educational and social revolutionary.' *Twentieth-Century China* 27, no. 2 (2002): 79–120.

[35] Sor-Hoon Tan, 'China's pragmatist experiment in democracy: Hu Shih's pragmatism and Dewey's influence in China.' *Metaphilosophy* 35: 1-2, (2004): 44–64.

[36] Kok Chung Hou, 'Hu Shi: A Chinese pragmatist and reformist', PhD diss. (London: University of London, School of Oriental and African Studies, 1998).

[37] Wa An, Xiangyang Xin, Xiong Ding and Yi Liu, 'Lifestyle as the Object of Design: Elements Exploration from Experience Perspective.' In *Design, User Experience, and Usability. Interaction Design: 9th International Conference, DUXU 2020*, Held as Part of the 22nd HCI International Conference, HCII 2020, Copenhagen, Denmark, July 19–24, 2020, Proceedings, Part I, edited by Aaron Marcus and Elizabeth Rosenzweig: 311–23. (Dordrecht: Springer International Publishing, 2020).

South Korea, who looks at the role of dignity in service design.[38]

Addams and her fellow feminist pragmatists have also been drawn into alignment with Buddhism, specifically with what has been referred to as 'engaged Buddhism'.[39] Engaged Buddhism denotes a repositioning of Buddhist thought such that it 'accommodates' ideas of 'radical social engagement', i.e. social practices that aim to transform situations for the better. This is seen to have been progressed by twentieth-century Buddhist writers such as Thich Nhat Hanh and Chan Khong, who are said to have 'reconstructed Buddhism to place primary emphasis on social action', leading to a 'religious philosophy of interdependence and engagement'.[40]

These threads are, of course, non-comprehensive. They offer only a glimpse of the possible connections one might surface in and beyond such perspectives as Buddhism.[41] Nevertheless, they also provide evidence of both alignment and relationship – a two-way exchange which is already there, ready to be explored. The overall point that can be drawn out here is that there is a line that leads beyond the Euro-American, Global North perspective from which we commenced; we can trace it and draw further lines ourselves should we wish.

---

[38] See e.g. Miso Kim, 'Designing for participation: Dignity and autonomy of service (Part 2).' *Design Issues* 34:3, (2018): 89–102.

[39] Judy Whipps, 'Philosophy and Social Activism: An Exploration of the Pragmatism and Activism of Jane Addams, John Dewey and Engaged Buddhism', PhD diss. (Cincinnati, OH: The Graduate School of Union Institute, 1998).

[40] Ibid, 13.

[41] On this latter aspect, Dewey scholar Thomas Alexander not only notes an alignment between Dewey's philosophy and the perspectives of Buddhism but also looks outwards to alignments that can be drawn with Native American traditions. The connection here again is based on the changeability of people and things. In drawing this link, Alexander envisions the potential for an 'eco-ontology' – that is, an environmentally grounded understanding of being linking meaning, value, culture and ecology together as one. This notion of eco-ontology relies on a coming together of personal meaning and value (what Alexander refers to as the 'human eros') and a broader cultural coalescing of meaning and value (referred to as 'spiritual ecologies'), Alexander, *The Human Eros*, 7.

However, it is also important to underscore again that such tracings cannot just be pursued for their own sake. Given its basis in experience, even if outward-facing, a philosophy through design will need to relate to the cultural contexts in which any questions have emerged. If one is moving beyond one's context, there must be a rationale, a need to seek an answer, which will relate back to context. Returning to the notion of situational concerns or points of intrigue, it may be that one wishes to open up discussions across cultures and ways of seeing to compare or extend a given frame of reference. It may be that we wish to question our own way of seeing. Ultimately, as per the denotative method, our starting point must reference things in our experience, that which can be pointed to. It is here we must begin and here we must end.

This rounds out our consideration of what a philosophy through design might become. We will now close by turning to briefly consider the possible wider implications of a philosophy through design.

THE WIDER VALUE OF A PHILOSOPHY THROUGH DESIGN

Philosophy today is much diminished as compared with its historical position. In antiquity, it functioned as the ultimate form of understanding, the means by which the world and our place in it was to be apprehended. In the modern era, this shifted; a focus on knowledge and matters of knowing became key. More recently, prior to the present situation, the nineteenth century saw the ceding of philosophic authority to science as one by one, field after field was hived off from philosophy. Whether relating to the natural or the social sciences, the fields we know today established themselves as standalone disciplines in their own right through philosophy.[42] This has led us to the present where philosophy, as a discipline, restricts itself to the pursuit of furthering

---

[42] Gaukroger, *The Failures of Philosophy*, provides a thorough account of these point of crisis from antiquity to the present.

technical programmes in areas such as logic or else exploring other specific agendas remote from present-day daily concerns (e.g. the present-day outworkings of deconstruction).

Writing in 1976, seeking to reprise a contemporary pragmatist perspective after some fifty years of neglect, American philosopher John McDermott noted that 'the development of "aesthetic sensibility" is a primary concern of our time and is as central to our ameliorative efforts as are the more commonly accepted political, sociological, economic, and psychological diagnoses and strategies'. Aesthetic sensibility here was applied in a Deweyan sense; it was about 'how we and others *feel our situation* and *feel about our situation*'. McDermott proposes that such a sensibility should 'become central to all our evaluations and judgements, especially those which pertain to our adopted strategies for social and political change'.[43]

However, like Dewey's reconstruction proposals, McDermott's vision was not carried forward and voices such as his remained relatively peripheral through the late twentieth century. Accordingly, we have a tracing of how pragmatist philosophy *might* have informed the late twentieth century, not a position on how it did. Nonetheless it does still provides us with a sense of how it can.

This brings us back to design and philosophy today. If philosophy can support design as it seeks to respond to its new-found, extended responsibilities, if we may eventually see designer philosophers, what might design offer the present and future of philosophy?

In answering this, I turn back to Dewey's reconstruction proposals.

It is true that these proposals are historic – over a century old, in fact – but they arose from an early diagnosis of the field's contemporary challenges (at least as they are perceived by some). Dewey's issue was our issue at its point of origin. Furthermore, as noted in Chapter 1, it is possible to see a response to philosophy's present issues in Dewey's 1920s work. We have seen that Philip Kitcher makes this very point.[44] Equally, Dewey's work underpins

---

[43] John J. McDermott, *The Culture of Experience: Philosophical Essays in the American Grain* (New York: New York University Press, 1976), xiii.
[44] Kitcher, *What's the Use of Philosophy*.

Thomas Alexander's call for a return wisdom and a renewed focus on critique.[45] Their work suggests that, just as in McDermott's time, there remains a need to explore 'ameliorative efforts' in the context of 'strategies of social and political change' via philosophy.

Kitcher's proposals are in keeping with Dewey's general agenda and reconstruction call when he argues that present-day philosophy should aim to support methodological clarification and synthesis across disciplines and, equally, must engage directly in the problems of the world, contributing to the framing of solutions. In making these proposals, Kitcher sees himself as removing the core of philosophy-as-is, decentring activities generally such that there is the possibility of moving away from technical abstraction and returning to lived experience. This, he argues, is a path towards the preservation and renewal of the field, one with which he hopes emerging philosophers will want to engage.

Alexander is not as specific as Kitcher in outlining a revised set of tasks for philosophy, nor is he focused on preserving the field. His concern is directed towards ensuring philosophy's relevance for the world of today. In this, as we have seen, he foregrounds the historical ideal of wisdom and notes the discipline's ontological and speculative capacity. He sees a clear role for the field in supporting intelligent action – a key Deweyan term for transformational inquiry.

Like my own proposal, these are visions for a philosophy that is engaged and engages, that transforms as it is enacted, just as Addams and her feminist colleagues practised over a century ago. In both cases, philosophy is repositioned in relation to life and the world, operating in direct terms, responding to the context. The claim of both would be that, if practised in this way, philosophy could carry a fresh immediacy and, ultimately, bring about real and lasting impact, serving both people and life generally. It might even allow for a centring of aesthetic sensibility as suggested by McDermott.

---

[45] Alexander, *The Human Eros*.

The difference, of course, between Kitcher's and Alexander's visions, and indeed McDermott's historic pitch, and my own is that mine originates from within design and involves design in definite terms; theirs comes from philosophy and alludes to design or, at least, design-like activities, but does not align with it directly. A careful translation would undoubtably be necessary if any proper transfer and truly *philosophic* realization of a philosophy through design were to be considered next to these. Nonetheless, the commitment to supporting transformation in relation to contemporary problems and issues opens up a route to design within the process. This is ontological and speculative inquiry combined with experimental testing.

Arguably, this is latent in the morally focused, materially grounded philosophy of technology work of Peter-Paul Verbeek and others, referenced in Chapter 2. Recently, Verbeek has suggested that the perspective he helped to shape has 'laid the foundation' for a philosophy of technology, which can 'combine profound philosophical innovation with empirical and societal engagement', as well as expanding to enfold areas such as multiculturalism and ecology.[46]

In the best-case scenario, what has been sketched out here would link to but also complement such a vision, amounting to the framing of a novel approach to philosophy that marries a *creative* empiricism (i.e. one bound to making and testing) to societal engagement. It would be an approach that with the right supports, philosophers could learn to work with. This would be tentative, faltering and unclear at times, but it would still provide something to work with and work out from.

In the end, the only way a philosophy through design will come to pass is if there is a perceived need, within design itself but also in philosophy. If individuals in both fields come to believe in the idea, they will be able to find a means of bringing it about.

---

[46] Peter-Paul Verbeek, 'The Empirical Turn.' In *The Oxford Handbook of the Philosophy of Technology*, edited by Shannon Vallor (Oxford: Oxford University Press, 2022), 35–54.

The existence of a latent approach or perspective no doubt helps to realize something more formal and recognizable, to progress it into being. Ultimately, our cases and pointings suggest that it is there as a possibility, as something which is but is not quite. The choice from here is whether to press ahead, to see if it can indeed yield value. This itself is a matter of argument and one the field would do well to engage in.

Here we return to our starting point in design's responsibilities. On a fundamental level, these are a given. The depth and reach of the various existential crises we face as a collective – that is, as a species and as a planetary community – mean responsibility can no longer be ignored. It is how we address and manage our responsibilities that is in question. Looking to the work of individuals such as Kitcher and Alexander, it would also appear that philosophies present difficulties is also a given, a disciplinary problem that also needs addressing.

I believe that philosophy-in-design and design-in-philosophy as a *philosophy through design* can be *one* answer for both disciplines simultaneously. There is the potential here to change both for the better such that they become paths by which 'goods' – human and more-than human – are knowingly created and sustained, as per Dewey's proposals. Here, we would have an active way of exploring meaning, value and the desirability of certain actions directly, collectively. This would amount to a reconstruction not only of design and philosophy, but also of what is possible and what might become possible. There is no other reconstruction more urgent and important.

REFERENCES

Abbinnett, Ross, *The Thought of Bernard Stiegler: Capitalism, Technology and the Politics of Spirit*. Abingdon, Oxon: Routledge. 2018.

Abrams, David, *Becoming Animal: An Earthly Cosmology*. New York: Vintage. 2010.

Ackermann, Rebecca, 'Design thinking was supposed to fix the world. Where did it go wrong', MIT Technology Review, 9 February 2023, https://www.technologyreview.com/2023/02/09/1067821/design-thinking-retrospective-what-went-wrong/

Addams, Jane, *Democracy and Social Ethics*. Urbana: University of Illinois Press. 2002 [1905].

Addams, Jane, *Democracy and Social Ethics*. New York: The Macmillan Company. 1905.

Adorno, Theodor, *The Culture Industry: Selected Essays on Mass Culture*. Abingdon, Oxon: Routledge. 2001.

Agamben, Giorgio, *What is an apparatus? And other essays*. Redwood City: CA: Stanford University Press. 2009.

Agnew, Elizabeth N., 'A will to peace: Jane Addams, World War I, and 'pacifism in practice.' *Peace & Change* 42, no. 1 (2017): 5–31.

Ahmed, Sara, *What's the Use? On the uses of use*. Durham, NC: Duke University Press. 2019.

AHRC, 'Design Research', Accessed 11 November 2024. https://www.ukri.org/what-we-do/browse-our-areas-of-investment-and-support/design-research/

Akama, Yoko, 'Being awake to Ma: designing in between-ness as a way of becoming with.: *CoDesign* 11, no. 3–4 (2015), 262–74.

Akama, Yoko, 'Archipelagos of Designing through Ko-ontological Encounters.' In *Arts-Based Methods for Decolonising Participatory Research*, edited by Tiina Seppälä, Melanie Sarantou and Satu Miettinen, 101–22. New York: Routledge. 2021.

Alexander, Thomas M., *The Human Eros: Eco-ontology and the Aesthetics of Experience*. Carbondale, IL: University of Southern Illinois Press. 2017.

An, Wa, Xiangyang Xin, Xiong Ding and Yi Liu, 'Lifestyle as the Object of Design: Elements Exploration from Experience Perspective.' In *Design, User Experience, and Usability. Interaction Design: 9th International Conference, DUXU 2020, Proceedings, Part I,* edited by Aaron Marcus and Elizabeth Rosenzweig, 311–23. Springer International Publishing. 2020.

Babich, Babette, *Günther Anders' Philosophy of Technology*. London: Bloomsbury. 2022.

Bacovic, Maja, Zivko Andrijasevic and Bojan Pejovic, 'STEM education and growth in Europe.' *Journal of the Knowledge Economy* 13, no. 3 (2022): 2348–71.

Ball, Brian, and Patrycja Kaszynska, 'We should lament the demise of philosophy departments', Times Higher Education, 24 June 2024, https://www.timeshighereducation.com/blog/we-should-lament-demise-philosophy-departments

Bang, Anne Louise, and Mette Agger Eriksen, 'Experiments all the way in programmatic design research.' *Artifact: Journal of Design Practice* 3, no. 2 (2014): 4–11.

Bang, Anne Louise, Peter Krogh, Martin Ludvigsen and Thomas Markussen, 'The Role of Hypothesis in Constructive Design Research.' Paper presented at the 4th The Art of Research: Making, Reflecting and Understanding. Aalto University School of Arts, Design and Architecture, Helsinki, Finland, 28–29 Nov 2012.

Bardzell, Shaowen, 'Feminist HCI: taking stock and outlining an agenda for design.' In Proceedings of the SIGCHI conference on Human Factors in Computing Systems: 1301–10. New York: ACM. 2010.

Bardzell, Shaowen, and Jeffrey Bardzell, 'Towards a feminist HCI methodology: social science, feminism, and HCI.' In *Proceedings of the SIGCHI conference on human factors in computing systems*: 675–84. New York: ACM. 2011.

Bashour, Bana, and Hans D. Muller (eds), *Contemporary Philosophical Naturalism and its Implications*. London: Routledge. 2014.

Bason, Christian, *Design for Policy*. London: Routledge. 2016.

Beck, Cheryl, Tatano, Barbara A. Keddy and Marlene Zichi Cohen, 'Reliability and validity issues in phenomenological research.' *Western Journal of Nursing Research* 16, no. 3 (1994): 254–67.

Biggs, Michael, 'The role of the artefact in art and design research.' *International Journal of Design Sciences and Technology*, 10 no. 2 (2002): 19–24.

Binder, Thomas, Giorgio De Michelis, Pelle Ehn, Giulio Jacucci and Per Linde. *Design Things*. Cambridge, MA, The MIT Press. 2011.

Bjögvinsson, Erling, Pelle Ehn and Per-Anders Hillgren, 'Design things and design thinking: Contemporary participatory design challenges.' Design issues 28, no. 3 (2012): 101–16.

Boden, Margaret A., *Mind as Machine: A History of Cognitive Science, Volume 1*. Oxford: Oxford University Press. 2006.

Boehnert, Joanna, *Design, Ecology and Politics: Towards the Ecocene*. London: Bloomsbury. 2018.

Boghossian, Peter, 'Philosophy that matters.' *The Philosophers' Magazine* 72 (2016): 29–30.

Bolvig Poulsen, Søren, and Ulla Thøgersen, 'Embodied design thinking: a phenomenological perspective.' *CoDesign* 7, no. 1 (2011): 29–44.

Bonsiepe, Gui, *The Disobedience of Design*, edited by Lara Penin. London: Bloomsbury. 2022.

Boon, Boudewijn, Ehsan Baha, Abhigyan Singh, Frithjof E. Wegener, Marco C. Rozendaal and Pieter Jan Stappers, 'Grappling with diversity in research through design'. In *Synergy – DRS International Conference 2020, Vol. 5: Situations*, edited by Stella Boess, Ming Cheung and Rebecca Cain, 139–51. London: The Design Research Society. 2020.

Borgmann, Albert, *Technology and the Character of Contemporary Life*. Chicago: University of Chicago Press. 1984.

Bousbaci, Rabah, *L'Homme comme un «être d'habitude». Essai d'anthropologie et d'épistémologie pour les Sciences du design*. Québec City: Presses de l'Université Laval. 2020.

Brassett, Jamie, 'Poised and complex: The becoming each other of philosophy, design and Innovation.' In *Deleuze and Design*, edited by Betti Marenko and Jamie Brassett, 31–57. Edinburgh: Edinburgh University Press. 2015,

Brennan, Andrew, and Yeuk-Sze Lo, *Understanding Environmental Philosophy*. Abingdon, Oxon: Routledge. 2014.

Bridle, James, *Ways of Being, Animals, Plants and Machines: The Search for a Planetary Intelligence*. London: Penguin Books. 2023.

Briggle, Adam, 'The Professionalization of Philosophy from Athens to the APA and Beyond'. In *A Companion to Public Philosophy*, edited by Lee McIntyre, Nancy McHugh, Ian Olasov, 9–17. London: John Wiley and Sons, 2022.

Bryant, Levi R., *The Democracy of Objects*. Ann Arbor: Open Humanities Press. 2011.

Buchanan, Richard, 'Declaration by design: Rhetoric, argument, and demonstration in design practice' *Design Issues*, 2, no. 1 (1985), 4–22.

Buchanan, Richard, 'Design and the new rhetoric: Productive arts in the philosophy of culture.' *Philosophy & Rhetoric* 34, no. 3 (2001): 183–206.

Büchs, Milena and Max Koch, 'Challenges for the degrowth transition: The debate about wellbeing' Futures 105 (2019): 155–65.

Bunge, Mario, *Philosophy in Crisis: The Need for Reconstruction*. Buffalo, NY: Prometheus Books. 2001.

Burik, Steven, The End of Contemporary Philosophy and the Task of Comparative Thinking: Heidegger, Derrida, and Daoism. Albany, NY: State University of New York Press. 2009.

Butler, Judith, *Gender Trouble*. Abingdon, Oxon: Routledge. 1990.

Buwert, Peter, and Matt Sinclair, 'Thought Experiments In The Ethics Of Designing For Future People.' Paper presented at 'DRS2024: Boston' 23–28 June 2024, Boston, USA. https://doi.org/10.21606/drs.2024.518

Campbell, James, *A Thoughtful Profession*. Peru, IL: Open Court. 2006.

Campbell, James, 'A History of Pragmatism.' In *The Bloomsbury Handbook of Pragmatism*, edited by Sami Pihlström, 85–99. London: Bloomsbury. 2024 [2011].

Cherry, Myisha, 'Coming Out of the Shade' In *Philosophy's Future: The Problems of Philosophical Progress*, 21–30. London: John Wiley and Sons. 2017.

Claver Fine, Peter, *The Design of Race How Visual Culture Shapes America*. London: Bloomsbury. 2021.

Community Philosophy, 'What is Community Philosophy', accessed 26 November 2024, https://communityphilosophy.co.uk/what-is-community-philosophy/

Community Philosophy, 'Philosophy Walks', accessed 26 November 2024, https://communityphilosophy.co.uk/philosophy-walks/

Coseru, Christian, *Perceiving Reality: Consciousness, Intentionality and Cognition in Buddhist Philosophy*. Oxford: Oxford University Press. 2012.

Costanza-Chock Sasha, *Design Justice: Community-led Practices to Build the Worlds We Need*. Cambridge, MA: The MIT Press. 2020.

Coyne, Lewis, *Hans Jonas: Life, Technology and the Horizons of Responsibility*. London: Bloomsbury. 2022.

Crilly, Nathan, David Good, Derek Matravers and P. John Clarkson, 'Design as communication: exploring the validity and utility of relating intention to interpretation.' *Design Studies* 29, no. 5 (2008): 425–57.

Crosby, Alexandra, 'Design activism in an Indonesian village.' *Design Issues* 35, no. 3 (2019): 50–63.

Cross, Nigel, 'Developing design as a discipline,' Journal of Engineering Design 29, no. 12 (2018): 691–708.

Culler, Jonathan, *On Deconstruction: Theory and Criticism after Structuralism (25th anniversary edn)*. Ithaca, NY: Cornell University Press. 2007 [1982].

D'Alisa, Giacomo, Frederico Demaria and Giorgos Kallis, Degrowth: A vocabulary for a new era. Abingdon, Oxon: Routledge. 2015.

Dallery, Arleen, Charles E. Scott and P. Holley Roberts, 'Introduction', in *Crisis in Continental Philosophy*, edited by Arleen Dallery, Charles E. Scott and P. Holley Roberts. Albany, NY: State University of New York Press. 1990.

Dalsgaard, Peter, 'Pragmatism and Design Thinking.' *International Journal of Design* 8, no. 1 (2014): 143–55.

d'Eaubonne, Francoise, 'Le Feminisme ou la mort' In *New French Feminisms: An Anthology*, edited by Elaine Marks and Isabelle de Courtivron. Amherst, MA: University of Massachusetts Press. 1980.

Decolonising Design, 'Editorial Statement', 18 December 2021, https://www.decolonisingdesign.com/statements/2016/editorial/

Deegan, Mary Jo, and Christopher W. Podeschi, 'The Ecofeminist Pragmatism of Charlotte Perkins Gilman.' *Environmental Ethics* 23, no. 1 (2001): 19–36.

de Freitas, Netto, Sebastião Vieira, Marcos Felipe Falcão Sobral, Ana Regina Bezerra Ribeiro and Gleibson Robert da Luz Soares, 'Concepts and forms of greenwashing: A systematic review,' *Environmental Sciences Europe* 32, no. 1 (2020): 1–12.

Deleuze, Gilles, and Félix Guattari, *One Thousand Plateaus: Capitalism and Schizophrenia*, translated by Brian Massumi. London: Continuum. 2004 [1980].

DelSesto, Matthew, *Design and the Social Imagination*. London: Bloomsbury. 2022.

Department of Industrial Design, TU Eindhoven, 'Systematic Change', accessed 29 April 2023. https://www.tue.nl/en/research/research-groups/systemic-change

Derrida, Jacques, *Of Grammatology*. Baltimore: The John Hopkins University Press. 1997 [1974].

Dewey, Jane, 'Biography of John Dewey.' In *The Philosophy of John Dewey*, edited by Paul Arthur Schilpp, 3–45. Evanston: Northwestern University Press. 1939.

Dewey, John, *The Middle Works, 1899–1924, Volume 4: 1907–1909, Essays on Pragmatism and Truth*, edited by Jo Ann *Boydston*. Carbondale, IL: Southern Illinois University Press. 1977.

Dewey, John, *The Middle Works, 1899–1924, Volume 9: 1916, Democracy and Education*, edited by Jo Ann Boydston. Carbondale: Southern Illinois University Press. 2008 [1980].

Dewey, John, *The Middle Works, 1899–1924, Volume 12: 1920, Essays, Miscellany, and A Reconstruction in Philosophy*, edited by Jo Ann Boydston. Carbondale, IL: Southern Illinois University Press. 2008 [1982].

Dewey, John, *The Later Works, 1925–1953, Volume 1: 1925, Experience and Nature*, edited by Jo Ann Boydston. Carbondale, IL: Southern Illinois University Press. 2008 [1981].

Dewey John, *The Later Works, 1925–1953, Volume 2: 1925–1927, Essays, Reviews, Miscellany, and The Public and its Problems*, edited by Jo Ann Boydston. Carbondale, IL: Southern Illinois University Press. 2008 [1984].

Dewey, John, *The Later Works, 1925–1953, Volume 4: 1929, The Quest for Certainty*, edited by Jo Ann Boydston. Carbondale, IL: Southern Illinois University Press. 2008 [1984].

Dewey, John, *The Later Works, 1925–1953, Volume 5: 1925–1927, Essays, The Sources of a Science of Education, Individualism, Old and New, and Construction and Criticism*, edited by Jo Ann Boydston. Carbondale, IL: Southern Illinois University Press. 2008 [1984].

Dewey, John, *The Later Works, 1925–1953, Volume 7: 1932, Ethics*, edited by Jo Ann Boydston. Carbondale, IL: Southern Illinois University Press. 2008 [1985].

Dewey, John, *The Later Works, 1925–1953, Volume 12: 1938, Logic: The Theory of Inquiry*. Edited by Jo Ann Boydston. Carbondale, IL: Southern Illinois University Press. 2008 [1986].

Dines Johansen, Jørgen, and Scend Erik Larsen, *Signs in Use: An introduction to semiotics*, translated by Dinda L. Gorlée and John Irons. London: Routledge. 2002.

DiSalvo, Carl, 'Design and the Construction of Publics.' *Design Issues* 25, no. 1 (2009): 48–63.

DiSalvo, Carl, *Design as Democratic Inquiry: Putting Experimental Civics into Practice*. Cambridge, MA: The MIT Press. 2022.

Dixon, Brian, 'Experiments in Experience: Towards an Alignment of Research through Design and John Dewey's Pragmatism.' *Design Issues* 35, no. 2 (2019): 5–16.

Dixon, Brian, *Dewey and Design: A Pragmatist Perspective for Design Research*. Springer: Cham. 2020.

Dixon, Brian 'From making things public to the design of creative democracy: Dewey's democratic vision and participatory design.' CoDesign, 16, no. 2 (2020): 97–110.

Dixon, Brian, *Design, Philosophy and Making Things Happen*. Abingdon, Oxon: Routledge. 2023.

Dixon, Brian, and Tara French, 'Processing the method: Linking Deweyan logic and design-in-research.' *Design Studies* 70 (2020): 100962.

Dixon, Brian, Anna Rylander Eklund and Frithjof Wegener, 'Introduction: Pragmatism, Dewey, and Design Inquiry.' *Design Issues* 39, no. 4 (2023): 3–8.

Dourish, Paul, *Where the Action Is*. Cambridge, MA: The MIT Press. 2001.

Dunne, Antony, *Hertzian Tales Electronic Products, Aesthetic Experience, and Critical Design*. Cambridge, MA: The MIT Press. 2008.

Dunne, Antony, and Fiona Raby, *Speculative Everything: Design, Fiction and Social Dreaming*. Cambridge, MA: The MIT Press. 2013.

Duran, Jane, 'Ellen Gates Starr and Julia Lathrop: Hull House and Philosophy', *The Pluralist*, 9, no. 1, (2014): 1–13.

Dykhuizen, George, *The Life and Mind of John Dewey*. Carbondale, IL: Southern Illinois University Press. 1973.

Ehn, Pelle, 'Work-oriented design of computer artifacts.' PhD diss. Arbetslivscentrum: Stockholm. 1988.

Ehn, Pelle, 'Learning in participatory design as I found it (1970–2015).' In *Participatory Design for Learning*, edited by Betsy DiSalvo, Jason Yip, Elizabeth Bonsignore and Carl DiSalvo, 7–21. Abingdon, Oxon: Routledge. 2017.

Escobar, Arturo, *Designs for the Pluriverse: Radical Interdependence, Autonomy, and the Making of Worlds*. Durham, NC: Duke University Press. 2018.

Falconer, Tara, and Marcos Mortensen Steagall, 'Grounding: A Practice-led Graphic Exploration of Ecofeminism, Wellbeing and

Ecological Consciousness for Young Women' DAT Journal, 8 no. 1 (2023): 101–34. https://doi.org/10.29147/datjournal.v8i1.689

Farías, Ignacio, Anders Blok and Celia Roberts, 'Actor network theory as a companion: an inquiry into intellectual practices.' In *The Routledge Companion to Actor–Network Theory*, edited by Ignacio Farías, Anders Blok and Celia Roberts, xx–xxxv. Abingdon, Oxon: Routledge. 2019.

Felton, Emma, Oksana Zelenko and Suzi Vaughan (eds), *Design and Ethics: Reflections and Practice*. Abingdon, Oxon: Routledge. 2012.

Fesmire, Steven, 'Dewey and Animal Ethics.' In *Animal Pragmatism: Rethinking Human-Nonhuman Relationships*, edited by Erin McKenna and Andrew Light, 43–62. Bloomington, IN: Indiana University Press. 2004.

Findeli, Alain, 'Moholy-Nagy's design pedagogy in Chicago (1937–46).' Design Issues 7, no. 1 (1990): 4–19.

Fischer, Marilyn, *Jane Addam's Evolutionary Theorizing: Constructing 'Democracy and Social Ethics'*. Chicago: University of Chicago Press. 2019.

Fletcher, Kate, and Mathilda Tham (eds), *Routledge Handbook of Sustainability and Fashion*. Abingdon, Oxon: Routledge. 2015.

Flusser, Vilém, *The Shape of Things: A Philosophy of Design*. London: Reaktion Books. 1999.

Flusser, Vilém, *Towards a Philosophy of Photography*. London: Reaktion Books. 2000.

Forlizzi, Jodi and Katja Battarbee 'Understanding experience in interactive systems.' In *Proceedings of the 5th Conference on Designing Interactive Systems: Processes, practices, methods, and techniques*, 261–8. New York: ACM, 2004.

Fowler, Bridget, *Pierre Bourdieu and Cultural Theory: Critical Investigations*. London: Sage. 1997.

Frayling, Christopher, 'Research in art and design.' *Royal College of Art Research Papers* 1 (1993): 1–5.

Fry, Tony, *A Design Philosophy: An Introduction to Defuturing*. Sydney: University of New South Wales Press. 1999.

Fry, Tony, *Design Futuring: Sustainability, Ethics and New Practice*. Oxford: Berg, 2009.

Fry, Tony, *Design as Politics*. Oxford: Berg. 2010.

Fry, Tony, *Writing Design Fiction: Relocating a City in Crisis*. London: Bloomsbury, 2021.

Fuad-Luke, Alastair, *Design Activism: Beautiful Strangeness for a Sustainable World*. Earthscan: London. 2009.

Fuad-Luke, Alastair, *EcoDesign: The Sourcebook*, 3rd edn. San Francisco: Chronicle Books, 2010.

Fuller, Buckminster, *Utopia or Oblivion: Prospects for Humanity*. London: Allen Lane 1970.

Gaard, Greta (ed.), *Ecofeminism*. Philadelphia: Temple University Press. 1993.

Gaard, Greta, 'From 'cli-fi' to critical ecofeminism: narratives of climate change and climate justice.' In *Contemporary Perspectives on Ecofeminism*, edited by Mary Phillips and Nick Rumens, 169–92. London: Routledge. 2015.

Gal, John, Stefan Köngeter and Sarah Vicary (eds), *The Settlement House Movement Revisited: A Transnational History*. Bristol: Policy Press. 2021.

Galle, Per, 'Design as intentional action: a conceptual analysis,' *Design Studies* 20, no. 1 (1999): 57–81.

Gare, Arran, 'Process Philosophy and Ecological Ethics', In *Applied Process Thought: Initial Explorations in Theory and Research*, edited by Mark Dibben and Thomas Kelly, 363–82. Frankfurt: Ontos Verlag. 2008.

Gaukroger, Stephen, *The Failures of Philosophy: A Historical Essay*. Princeton, NJ: Princeton University Press. 2020.

Gaver, Bill, and John Bowers, 'Annotated portfolios.' *interactions* 19, no. 4 (2012): 40–9.

Gaver, Eugene, and Richard Buchanan, *Pluralism in Theory and Practice: Richard McKeon and American Philosophy*. Nashville TN: Vanderbilt University Press. 2000.

Gentes, Anne, *The In-Discipline of Design: Bridging the Gap between the Humanities and Engineering*. Cham: Springer. 2017.

Ghimire, Shurendra, 'Buddhist Pragmatism or Pragmatic Buddhism: What is the relationship between Buddhism and Pragmatism?' *BMC Journal of Scientific Research* 4, no. 1 (2021): 49–64.

Grant, Edward, *A History of Natural Philosophy: From The Ancient World To The Nineteenth Century*. Cambridge: Cambridge University Press. 2007.

Grayling, Antony C., *The History of Philosophy: Three Millenia of Thought From the West and Beyond*. London: Penguin. 2019.

Greenough, Horatio, *Form and Function: Remarks on Art, Design and Architecture*, edited by Harold A. Small. Berkeley: University of California Press. 1966 [1947].

Groth, Camilla, *Making Sense through Hands*. Helsinki: Aalto University. 2017.
Gueudet, Ghislaine, Laetitia Bueno-Ravel, Simon Modeste and Luc Trouche, 'Curriculum in France: A national frame in transition.' In *International Perspectives on Mathematics Curriculum*, edited by Denisse R. Thompson, Mary Ann Huntley and Christine Suurtamm, 41–70. Charlotte, NC: Information Age Publishing. 2017.
Haines Lyon, Charlotte, 'Exploring Community Philosophy as a tool for parental engagement in a primary school.' *International Journal for Transformative Research* 2, no. 2 (2015): 39–48.
Hamington, Maurice, 'Jane Addams and a politics of embodied care.' *The Journal of Speculative Philosophy* 15, no. 2 (2001): 105–21.
Han, Byung-Chul, *Psychopolitics: Neoliberalism and New Technologies of Power*, translated by Erik Butler. London: Verso. 2017.
Harman, Graham, *Object-Orientated Ontology: A New Theory of Everything*. London: Penguin. 2018.
Harold, James A. *An Introduction to the Love of Wisdom: An Essential and Existential Approach to Philosophy*. Oxford: University Press of America. 2004.
Heft, Harry, 'William James' psychology, radical empiricism, and field theory: Recent developments.' *Philosophical Inquiries* 5, no. 2 (2017): 111–30.
Heidegger, Martin, *The Question Concerning Technology and Other Essays*, translated by William Lovitt. New York: Harper and Row. 1977.
Heidegger, Martin, *Being and Time*, translated by Joan Stambaugh. Albany, NY: State University of New York Press. 2010 [1927].
Hepworth, Katherine, 'Governmentality, Technologies & Truth Effects in Communication Design.' In *Advancements in the Philosophy of Design*, edited by, Pieter E. Vermaas and Stéphane Vial, 497–522. Cham: Springer. 2018.
Hickman, Larry, A., *Tools for a Philosophical Culture: Putting Pragmatism to Work*. Bloomington, IN: Indiana University Press. 2001.
Hickman, Larry A., *Pragmatism as Post-Postmodernism: Lessons from John Dewey*. New York: Fordham University Press. 2007.
Higgins, Andrew, and Alexis Dyschkant, 'Interdisciplinary collaboration in philosophy.' Metaphilosophy 45, no. 3 (2014): 372–98.

Homem, Luís, and Bruno Rego, 'Deep Ecology and Utopia: Eco-centric Nowhere.' International Journal of Critical Cultural Studies 13, no. 1 (2015): 9–19.

Hook, Sydney, 'Introduction.' In John Dewey, *The Later Works, 1925–1953, Volume 1: 1925, Experience and Nature*, edited by Jo Ann Boydston, vii–xxiii. Carbondale, IL: Southern Illinois University Press. 2008 [1981].

Hou, Kok Chung, 'Hu Shi: A Chinese pragmatist and reformist', PhD diss. University of London, School of Oriental and African Studies. 1998.

Houtbeckers, Eeva and Gaziulusoy, Idil, 'Ecofeminist Understandings of Care and Design for Sustainability Transitions: Towards a theoretical framework of work for the degrowth movement.' *Proceedings of the Bi-Annual Nordic Design Research Society Conference, Nordes, Who Cares?, 2–4 June. 2019*. Alto: Alto University.

Hudson, Cheryl, 'The 'Un-American' Experiment: Jane Addams's Lessons from Pullman.' Journal of American Studies 47, no. 4 (2013): 903–23.

Hui, Yuk, *Art and Cosmotechnics*. Minneapolis: University of Minnesota Press. 2021.

Hummels, Caroline, and Pierre Lévy, 'Matter of transformation: Designing an alternative tomorrow inspired by phenomenology.' *Interactions* 20, no. 6 (2013): 42–9.

Hummels, Caroline, Sander van der Zwan, Maarten Smith and Jelle Bruineberg, 'Non-discursive philosophy by imagining new practices through design.' *Adaptive Behavior* 30, no. 6 (2022): 537–40.

Ihde, Don, *Technology and Lifeworld: From Garden to Earth*. Bloomington, IN: Indiana State University Press. 1990.

Ihde, Don, *Postphenomenology and Technoscience: The Peking University Lectures*. Albany, NY: State University of New York Press. 2009.

Imarhiagbe, Miriam, 'The Right to Repair in EU Competition Law.' *Nordic Journal of European Law* 5, no. 1 (2022), 166–72.

Inada, Kenneth K., and Nolan Pliny Jacobson (eds), *Buddhism and the American Thinkers*. Albany, NY: State University of New York Press. 1984.

Irwin, Terry, 'Transition design: A proposal for a new area of design practice, study, and research.' *Design and Culture* 7, no. 2 (2015), 229–46.

Irwin, Terry, Gideon Kossoff and Peter Scupelli, *Transition Design 2015*. Pittsburgh, PA: Carnegie Mellon University. 2015.

Jacobson, Nolan Pliny, *The Heart of Buddhist Philosophy*. Carbondale, IL: Southern Illinois University Press. 1988.

James, Meredith, 'Advancing design thinking towards a better understanding of self and others: A theoretical framework on how Buddhism can offer alternate models for design thinking.' *Form Akademisk* 10, no. 2 (2017): 1–14.

James, William, *The Collected Works of William James: A Pluralistic Universe*, edited by Fredson Bowers, Ignas K Skrupkelis, Frederick Burkhardt. Cambridge, MA: Harvard University Press. 1977 [1909].

Jonas, Hans, *The Imperative of Responsibility: In Search of Ethics for the Technological Age*, translated by Das Prinzip Verantwortung. Chicago: University of Chicago Press. 1984.

Kahn, Charles H., *The Art and Thought of Heraclitus: An edition of fragments with translation and commentary*. Cambridge: Cambridge University Press. 1979.

Kahn, Sholom J., 'Experience and existence in Dewey's naturalistic metaphysics.' *Philosophy and Phenomenological Research* 9, no. 2 (1948): 316–21.

Kalupahana, David J., *A History of Buddhist Philosophy: Continuities and Discontinuities*. Honolulu, HI: University of Hawaii Press. 1992.

Kaplan, David M. (ed.), *Readings in the Philosophy of Technology*. Plymouth, UK: Rowman and Littlefield Publishers.

Kaptelinin, Victor, and Bonnie A. Nardi, *Acting with Technology: Activity Theory and Interaction Design*. Cambridge, MA: The MIT Press. 2009.

Keats, Jonathan, *You Belong to the Universe: Buckminster Fuller and the Future*. Oxford: Oxford University Press. 2016.

Keller, David R. (ed.), *Environmental Ethics*. Chichester: Wiley Blackwell. 2010.

Kellogg, Frederic R., 'Moral Dilemmas, Ethical Particularism, and Dewey's Continuum of Normative Inquiry.' *European Journal of Pragmatism and American Philosophy* 13, no. XIII–2 (2021).

Kennedy, Emily, Daphne Fecheyr-Lippens, Bor-Kai Hsiung, Peter H. Niewiarowski and Matthew Kolodziej, 'Biomimicry: A path to sustainable innovation.' *Design Issues* 31, no. 3 (2015): 66–73.

Kim, Miso, 'Designing for participation: Dignity and autonomy of service (Part 2).' *Design Issues* 34:3, (2018): 89–102.

Kimbell, Lucy, 'Logics of social design.' Paper presented at *Design as Common Good*, Online, March 25–16. 2021.

Kimbell, Lucy and Jocelyn Bailey, 'Prototyping and the new spirit of policy-making', *CoDesign* 13, no. 3 (2017): 214–26.

Kimbell, Lucy, Catherine Durose, Ramia Mazé and Liz Richardson, *Design and Policy: Current Debates and Future Directions for Research in the UK: Report of the AHRC Design Policy Research Network*. London: University of the Arts London. 2023.

Kiran, Asle, 'Four Dimensions of Technological Mediation', In *Postphenomenological Investigations: Essays on Human-Technology Relations*, edited by Robert Rosenburg Peter-Paul Verbeek, 123–40. Lanham, MD: Lexington Books. 2015.

Kirby, William, *Empires of Ideas: Creating the Modern University from Germany, to America to China*. Cambridge, MA: Harvard University Press. 2022.

Kirlik, Alex, and Peter Storkerson, 'Naturalizing Peirce's semiotics: Ecological psychology's solution to the problem of creative abduction.' In *Model-Based Reasoning in Science and Technology: Abduction, Logic, and Computational Discovery*, edited by Lorenzo Magnani, Walter Carnielli and Claudio Pizzi, 31–50. Berlin: Springer. 2010.

Kitcher, Philip, *What's the Use of Philosophy*. New York: Oxford University Press. 2023.

Kloppenberg, James T., *Social Democracy and Progressivism in European and American Thought, 1870–1920*. Oxford: Oxford University Press. 1986.

Knoll, Michael, *John Dewey's Laboratory School: The Rise and Fall of a World-Famous Experiment*. London: Palgrave Macmillan. 2024.

Koskinen, Ilpo, 'Agonistic, convivial, and conceptual aesthetics in new social design.' Design Issues 32, no. 3 (2016): 18–29.

Koskinen, Ilpo and Gordon Hush, 'Utopian, molecular and sociological social design.' *International Journal of Design* 10, no. 1 (2016): 65–71.

Koskinen, Ilpo and Peter Gall Krogh, *Drifting by Intention: Four Epistemic Traditions from within Constructive Design Research*. Cham: Springer. 2020.

Koskinen, Ilpo, John Zimmerman, Thomas Binder, Johan Redström and Stephan Wensveen, *Design Research Through Practice: From the Lab, Field, and Showroom*. Amsterdam: Elsevier. 2011.

Kossoff, Gideon, 'Holism and the Reconstitution of Everyday Life: a Framework for Transition to a Sustainable Society' PhD diss. Dundee: University of Dundee. 2011.

Krippendorff, Klaus, *The Semantic Turn: A new foundation for design*. Boca Raton, FL: The CRC Press. 2004.

Kyng, Morten, 'Bridging the Gap Between Politics and Techniques: On the next practices of participatory design.' *Scandinavian Journal of Information Systems* 22, no. 1 (2010): 49–68.

Lagerlund, Henrik, 'Material Substance'. In *The Oxford Handbook of Medieval Philosophy*, edited by John Marenbon, 468–85. Oxford: Oxford University Press. 2012.

Lake, Danielle, 'Jane Addams, Social Design, and Wicked Problems: Designing in, with, and across.' In *The Oxford Handbook of Jane Addams*, edited by Patricia M. Shields, Maurice Hamington and Joseph Soeters. Oxford: Oxford University Press. 2022.

Lake, Danielle, and Judy Whipps, 'Feminist Pragmatist Design: Evolutionary Systems Change.' *Design Issues* 39, no. 4 (2023): 21–34.

Latour, Bruno, *Reassembling the Social: An Introduction to Actor Network Theory*. Oxford: Oxford University Press. 2005.

Latour, Bruno, 'From Realpolitik to Dingpolitik or How to Make Things Public.' In *Making Things Public: Atmospheres of Democracy*, edited by Bruno Latour and Peter Weibel, 14–41. Cambridge, MA: The MIT Press, ZKM/Center for Art and Media in Karlsruhe. 2005.

Latour, Bruno, 'A cautious Prometheus? A few steps toward a philosophy of design (with special attention to Peter Sloterdijk)'. In *Networks of Design: Proceedings of the 2008 Annual International Conference of the Design History Society*, edited by Fiona Hackney, Jonathan Glynne and Viv Minton, 2–10. London: Design History Society. 2009.

Lee, Mordecai, *The Philosopher Lobbyist: John Dewey and the People's Lobby, 1928–1940*. Albany NY: State University of New York Press. 2015.

Leopold, Aldo, *A Sand Country Almanac*. Oxford: Oxford University Press. 1966 [1949].

Light, Andrew, and Eric Kratz (eds), *Environmental Pragmatism*. Abingdon, Oxon: Routledge. 1996.

Light, Ann, 'HCI as heterodoxy: Technologies of identity and the queering of interaction with computers.' *Interacting with Computers* 23, no. 5 (2011): 430–8.

Lincoln, Yvonna, and Egon Guba, *Naturalistic Inquiry*. London: Sage. 1985.

Lindström, Kristina, and Åsa Ståhl, 'Making private matters public in temporary assemblies,' *CoDesign* 8, no. 2–3 (2012): 145–61.

Lindström, Kristina, and Åsa Ståhl, 'Un/Making the Plastic Straw: Designerly Inquiries into Disposability,' Design and Culture (2023): 1–23.

Malpass, Matt, *Critical Design in Context: History, Theory and Practice*. London: Bloomsbury. 2017.

Manning, Erin, and Brian Massumi, *Thought in the Act: Passages in the Ecology of Experience*. Minneapolis, MN: University of Minnesota Press. 2014.

Manzini, Ezio, *Design when Everyone Designs*. Cambridge, MA: The MIT Press. 2015.

Marenko, Betti and Jamie Brassett (eds), *Deleuze and Design*, Edinburgh: Edinburgh University Press. 2015.

Marres, Noortje, *Material Participation: Technology, the Environment and Everyday Publics*. London: Palgrave Macmillan. 2012.

Marx, Karl, 'Thesis on Feuerbach'. In *Ludwig Feuerbach and the Outcome of Classical German Philosophy*, edited by Frederic Engels, 82–4. New York: International Publishers. 1941 [1888].

Mathews, Freya, 'Towards a deeper philosophy of biomimicry.' *Organization & Environment* 24, no. 4 (2011): 364–87.

Mathur, Dinesh Chandra 'The historical Buddha (Gotama), Hume, and James on the self: Comparisons and evaluations.' *Philosophy East and West* 28, no. 3 (1978): 253–69.

Matthews, Ben, and Margot Brereton, 'Navigating the Methodological Mire: Practical Epistemology in Design Research'. In *The Routledge Companion to Design Research*, edited by Paul A. Rodgers and Joyce Yee, 151–62. Abingdon: Routledge. 2015.

Maturana, Humberto R., and Francesco J. Varela, *The Tree of Knowledge: The Biological Roots of Human Understanding*, translated by Robert Paolucci. Boston: Shambhala/New Science Press. 1987.

Mauro-Flude, Nancy and Yoko Akama, 'A feminist server stack: co-designing feminist web servers to reimagine Internet futures.' *CoDesign* 18, no. 1 (2022): 48–62.

May, Todd, 'When is a Deleuzian becoming?' *Continental Philosophy Review* 36, no. 2 (2003): 139–53.

McCarthy, John and Peter Wright, *Technology as Experience*. Cambridge, MA: The MIT Press. 2004.

McDermott, John J., *The Culture of Experience: Philosophical Essays in the American Grain*. New York: New York University Press. 1976.

McDonald, Hugh P., *John Dewey and Environmental Philosophy*. Albany, NY: State of New York University Press. 2004.

McDonald, Hugh P. (ed.), *Environmental Pragmatism*. New York: Rodopi. 2012.

McKenna, Erin and Andrew Light (eds), *Animal Pragmatism: Rethinking Human-Nonhuman Relationships*. Bloomington, IN: Indiana University Press. 2004.

Mies, Maria and Vandana Shiva, *Ecofeminism*. London: Zed Books. 1993.

Misak, Cheryl, *The American Pragmatists*. Oxford: Oxford University Press. 2013.

Miscevic, Nenad, *Thought experiments*. Cham: Springer. 2022.

Molesworth, Helen, and Ruth Erickson, Look Before you Leap: Black Mountain College 1933–1957. New Haven, CT: Yale University Press. 2015. 33.

Moran, Dermot, *Introduction to Phenomenology*. Abingdon, Oxon: Routledge. 2000.

Myers, William T, 'Is Whitehead a Pragmatist? On the Pragmatic Elements in Whitehead's Metaphysics.' In *Thinking with Whitehead and the American Pragmatists: Experience and Reality*, edited by Brian G Henning, William T Myers and Joseph D. John, 3–24. London: Lexington Books. 2015.

Myers, William T., 'Dewey, Whitehead and Process Metaphysics.' In *The Oxford Handbook of John Dewey*, edited by Steven Fesmire, 53–72. Oxford: Oxford University Press. 2017.

Naess, Arne, *Ecology, Community and Lifestyle: Outline of an Ecosophy*. Cambridge: Cambridge University Press. 1990.

Naess, Arne and George Sessions, 'The Deep Ecology Platform' In *Clearcut: The Tragedy of Industrial Forestry*, edited by Bill Devall. San Francisco: Sierra Club Books and Earth Island Press. 1993.

Nancy, Jean-Luc, *The Pleasure in Drawing*. New York: Fordham University Press. 2013.

Nealon, Jeffrey, *Double Reading: Postmodernism After Deconstruction*. Ithaca, NY: Cornell University Press. 2019 [1993].

Noë, Alva, *Strange Tools: Art and Human Nature*. New York: Farrar, Straus and Giroux. 2016.

Nold, Christian, Patrycja Kaszynska, Jocelyn Bailey and Lucy Kimbell, 'Twelve potluck principles for social design.' *DISCERN: International Journal of Design for Social Change, Sustainable Innovation and Entrepreneurship* 3, no. 1 (2022): 31–43.

Norman, Don, *The Design of Everyday Things*. New York: Basic Books. 2013 [1986].

Olasov, Ian, *Ask a Philosopher: Answers to Your Most Important and Unexpected Questions*. London: Hachette Press. 2020.

Overbeeke, Kees, *The Aesthetics of the Impossible*, TU Eindhoven, 11 Feb 2020, research.tue.nl https://research.tue.nl/en/publications/the-aesthetics-of-the-impossible

Overbeeke, Kees, Steven S. Wensveen, Caroline Hummels, Joep Frens and Philip Ross, 'DQI Interaction Design Research'. In *Entwerfen-Wissen-Produzieren*, edited by Claudia Mareis, Gesche Joost and Kora Kimpel, 93–206. Bielefeld, Germany: Transcript-Verlag. 2010.

Palmås, Karl, and Otto Von Busch, 'Quasi-Quisling: co-design and the assembly of collaborateurs.' *CoDesign* 11, no. 3–4 (2015): 236–49.

Papanek, Victor, *Design for the Real World*. London: Thames and Hudson. 1971.

Papanek, Victor, *Design the Real World*, 3rd edn. London: Thames and Hudson. 2019 [1971].

Parker Follett, Mary, *Prophet of Management: A Celebration of Writings from the 1920s*, edited by Pauline Graham. Washington, DC: Beard Books. 1995.

Parsons, Glenn, *The Philosophy of Design*. Cambridge: Polity. 2015.

Perkins Gilman, Charlotte, *Herland*. New York: Dover Publications. 1998 [1915].

Phillips, Mary, and Nick Rumens (eds), *Contemporary Perspectives on Ecofeminism*. London: Routledge. 2015.

Place, Alison (ed.), *Feminist Designer: On the Personal and the Political in Design*. Cambridge, MA: The MIT Press. 2023.

Platt, Harold L., 'Jane Addams and the Ward Boss Revisited: Class, politics, and public health in Chicago, 1890–1930.' *Environmental History* 5, no. 2 (2000): 194–222.

Poceski, Mario, 'Philosophical Reflections, Identity formations, Buddhist Responses to Religious Diversity'. In *Buddhism in Dialogue with Contemporary Societies*, edited by Carola Roloff, Michael Zimmermann, Wolfram Weiße, 85–100. München, Bayern: Waxmann. 2020.

Potter, Norman *What Is a Designer: Things, Places, Messages*. London: Studio Vista. 1969.

Preston, Aaron, *Analytic Philosophy: The History of an Illusion*. London: Continuum. 2007.

Price, Rebecca Anne, and Peter Lloyd, 'Asking effective questions: awareness of bias in designerly thinking.' In *Handbook of*

Engineering Systems Design, edited by Anja Maier, Josef Oehmen and Pieter E. Vermaas, 1–16. Cham: Springer International Publishing. 2022.

Prochner, Isabel, and Danny Godin, 'Quality in research through design projects: Recommendations for evaluation and enhancement.' *Design Studies* 78 (2022): 101061.

Pye, David, *The Nature and Aesthetics of Design*. London: Barrie and Jenkins. 1978.

Quijano, Anibal, 'Coloniality of Power and Eurocentrism in Latin America'. *International Sociology*, 15, no. 2 (2000): 215–32.

Ramakrishna, Seeram, and Rajan Jose, 'Addressing sustainability gaps.' Science of The Total Environment 806 (2022): 151–208.

Rescher, Nicholas, *Process Metaphysics: An Introduction to Process Philosophy*. 'Albany, NJ: State University of New York Press. 1996.

Rogers, Yvonne, *HCI Theory: Classical, Modern, Contemporary*. San Rafael: Morgan and Claypool. 2012.

Rolston III, Holmes, 'Challenges in Environmental Ethics.' In *The Environment in Question, 2nd edn*, edited by David E. Cooper and Joy A. Palmer, 144–54. Abingdon, Oxon: Routledge. 2005.

Rorty, Richard, *The Linguistic Turn: Essays in Philosophical Method, With Two Retrospective Essays*. Chicago: University of Chicago Press. 1992 [1967].

Rosenthal, Sandra B., and Rogene A. Buchholz, 'How Pragmatism *is* an Environmental Ethic', In *Environmental Pragmatism*, edited by Andrew Light and Eric Kratz, 38–49. Abingdon, Oxon: Routledge. 1996.

Ross, Philip, 'Ethics and aesthetics in intelligent product and system design.' PhD diss. Eindhoven: University of Technology Eindhoven. 2008.

Rossman, James Robert, and Mathew D. Duerden, *Designing Experiences*. New York: Columbia University Press. 2019.

Russell, Daniel, *Pleasure and Good Life*. Oxford: Oxford University Press. 2005.

Rust, Chris, Judith Mottram and Jeremy Till, *Review of Practice-led Research in Art, Design and Architecture*. London: The Arts and Humanities Research Council. 2007.

Rynbrandt, Linda J., and Mary Jo Deegan, 'The ecofeminist pragmatism of Caroline Bartlett Crane, 1896–1935.' *The American Sociologist* 33, no. 3 (2002): 58–68.

Salleh, Ariel, *Ecofeminism as Politics: Nature, Marx and the Postmodern*, 2nd Edition. London: Bloomsbury. 2017.

Sandel, Michael J., *Public Philosophy: Essays on Morality in Politics*. Cambridge, MA: Harvard University Press. 2005.

Sanders, Elizabeth B.-N., and Pieter Jan Stappers, 'Co-creation and the new landscapes of design.' *Co-design* 4, no. 1 (2008): 5–18.

Schirato, Tony, and Susan Yell, *Communication and Culture: An Introduction*. London: Sage, 2000.

Schneiderhan, Erik, 'Pragmatism and empirical sociology: the case of Jane Addams and Hull House, 1889–1895.' *Theory and Society* 40 (2011): 589–617.

Schultz, Tristan, Danah Abdulla, Ahmed Ansari, Ece Canlı, Mahmoud Keshavarz, Matthew Kiem, Luiza Prado de O. Martins and Pedro J. S. Vieira de Oliveira, 'What is at stake with decolonizing design? A roundtable.' *Design and Culture* 10, no. 1 (2018): 81–101.

Scott, David, 'William James and Buddhism: American pragmatism and the orient.' *Religion* 30, no. 4 (2000): 333–52.

Shi, Xiaoyi, 'Deep Ecology in the Perspective of Whitehead's Process Philosophy'. *Journal of Humanities, Arts and Social Science*, 7 no. 5 (2023): 922–6.

Siegfried, Charlene Haddock, *Reweaving the Social Fabric: Pragmatism and Feminism*. Chicago: University of Chicago Press. 1996.

Siegfried, Charlene Haddock, 'Introduction.' In Jane Addams, *Democracy and Social Ethics*. Urbana: University of Illinois Press. 2002 [1905].

Simonsen, Jasper, and Toni Robertson (eds), *Routledge International Handbook of Participatory Design*. Abingdon, Oxon: Routledge. 2012.

Skaggs, Steven, *FireSigns: A Semiotic Theory for Graphic Design*. Cambridge, MA: The MIT Press. 2017.

Sleeper, Ralph, *The Necessity of Pragmatism: John Dewey's Conception of Philosophy*. New Haven, CT: Yale University Press. 1986.

Smith, Rachel Charlotte, Kasper Tang Vangkilde, and Mette Gislev Kjaersgaard, Design Anthropological Futures. Abingdon, Oxon: Routledge. 2020.

Smits, Merlijn, Geke Ludden, Ruben Peters, Sebastian J. H. Bredie, Harry Van Goor and Peter-Paul Verbeek. 'Values that matter: A new method to design and assess moral mediation of technology.' *Design Issues* 38, no. 1 (2022): 3 9–54.

Steen, Marc, 'Co-design as a process of joint inquiry and imagination.' *Design Issues* 29, no. 2 (2013): 16–28.

St John, Nicola, and Yoko Akama, 'Reimagining co-design on Country as a relational and transformational practice.' *CoDesign* 18, no. 1 (2022): 16–31.

Stompff, Guido, Ties van Bruinessen and Frido Smulders, 'The generative dance of design inquiry: Exploring Dewey's pragmatism for design research.' Design Studies 83 (2022): 101136.

Takeda, Ryusei, 'Mahayana Buddhism and Whitehead's Philosophy.' *Process Studies* 23, no. 2 (1994): 72–86.

Tan, Sor-Hoon, 'China's pragmatist experiment in democracy: Hu Shih's pragmatism and Dewey's influence in China.' *Metaphilosophy* 35:1-2, (2004): 44–64.

Tanner, Laurel, *Dewey's Laboratory School: Lessons for Today.* New York: Teachers College Press, Columbia University. 1997.

The Studio at the Edge of the World, 'Edgewords', accessed 18 November 2024, https://www.thestudioattheedgeoftheworld.com/archive1.html

Thomas-Fogiel, Isabelle, *The Death of Philosophy: Reference and Self-Reference in Contemporary Thought.* New York: Columbia University Press. 2011.

Tonkinwise, Cameron 'Designing Philosophically: Review of Vilem Flusser The Shape of Things: A Philosophy of Design.' Design Philosophy Papers 1, no. 6 (2003): 363–70.

Tonkinwise, Cameron, 'Is Social Design a Thing?' In *The Social Design Reader*, edited by Elizabeth E. Resnick, 9–16. London: Bloomsbury. 2015.

Tonkinwise, Cameron, '"I Prefer Not To": Anti-Progressive Designing.' In *Undesign: A Critical Practice at the Intersection of Art and Design*, edited by Gretchen Coombs, Andrew McNamara and Gavin Sade, 74–84. Abingdon, Oxon: Routledge, 2019.

Torres Aldave, Mikel 'Who owns nature? Sentience, environmental ethics and intervention in nature.' *Estudios de Filosofía* 65 (2022): 7–29.

Trotto, Ambra, 'Rights Through Making.' PhD diss. Eindhoven: Eindhoven University of Technology. 2011.

University of Cambridge, Faculty of Philosophy, 'About Us Overview', accessed November 9 2024. https://www.phil.cam.ac.uk/aboutus

van Belle, Jonne, Jelle van Dijk and Wouter Eggink, 'Towards a Tangible Philosophy through Design; Exploring the question of being-in-the-world in the digital age.' In *Proceedings of the Academy for Design Innovation Management conference*, Loughborough University, 19–21 June.

van der Zwan, Sander, Maarten Smith, Jelle Bruineberg, Pierre Levy and Caroline Hummels 2020, 'Philosophy at work: Postphenomenology as a generative lens in design research and practice.' In *Proceedings of DRS2020 International Conference, Volume 4: Education*, edited by Stella Boess, Ming Cheung and Rebecca Cain, 1691–1706. London: The Design Research Society.

Vaughan, Laurene (ed.), *Practice-Based Design Research*. London: Bloomsbury. 2017.

Verbeek, Peter-Paul, *What Things Do: Reflections on Technology, Agency and Design*. University Park, PN: Pennsylvania State University Press. 2005.

Verbeek, Peter-Paul, *Moralizing Technology: Understanding and Designing the Morality of Things*. Chicago: University of Chicago Press. 2011.

Verbeek, Peter-Paul, 'The Empirical Turn.' In *The Oxford Handbook of the Philosophy of Technology*, edited by Shannon Vallor, 35–54. Oxford: Oxford University Press. 2022.

Verganti, Roberto, Claudio Dell'Era and Kenneth Scott Swan, 'Design thinking: Critical analysis and future evolution.' *Journal of Product Innovation Management* 38, no. 6 (2021): 603–22.

Vermaas, Pieter E., and Stéphane Vial (eds), *Advancements in the Philosophy of Design*. Cham: Springer. 2018.

Vermaas, Pieter E., Peter Kroes, Andrew Light and Steven Moore (eds), *Philosophy and Design: From Engineering to Architecture*. Dordrecht: Springer. 2007.

Vial, Stéphane, 'The effect of design: A phenomenological contribution to the quiddity of design presented in geometrical order,' *Artifact: Journal of Design Practice* 3, no. 4 (2015): 1–6.

von Busch, Otto, 'Fashion-able. Hacktivism and engaged fashion design.' PhD diss. Gothenburg: University of Gothenburg, 2008.

Wagler, Ron, 'The sixth great mass extinction.' Science Scope 35, no. 7 (2012): 48–55.

Wahl, Daniel Christian, *Designing Regenerative Cultures*. Axminister: Triarchy Press. 2016.

Wakkary, Ron, *Things we Could Design: For More Than Human Centered Worlds*. Cambridge, MA: The MIT Press. 2021.

Wakkary, Ron, Doenja Oogjes, Henry W. J. Lin and Sabrina Hauser, 'Philosophers living with the tilting bowl.' In *Proceedings of the 2018 CHI Conference on Human Factors in Computing Systems*, 94, 1–12. New York: ACM, 2018.

Wakkary, Ron, William Odom, Sabrina Hauser, Garnet Hertz and Henry Lin, 'Material speculation: Actual artifacts for critical inquiry.' In *Proceedings of The Fifth Decennial Aarhus Conference on Critical Alternatives*, 97–108. New York: ACM. 2015.

Wakkary, Ron, Doenja Oogjes, Sabrina Hauser, Henry W. J. Lin, Cheng Cao, Leo Ma and Tijs Duel, 'Morse Things: A Design Inquiry into the Gap Between Things and Us' In *Conference on Designing Interactive Systems*, 503–14. New York: ACM, 2017.

Walker, Stuart, *Sustainable by Design: Explorations in Theory and Practice*. London: Earthscan. 2006.

Walker, Stuart, *Design for Resilience: Making a Future We Leave Behind*. Cambridge, MA: The MIT Press. 2023.

Wallace-Wells, David, *The Uninhabitable Earth*. London: Penguin. 2020.

Weber Linn, James, *Jane Addams: A Biography*. Chicago: University of Illinois Press. 2000.

Wechsler, Harold S., Lester F. Goodchild and Linda Eisenmann (eds), *The History of Higher Education*. Boston, MA: Pearson. 2006.

Weston, Anthony, 'Beyond intrinsic value: Pragmatism in environmental ethics.' *Environmental Ethics* 7, no. 4 (1985): 321–39.

Whipps, Judy, 'Philosophy and Social Activism: An Exploration of the Pragmatism and Activism of Jane Addams, John Dewey and Engaged Buddhism', PhD diss. The Graduate School of Union Institute. 1998.

White, Morton, *A Philosophy of Culture: The Case for Holistic Pragmatism*. Princeton, NJ: The Princeton University Press. 2002.

Whitely, Nigel, *Design for Society*. London: Reaktion Books. 1993.

Wilkie, Alex, 'How well does ANT equip designers for socio-material speculations?' In *A Routledge Companion to Actor-Network Theory*, edited by Ignacio Farías, Anders Blok and Celia Roberts, 389–99. Abingdon: Routledge. 2019.

Williams, Jeffrey, 'The Death of Deconstruction, the End of Theory, and Other Ominous Rumors.' *Narrative* 4, no. 1 (1996): 17–35.

Williamson, Bess, and Elizabeth Guffey (eds), *Making Disability Modern: Design Histories*. London: Bloomsbury. 2020.

Willis, Anne-Marie, 'Ontological designing.' *Design Philosophy Papers* 4, no. 2 (2006): 69–92.

Willis, Anne-Marie, 'Editorial.' *Design Philosophy Papers* 15 no. (2017): 95–97.

Willis, Anne-Marie, 'Introduction'. In *The Design Philosophy Reader*, edited by Anne-Marie Willis, 1–10. London: Bloomsbury, 2019.

Winograd, Terry, and Ferando Flores, *Understanding Computers and Cognition: A New Foundation for Design*. Norwood, NJ: Albex. 1986.

Wood, David, 'What is ecophenomenology?' *Research in Phenomenology* 31, no. 1 (2001): 78–95.

Wright, Peter and John McCarthy, 'Experience-centered design: Designers, users, and communities in dialogue.' *Synthesis Lectures on Human-Centered Informatics* 3, no. 1 (2010): 1–123.

Yao, Yusheng, 'Rediscovering Tao Xingzhi as an educational and social revolutionary.' Twentieth-Century China 27, no. 2 (2002): 79–120.

Zimmerman, John, Erik Stolterman and Jodi Forlizzi, 'An analysis and critique of Research through Design: Towards a formalization of a research approach.' In *Proceedings of the 8th ACM Conference on Designing Interactive Systems* (2010), pp. 310–19.

Zitouni, Benedikte, 'Planetary destruction, ecofeminists and transformative politics in the early 1980s.' *Interface* 6, no. 2 (2014): 244–70.

INDEX

Abrams, David 157
accessibility 32, 138
accountability 43
activism 104, 117
activity theory 75
actor network theory (ANT) 11–12, 17, 120–4, 150
adaption 131
Addams, Jane 13, 20–2, 134
   continued calls for reconstructions 60–3
   feminist pragmatists 48–52
   linking and comparing feminist pragmatists 52–4
   linking with Dewey 63–7
   philosophy today 56–60
   as proto-designer philosopher 39–42
   social horizon 99, 100–5, 118, 125
   technical horizons 73, 94
   see also philosophy through design
Adorno, Theodor 107
advocacy, environmental 134
aesthetic sensibility 198
affordances 82
agency 93, 119, 150
Ahmed, Sara 20
Akama, Yoko 111, 115, 126
Alexander, Thomas 61, 174, 199, 200
alignment 196
alternatives 148
American Philosophic Association (APA) 56
analytic philosophy 15
Anders, Günther 18–19
animals 135
anma 112
annotated portfolio 172, 179
anthropology 105
argumentation 45, 170, 171, 178, 188, 189

artefacts 11, 25, 107
   ecological horizon 148, 163
   philosophy through design 169, 171–2, 180
   technological horizon 71, 84, 92
artificial intelligence (AI) 5, 69–70, 71, 74, 94
Ask a Philosopher 63
assembly, temporary 145
attention 75
audiences 107, 179, 182
autonomous design 110
awareness 194

Bang, Anne Louise 28
Bardzell, Shaowen and Jeffery 78
Bartlett Crane, Caroline 153, 164
becoming, ways of 112
being 142
being-in-the-world 84
being-knowing 112
biases 2
biocentrism 158–9, 160, 164, 165
biodiversity 130, 158
biosphere 131
Black Mountain College 65
Boehnert, Joanna 142
Boghossian, Peter 57–8
Bonsiepe, Gui 7
Bourdieu, Pierre 107
brands 136
Brindle, James 157–8
Buchanan, Richard 171, 173
Buddhism 191–3, 194, 196
Bunge, Mario 60
Buwert, Peter 89

capitalism 142
care 16
Chicago Bauhaus 65
China 194–5
citizens 101, 102, 117
climate change 149, 153

climate emergencies (crisis) 130, 158, 161, 170
co-authorship 184
co-creation 99, 178
co-design 4, 99, 112, 114, 121
co-development 84
collaboration 25, 144
  philosophy through design 178, 180, 184, 189
  social horizon 103, 112, 122, 127
collage 155
collective actions 201
  see also collaboration
communicability 26, 179
communication 32, 39, 47, 105–11, 125, 180
communities 50–2, 83, 170
  ecological horizon 134, 144, 163
  social horizon *see* social horizon
  see also digital communications
communities of practice 3, 41, 189
Community Philosophy 63
complexity 84
concerns, emergent 74
consequences, potential 90, 171, 193
Constanza-Chock, Sasha 7, 107, 116
consumers (consumption) 136, 137, 138, 139, 142
contexts 24, 27, 117, 144
  Dewey and Addams 44–5, 51–2, 54
  meaning 190
  philosophy through design 168, 172, 176, 178
  technological horizon 85, 92
contextualization 179
continental philosophy 15, 58–9
cooperation 52
co-shaping 84
country 112
creativity 163, 171
crises 130, 158, 162, 170, 201
critical design 121–2
criticism 47

culture 105–11, 125, 168
curricula, national 57, 65
customer design (CX) 3
  see also user-centred design; user experience design (UX)
customs 102, 125

Darwin, Charles 132
debates 118, 162
decisions 171, 194
decolonialism 39, 41, 94, 108–10, 126–7, 190
Decolonising Design Group 109
deep ecology 151–2, 164, 165
defuturing 140, 141
degradation, environmental 142
degrowth 139, 154
Deleuze, Gilles 88, 107
deliberation 125
DelSesto, Matthew 66, 104
democracy 52, 101, 103, 105, 125, 190
Democracy and Social Ethics 51
denotation 46, 172–3, 175
Descartes, René 149
design curricula 6
design dimensions 84
designer philosophers 187–9
designers 113–20, 126
Design for the Real World 136
designing 84, 176
Designing for Quality Interactions (DQI) 82, 83–5, 158
design modelling 2
design outcomes 74
Design Philosophy Papers 10
design research 91, 168, 187
  distinctions with philosophy through design 181–2
  similarities with philosophy through design 180–1
desirability 169, 178, 201
devices 122
Dewey, John 13, 20–2, 37–8, 42–8
  concerns 54–6

continued calls for reconstructions 60–3
ecological horizon 133, 135
linking and comparing feminist pragmatists 52–4
linking with Addams 63–7
philosophy today 56–60
as proto-designer philosopher 38–42
social horizon 99, 100–5, 118, 125
technological horizon 71–2, 76, 80, 93–4
see also philosophy through design
dialogues 63
see also debates
difference 66, 190
digital communications 57
digital technologies 5
see also ontologizing, digital
Dingpolitik 121
disabilities 115–16
DiSalvo, Carl 66, 104
disciplines 47, 199
displays 11
disposability 148
diversity 66, 190
Dunne, Antony 10, 88
Dutch Ministry of Infrastructure and Water Management 86, 163
dwelling 16

EcoDesign 137
ecofeminism 134, 150, 152–6, 164
ecological literacy 143
ecology 5, 129–32, 170, 175
 deep ecology 151–2
 ecofeminism 152–6
 environmental ethics 158–61
 environmental philosophies 148–51
 expanding agenda 136–44
 Kristina Lindström and Åsa Ståhl 144–8

philosophy through design 161–5
in pragmatism 132–6
economic remodelling 140
ecophenomenology 150, 156–8, 164
ecosophy 151
education (schools) 99, 187
Eindhoven University of Technology 74, 81, 88–90, 94, 158, 182
 see also Designing for Quality Interactions (DQI)
elimination 140
embodied care 103
embodiment 92
empathic design 114
Energy Babble 122
engagement 62, 112, 113, 157, 196
environmental degradation 142
environmental ethics 158–61
environmental philosophies 148–51
 deep ecology 151–2
 ecofeminism 152–6
 ecophenomenology 156–8
environments 122–3, 150–2, 155, 161
errors 75
Escobar, Arturo 7, 109–10, 111, 125
ethics 5–6, 12, 17, 19, 29
 Dewey and Addams 51–2
 ecological horizon 150
 environmental 133–4, 158–61, 164–5
 philosophy through design 169, 177, 183, 188
 social horizon 103, 105, 125–7
 see also technologies (technology horizon)
ethnography 114
European Union 138
events, global 141
Everyday Design Studio 87, 88, 90, 94, 182
evidence 179
evolution 141
evolutionary theory 132
exhibitions 11
existence 46, 47

expectations 141
experience 44–6, 64, 175, 193
   technological horizon 75, 81, 91
Experience and Nature 44, 46, 61, 195
experience-centred design 77
experiences 76, 94
experimentation 24, 80, 131
   Dewey and Addams 39, 43–4, 64
   starting point 176, 178, 180, 190
expertise 189
exploitation 73

facts 171
Falconer, Tara 155
fashion industry 136, 138
feelings 76
feminism 20, 22, 116
   philosophy through design 169, 190, 196, 199
   pragmatists 48–54
   technological horizon 74, 78
   see also Addams, Jane
Feminist Server Stack 78
flexibility 122, 126
Flusser, Vilém 18–19
food 137
Fraser, Simon 89
Fry, Tony 7, 16, 109, 185, 190
   ecological horizon 140–2, 162
Fuad-Luke, Alastair 137
Fuller, Buckminster 115
functions 141
future generations 150
futures 89, 177, 181, 185–7, 189–97
   ecological horizon 140, 163

Gaukroger, Stephen 58
Gaziulusoy, Idil 154
gender 152, 161, 164
general public *see* public, members of (general)
generations, future 150
Gibson, James 82

Gilman Perkins, Charlotte 153–4, 164
Global North 189, 190, 196
goodness (goods) 47
great extinctions 130
greenwashing 138
Grounded 155, 156
groups 178, 179
Guattari, Félix 88, 107

habits 102, 125, 133
Hamington, Maurice 103
Han, Byung-Chul 19
handbooks 137
Heidegger, Martin 16, 79, 82, 142
Herland 154
hermeneutics 79
   see also meanings
Hickman, Larry 133–4
Houtbeckers, Eeva 154
Hui, Yuk 19
Hull House 40, 49–52, 64, 66, 73, 134
   social horizon 99, 102, 104
human-centred design 114
human experience 92
humanism 119, 149
humans (humanness) 87, 141, 160
Hu, Shih 195
Husserl, Edmund 79

identity 2
Ihde, Don 79, 81
images 11
impacts 193
inclusivity 78
indigenous communities 112
Industrial Revolution 2
inequalities 64
Ingold, Tim 86
inquiry, patterns of 43
insights 47, 127, 178, 179, 181, 182
   ecological 131
integration 54, 188, 191
intelligence 157, 164
intelligent actions 43

interactions 120, 192
interdependence 131, 159, 196
interdisciplinarity 144, 185, 187, 189
interrelationality 127, 157–8, 159, 162
intersubjectivity 171
invention 171
issues 176
iterations 43, 44, 179

Jacobson, Nolan 192
James, William 42, 48–9, 54, 110, 133, 192
Jaspers, Karl 79
Jonas, Hans 19
judgement 171, 177
justification 159

Kelley, Florence 134
Kimbell, Lucy 186
Kiran, Asle 84
Kitcher, Philip 60–1, 198, 199, 200
knowledge 134, 174, 197
    indigenous 190
    interdisciplinary 181
knowledge production 12, 23, 28, 30, 81
Koskinen, Ilpo 30
Kossoff, Gideon 143, 144
Krogh, Peter 28

Lake, Danielle 66, 104
land ethic 159
    see also biosphere
language 106, 123
Lathrop, Julia 49, 134
Latour, Bruno 11, 17–18, 102, 120–1
leadership 104
lectures 55
legacy 14
legitimacy 3, 4, 23
Leopold, Aldo 159–60
lifeforms 160
life patterns 139

Lindström, Kristina 132, 144–8, 162–3, 171
Linn, James Weber 50
listening 51, 102, 103
literacy, ecological 143
literature 191
logical positivism 56, 58
longevity 146
Lovejoy, Arthur 56
Ludvigsen, Martin 28

manufacturing 2, 73
Manzini, Ezio 118
mapping, resolution 177
marginalization 116
marketing 138
Markussen, Thomas 28
Marres, Noortje 102, 123
Marxism 74, 77
mass culture 107
mass production 2, 73
materials 136, 137, 139, 141
material speculation 87
McDermott, John 198, 199
McDonald, Hugh 133
McKeon, Richard 108, 110, 171
Mead, George Herbert 48–9, 54, 105
meaningfulness 32
meanings 169–70, 172, 174, 177–9, 181, 201
    contextual 190
    social horizon 98, 126
    see also ecology; technologies (technology horizon)
media engagement 55
mediation 120
memory 75
Merleau-Ponty, Maurice 82
metaphysical questions 46
microbiological health 146
mind mapping 155
Miso, Kim 195
morality 17, 102, 200
    ecological horizon 134, 160–1
    technological horizon 80, 92

more-than-human 150, 157, 161
  see also non-humans
Mortensen Steagall, Marco 155
motivational contexts 24, 180
museum exhibitions 172

Naess, Arne 151, 163
narratives 11
nature 150
needs 141, 194, 200
Netherlands 86
networks 150, 160
  see also actor network theory (ANT); social horizon
Newton, Isaac 149
nomad practices 88
non-humans 92, 119, 120, 124, 126, 150
norms 141

objectivity 171
object-orientated ontologies (OOO) 11, 17, 37, 57
objects 122, 148
obsolescence 138, 139
Odom, William 87
Olasov, Ian 63
ontological transformation 181
ontologizing, digital 69–74
  digital source point 91–5
  empirical philosophy 82–91
  philosophies of design 74–81
openness 94, 168, 194
opportunities 188
oppression 116, 126, 152
organizational structures 117
organizations, grassroots 138
outcomes 32, 75, 169–75, 177, 180, 193
Overbeeke, Kees 82

Pålmas, Karl 122
Papanek, Victor 1, 115, 136
Parson, Glen 15
participants, research 27

participation 66, 157
  see also social horizon
participatory design 4, 77, 78, 99, 114, 117
participatory practice 94
patchwork 144
perception 75, 79, 80
perspectives 51, 191
persuasion 171, 174
phenomenology 76
Philosophy of Design, The 15
philosophy through design 167
  collaborative philosophizing 184–5
  designer philosophers 187–9
  distinctions 181–2
  end 178–80
  futures 185–7
  middle 176–8
  pluralism from pragmatism 189–97
  processes and outcomes 170–5
  similarities 180–1
  start 175–6
  thought experiments 182–4
  tracing of 168–70
  wider value 197–201
philosophy today 56–60, 197–8
photographs 11
Pierce, Charles Sanders 42, 48–9, 132–3
plastic straws 145–6
plurality 30, 94, 161
pluriverse 109, 110
policy design 3
politics 117, 123
pollution 4, 136
possibilities 177
postconsumerism 140
posthumanism 80, 87
postphenomenology 16–17, 19
  Dewey and Addams 37, 57
  see also technologies (technology horizon)

potential 177
power 106, 107, 116, 122, 125, 127
practice functions 86
   see also communities of practice
pragmatism 39, 42, 45, 48, 186
   ecofeminism 164
   ecological horizon 161, 165
   ecology 132–6
   feminism 153
   technological horizon 74, 76
   see also Dewey, John
precedence 14
presentations 55, 189
printmaking 155
problem definition 177
problem solving 43, 50, 101–2, 168, 188, 200
processes 139, 148, 170–5
procomposition 122
professionalization 56
programmes 162
protocol, staged 174–9
prototypes 77, 183
psychoanalysis 59
psychology 6, 75
Public and its Problems, The 72
publications 11, 55
public health 146
public, members of (general) 113, 172, 179
public philosophy 55, 64
purpose 188

questioning 105, 174

Raby, Fiona 10, 88
race 116
readership 55
realities 46, 72, 74, 92, 192
recoding 141
recognition 3, 4
Reconstruction of Philosophy, A 43, 46
reconstructions 21–2, 40, 60–3
reflection 105, 169, 176
   see also Addams, Jane; Dewey, John; ecology
reflexivity 113
regeneration 118
relationality 88
relationships 55, 175, 192, 196
   ecological horizon 144, 153–4, 159
   human-nature 150 *see also* deep ecology
   social horizon 107, 111–13, 120
   technological horizon 89, 92, 94
   see also interrelationality
repair 137
repairability 138, 139
repurpose 137
research 12–13, 23–5, 27–8, 32, 43, 86
   see also design research
research data 114
researcher participation 66
resilience 140
resources 16, 137
responsibilities, design 4–8, 168, 188, 198, 201
restoration 157
retraceability 26, 180
retroscription 122
reuse 137
rituals 84
Ross, Philip 29

Salleh, Ariel 153
Scandinavia 23, 77, 117
Schön, Donald 65
schools *see* education (schools)
science 197
scrapbooking 155
seeing, ways of 191
selfhood 5
semiotics 106
sentience 160
sequence 171
service design 3, 117
Sessions, George 151

sewing 144
Shape of Things, The 19
Siegfried, Charlene Haddock 51, 53
significance 165
signs, theory of 132
Simon Fraser University 81, 87
Sinclair, Matt 89
situatedness 92, 157
situations 76
Sloterdijk, Peter 18
smartphones 71
social conditions 73
social contexts 169
social ethics 125
social horizon 97–100
 actor network theory (ANT) 120–4
 in design 113–20
 Dewey and Addams 100–5
 many ways of seeing 124–7
 rethinking relations 111–13
 social pragmatism 105–11
social imagination 119
social interactions 5
social networks 117–18
social norms 52
social pragmatism 105–11
social reforms 40
social responsibility 115
social understanding 73
social work 50
societal engagement 64
specialization, disciplinary 55
speculative design 121–2, 180
Ståhl, Åsa 132, 144–8, 162–3, 172
stakeholders 126, 163, 170
 see also communities
Starr, Ellen Gates 49
status 160
stereotypes 2
St. John, Nicola 111, 115, 126
storytelling 51
structures, organizational 117
support networks 97
sustainability 118, 136–40, 144–5

Sustainment 141
Systematic Change 82–3

Tao, Zingzhi 195
teaching models 41
technologies (technology horizon) 9, 12, 16, 19, 29, 69–74
 digital source point 91–5
 ecological horizon 142
 empirical philosophy 82–91
 philosophies of design 74–81
 philosophy through design 170, 175
 social horizon 119, 123
 see also digital technologies
technoscience 79
 see also perception
temporality 146
temporary assembly 145
texts 172, 179
Thing politics 121
things (thing-centredness) 87, 93, 119, 121, 150
thought experiments 89, 90, 182–4
thrownness 18
time periods 182
Tonkinwise, Cameron 19, 145
tools, generative 84, 88
trade unions 117
traditions 2
transdisciplinarity 144
transferability 27, 179, 180
transformations 200
Transforming Practices 82
transition design 143
transport 137
traumas 126
trolley experiment 183
Trotto, Ambra 29
trust building 112

uncertainty 66
understanding 131, 197
universities 57

un/making 145, 146, 147–8
Un/Making project 162, 172
unsustainability 140, 145
    see also sustainability
user-centred design 114, 116
user experience design (UX) 3, 75

validity 194
values
    social horizon 98, 126
    technological horizon 84, 87, 89–90
    see also ecology; philosophy through design
van Belle, Jonne 12, 86, 88
Van Busch, Otto 122
Verbeek, Peter-Paul 17, 119, 200
    see also technologies (technology horizon)
viability 32
visual scenarios 11
Von Busch, Otto 29
von Goethe, Johann Wolfgang 143

Wakkary, Ron 87, 119
Walker, Stuart 7, 137, 139, 140
ways of seeing 191
Whipps, Judy 66, 104
White, Morton 108
Wilke, Alex 122, 127
Willis, Anne-Marie 9, 93
wisdom 61, 199
Wood, David 156

Xin, Xiangyang 195

Young, Ella Flagg 53